Thought Patterns
for a
Successful Career™

THE PACIFIC INSTITUTE®

4300-520-0710

Copyright MMVI, The Pacific Institute, Inc.
1709 Harbor Avenue SW • Seattle, WA 98126-2049
(206) 628-4800 • (800) 426-3660 • Fax (206) 587-6007
www.thepacificinstitute.com
4300-520-0710

About Thought Patterns for a Successful Career™

The foundation of all human action is human thought. Our thought process forms the foundation upon which we build every facet of our lives. Therefore, it is important for each of us to understand how our minds work – how we got the habits and attitudes, the beliefs that may stand in the way of releasing our vast inner potential and leading fulfilling and purposeful lives. Our beliefs and expectations about ourselves, our families, our organizations – indeed, our world – are directly reflected in our "performance reality."

Thought Patterns for a Successful Career is designed to build your understanding, with a structured process, of how your mind works, and how you can control the way you think to achieve success – in any part of your life that you desire. Based on decades of research in the fields of cognitive psychology and social learning theory, the education presented here stands at the forefront, reflecting the qualities and characteristics of high-performance individuals and organizations.

Vividly presenting the concepts and education on video, Lou Tice provides revealing and productive insights into how you think and how your thoughts affect how you act. This information unlocks a toolbox of skills and applications that unleashes your potential in ways you never before thought possible. These tools and techniques can be applied immediately, to help you reach your goals easily and enjoyably. Life is propelled out of the ordinary and into an exciting adventure.

By your participation in this program, you join millions upon millions of people around the world who have discovered that the path to true success lies in their own thinking. From small business proprietors to Fortune 1000 executives; from clergy to the military; from educators to political leaders, the economically disadvantaged and prison inmates; from students to bureaucrats, athletes, healthcare professionals and high-tech industries – all are using this information, this education, to make a positive difference in the world around them.

About The Pacific Institute®, Inc.

The Pacific Institute was founded by Lou and Diane Tice, in 1971. Since then, the company has expanded onto six continents and into over 60 countries, and its programs have been translated into a multitude of languages. It has developed a reputation for offering the most practical and enlightening programs ever to come out of the fields of cognitive and self-image psychology and high-achiever research. International headquarters for The Pacific Institute is in Seattle, Washington.

The guiding principle of The Pacific Institute is that individuals have a virtually unlimited capacity for growth, change and creativity, and can adapt readily to the tremendous changes taking place in this fast-paced, technological age. Central to this is that individuals are responsible for their own actions, and can regulate their behavior through a structured process that includes goal-setting, self-reflection and self-evaluation, among other things.

By applying The Pacific Institute's education, people are able to develop their potential by changing their habits, attitudes, beliefs and expectations. This, in turn, allows individuals in an organizational setting to achieve higher levels of growth and productivity, as well as shifting the collective behavior. This shift leads to more constructive organizational cultures, and healthier, higher performing workplaces.

Solidly grounded in the latest research coming out of the fields of cognitive psychology and social learning theory, documented results clearly show measurable increases in organizational effectiveness and productivity after applying The Pacific Institute concepts.

About Lou Tice

He may have started out as a high school teacher and football coach, but a belief in "no limits" has led Lou Tice to become one of the most highly respected educators in the world today. His singular style of teaching – taking the complex concepts and current research results from the fields of cognitive psychology and social learning theory, and making them easy to understand and even easier to use – has brought him students from all over the globe.

Lou Tice believes that excellence is a process – an achievable, continuous process that inevitably results when we learn to control how we think, what we expect and what we believe. International business, political and military leaders consult with him on how to do more with less and bring out the best in those with whom they work. Top athletes come to him for help with mastering the psychological aspects of peak performance. He works with educators on strategies that motivate both staff and students to set and achieve meaningful goals.

Lou's experience in working with Fortune 1000 companies spans over 35 years. When working with organizations, Lou translates his message into practical applications that impact corporate culture and group performance.

Lou's ability as a consummate teacher and mentor has brought him to some of the world's hot spots: to the leaders of Northern Ireland, where he has worked since the mid-80's; to Guatemala, where he has worked since the signing of the Peace Accords in 1995; and to South Africa, from before the end of the era of apartheid to this very day. In 2004, he brought his considerable talents to bear in an on-going partnership with University of California head football coach, Pete Carroll, to make a positive difference in South Los Angeles.

Born and raised in Seattle, Washington where he and Diane, his wife, still make their home, Lou received his bachelor's degree from Seattle University. He went on to earn an MA in Education from the University of Washington, with a major focus in the mental health sciences. Lou is the internationally recognized author of the popular books, *Smart Talk for Achieving Your Potential* and *Personal Coaching for Results.* He is also co-editor, with Dr. Glenn Terrell, of the *Cultures of Excellence* book series.

In the final analysis, Lou Tice is a masterful teacher and educator who is remarkably successful at empowering individuals to achieve their full potential.

About Dr. Joe Pace

Dr. Joe Pace is a nationally known speaker who conducts seminars and workshops in areas of school management, faculty development, student retention, psychology, and motivation. He has instructed thousands of college-level students in the areas of psychology, personal development, and business administration.

He has earned a Doctorate in Education, a Masters degree in psychological counseling, and a Bachelors degree in business administration. His doctoral dissertation and over 30 years of research, concerning success concepts and innovative student retention and persistence techniques, have been the sources for his authoring numerous articles and lecturing internationally.

Dr. Pace, psychologist and former college president, currently serves as the Managing Partner of the Education Initiative for The Pacific Institute. He is the creator of the *Success Strategies for Effective Colleges and Schools* program, which has been implemented internationally by The Pacific Institute. He is also an educational and psychological consultant for various schools, colleges and organizations throughout the United States and Canada.

From 1974 to 1988, Dr. Pace was Chairman of the Board and President of Prospect Hall College in Hollywood, Florida. Before joining Prospect Hall College, he was the Director at Fort Lauderdale University; prior to relocating to Florida, he served as the Director of Jamestown Business College in Jamestown, New York.

Dr. Pace was appointed, by the Governor of Florida, to the Florida State Department of Education's nine-member licensing commission for private schools, serving on the commission for ten years, and elected chairman twice. Additionally, he is a former president of the Florida Association of Postsecondary Schools and Colleges.

On a national level, Dr. Pace served as Commissioner of the Accrediting Council for Independent Colleges and Schools in Washington, DC. He served on the Executive Committee of the Council and also on the Board of Directors of the Association of Independent Colleges and Schools, currently known as the Career College Association CCA).

About Dr. Glenn Terrell

Dr. Glenn Terrell earned his B.A. in Political Science from Davidson College, his M.S. in Psychology from Florida State University, and a Ph.D. from the University of Iowa.

Dr. Terrell served as Chairman of the Department of Psychology, University of Colorado, Dean of the College of Liberal Arts and Sciences and as Dean of Faculties at the University of Illinois in Chicago before an 18-year tenure as President of Washington State University. He also served as President of the National Association of State Universities and Colleges, Commissioner for the State of Washington on the Western Interstate Commission for Higher Education, served on the Board for General Telephone Northwest and West for 23 years, is a Member of the Society for Research in Child Development, and a Fellow for the American Psychological Association and the American Association for the Advancement of Science.

Dr. Terrell has received numerous honorary degrees and awards, among them a listing in Who's Who in America: American Men of Science, and Distinguished Graduate of the Department of Psychology, University of Iowa. His first book, *The Ministry of Leadership: Heart and Theory,* was published in December, 2002.

For the past 18 years, Dr. Terrell has been the Chairman of Curriculum and Research for The Pacific Institute, and is co-editor with Lou Tice of the *Cultures of Excellence* book series.

Using this Manual

This book is designed and written to supplement the video and audio programs. This investment in is yourself, and the manual is designed to enhance and expand those excellent qualities you already possess. Your active participation will cause a wealth of effective, practical, self-educating concepts to come alive for you.

The reflective questions in each unit are designed for just that – reflection. As the Greek philosopher Plato once said, "The unexamined life is not worth living." This course gives you time to think about what you think about – something most of us do not take the time to do. The reflective questions will help you see how the concepts can apply immediately to your quest for education, and to the way you run your life, your family, your team or organization.

In this process, you are the co-author with Lou. Thus, you are urged to not view this manual as a work designed for passive reading. It is a guide for your personal fulfillment and future purpose. Like you, it is a work in progress.

Introduction to Journal Writing

You are encouraged to keep a personal journal. A journal is similar to a diary. Here are some examples of the type of information you record in your journal:

- Successes
- Setbacks – particularly how you overcome them
- "Ah-ha's" (major learning moments)
- Life events
- Your beliefs
- Information from your classes, good books you read or wise people you meet
- Your feelings about situations, both past and present
- Information to identify where you are getting in your own way
- Your goals and affirmations
- Dialogues with yourself, so that you encourage you with positive self-talk when you feel discouraged
- Etc., etc., etc.

Keep your journal. Always date your journal entries. Review it often. You will be amazed at how much you discover about you. You may more easily recognize behavior patterns that are getting in your way, beliefs that no longer serve you well, scotomas to problems or solutions. Once you recognize a problem, you can overcome it by writing an affirmation.

For more information about The Pacific Institute's products and services, please call 1-800-426-3660 (U.S. and Canada) or visit our website at www.thepacificinstitute.com.

Note From Lou

We are going to deal with some very powerful material in this course. I am going to show you how to turn yourself loose in a way you have never been turned loose before. Do not think of this text as a workbook. Rather, think of it as an affirmative guide we are co-authoring. Think of this text as being your book, your chart, your guideline to personal growth and excellence – the kind of growth you never believed possible.

What I intend to help you do is to throw away many invalid, conditioned beliefs you now have. As we work together in this book, you will see how practical this information can be. A whole planned, positive way to enhance your life is open to you. You will not only grow yourself, but you will also show the people around you how they can grow too. You will learn how to achieve goals you never thought possible before – personal, family, spiritual, organizational, whatever you choose. There is no limit, I assure you. You will learn how to increase your self-efficacy – your ability to make things happen – both personally and professionally.

In this course, we will compare restrictive, negative ways of thinking with constructive, positive concepts we have always had at our disposal. These are live, vibrant concepts that will help you break out of old traps. I will show you that we have unlimited potential for growth and creativity.

By applying yourself to this program, by giving it your own reflective input, you will see that most barriers to personal growth and development are self-imposed. You will see that we live and work on partial beliefs, partial truths, and that sometimes we function with false beliefs. A wealth of sound psychological material has been condensed here. I have presented it in practical, easy-to-understand concepts. Our basic premise is this: we act, we work, we produce, we behave, not in accordance with the truth, but only with the truth as we perceive it to be. You will see throughout this curriculum and exercises it asks of you, that if we change the way we think, we can change the way we act.

So, let us now get on with your life. What you are about to learn is as practical as balancing your checkbook. Once you have learned these principles, you will be amazed at what you can really do and become.

Let us begin to open doors together.

Lou Tice

Acknowledgements

Program Development

Lou Tice, M.A. Education

Joe Pace, Ph.D. Education

Curriculum Advisors

Diane Tice, B.A. Education

Glenn Terrell, Ph.D. Psychology

Video Production and Editing

Christy A. Watson, B. A.

Written Text and Editing

Shawn Knieriem

Christy A. Watson, B.A.

Layout and Design

Courtney Cook Hopp, B.A.

Other Contributors

Our thanks to The Pacific Institute staff, project directors and many interested facilitators and seminar participants. A special "thank you" to our studio audience.

Table of Contents

Table of Contents

COURSE OVERVIEW
Looking Forward Safely

Unit Overview

Up until today, many of us have let a fear of new things, new places or new people keep us from moving toward the futures we want for ourselves and our families. No more. Throughout this course, we will gain the knowledge, and learn the tools and techniques that will help us attain our best futures.

Unit Objectives

By the end of this unit, I will:

- understand how to begin helping myself get ready for my future, in my imagination.

- know that this course will teach me what I need to know to be successful.

- know the importance of comfort zones.

It's **OK** to be afraid.
It's not **OK** to stay afraid.

COURSE OVERVIEW
Looking Forward Safely

Key Concepts

- Comfort Zones
- Visualization
- Anxiety
- Subconscious
- Potential
- Goal
- Negative Creativity

Notes

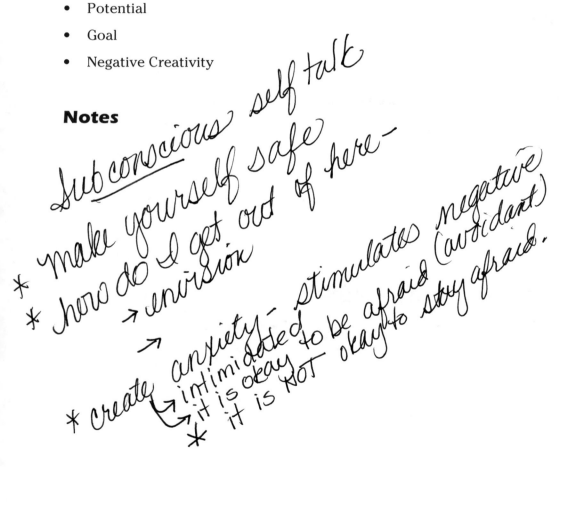

Subconscious self talk

* make yourself safe
* how do I get out of here —
→ envision
→ create anxiety — stimulates negative
↳ intimidated to be afraid (avoidant)
· it is okay to be afraid
* it is NOT okay to stay afraid.

COURSE OVERVIEW
Looking Forward Safely

Notes

COURSE OVERVIEW
Looking Forward Safely

Reflective Questions

What are some of the reasons I am going to school?

COURSE OVERVIEW
Looking Forward Safely

Reflective Questions

What do I want my life to look like when I finish school?

COURSE OVERVIEW
Looking Forward Safely

Summary

What we want to do is help you get yourself really ready for your future. I think what I'll start off with is a little bit about what happens when you go someplace that's unfamiliar. Do you remember when you started school? What would you think of a mother or a father who wanted school to be the surprise of their five year old's life? You know how you could do that? You never talk about school. You just keep it a secret. Then, on the first day, you put them in the car and you drive them to this building. You drop them off and you say, "Have a nice day! I'll be back to get you about 4 o'clock." What do you think would happen? Would that kid scream and yell? Absolutely. "What's wrong with that kid?" School is going to be good for him or her. Why would they be making such a fuss? It's too new.

See, what a good mother or a good father would do is talk about school. Now, what you're doing when you're talking about it, you're going to learn, is you're visualizing in your mind. You're using your imagination to take yourself into the future. Little children are very familiar and very confident as long as they can stay in their own house, in their own yard with their own friends. Am I right? But, if you uproot that child quickly and drop them into a place that is unfamiliar, that's what's called being out of your – and you're going to hear more about this – out of your comfort zone.

So a good mother or father talks about school. They even get the kids to play school. You may take them up and show them school, and they get to sit in the same seat that they may sit in. You talk them into it. You tell them, "Gee, you can learn your numbers. You're going to meet some new friends. You're going to learn how to spell and learn how to read." What you're doing is getting them to look forward safely – not just look forward. You need to learn to look forward and practice in your mind to take yourself into your future, even if it's the next day or the next week or into your new career. You need, in your mind, to take yourself there safely or you become just like that little five or six year old; it's a shock to your system. And you always want go back to where it's safe and familiar.

It's normal for people to always want to go back to their old friends or their old way, even if the old way isn't so good. Unfortunately, you don't let yourself go where you're capable of going. Sometimes, going to a new school, a new college for yourselves, if you don't look forward correctly, you'll scare yourself to death. Looking forward is one thing, but it's how you look forward. I'm going to teach you all this as we unfold this course.

Again, if we had this five year old and we were going to talk about school, but I'd say, "When you go to school, you better behave yourself; because if you don't behave, that teacher is going to slap you silly. Have a good day!" What do you think the kid would think? They can look forward, but if they look forward and scare themselves, they still don't want to go. And if they do go, they want to get home as fast as they can. I contend that, if you took that little five year old to school without talking about going to school, without getting them to feel safe in the new in their mind

COURSE OVERVIEW
Looking Forward Safely

to start with, then you could get in the car, drive home, and don't be surprised to see that little kid still attached to the bumper of your car! Am I right? Have you ever tried to take them to a new baby sitter's without telling them about the baby sitter?

Too often, you do this to yourself. So I'm going to show you how astronauts get themselves ready to go to the moon. How do people get themselves ready if they are great athletes? How do you keep your mind looking forward safely? That's a technique. Otherwise, your subconscious, you're going to see, scares the dickens out of you. It tells you to, "Go back. Go back. Go back," to what we might call your comfort zone. So we need to make your future – your new courses, your new career, school – more familiar and safe, or as familiar and safe as where you came from.

When you're out of your comfort zone, your anxiety gets up inside of you. When you feel out of place, you don't get what people are saying; you block it. Did you know that? Did you ever go someplace and somebody introduces you to somebody else and you forget their name by the time you have walked to the other side of the room? Well, it didn't even get through. So, when you're out of your comfort zone, you're not stupid and you're not dumb. When you're out of place, you block information. You must make yourself feel in place or you don't get what the person is talking about. You'll make the mistake of saying, "I'm just not good at this. I just can't get it."

The other thing that happens, when you're out of place for you (whatever out of place might be), things don't look good, don't look right, don't look familiar. You may get the information in, go to take the test, and it won't come out. So when you're out of your comfort zone, you need to know that you squeeze your recall to the point where your mind just doesn't retrieve what you thought you knew. Did you ever study for a test, go in and take the test and nothing comes out? It could be you're stupid. It could be, but let's just suppose you're not. If you're out of place and out of your comfort zone, then you have difficulty in remembering what you thought you knew – until you leave the class, and then it comes. "Geez, why didn't I get it when I needed it?"

When you're out of your comfort zone, all this happens and more. Most people then say, "I guess I'm just not cut out for school. I'm not good at this. I don't need to be here." Your subconscious says, "Go back where it's safe. Go back to the familiar. Go back to your old life." Well, we're not going to let that happen. What you're going to be able to do is learn to practice in your mind – make yourself familiar, make yourself safe – so that you can get the best out of yourself in your class and then in your future. Does that make sense? I'll show you how to do that. Do you want that? It would really be worth it, wouldn't it?

Now, if you really want to know about being out of place, let me ask you: Did you ever, when you were at a show theater or a ball game or airport, need to use a rest room and found your-self in the wrong one? What goes through your mind? "Oh, no, I hope nobody's looking." I hope nobody's looking, and how do I get out of there and go back where I belong. See, that happens to people when they're out of their comfort zone at school or around people that are not the same color or look more important. Whenever you're out of place, that's what goes through your

COURSE OVERVIEW
Looking Forward Safely

mind. "How do I get out of here and go back where I belong?" See, you could have the potential to use either rest room. It's just hard to use your potential when you're in the wrong one. I learned how to do that in my mind a long time ago. When I want to go someplace or let myself do something, I learn to practice in my mind, and just like the first grader, take myself there safely.

Now, one more piece. When you look at a goal or a problem in your life, here's what goes through your mind: Is this class, this school, this career bigger than me or am I bigger than it? Now what that really means is when you look at the goal, and we think this is too big for us, we create inside of ourselves anxiety. Do you know what anxiety is like? It's like you get uptight. You get tense. Now, what goes through your mind, when that occurs, is it stimulates inside of our brain negative ideas or negative creativity. Now negative doesn't mean bad. Negative means avoidant. When you look at something that you think is too big for you or too good for you or too hard for you, your subconscious starts coming up with reasons why you should quit, why you should go back, why you don't belong there. Your subconscious just comes up with ideas. You wake up at two in the morning with reasons why you should quit. You put obstacles in your way, but it's in your imagination because you're intimidated by the future goal.

What I want to teach you is don't back up your goal and don't quit. It's okay to be afraid. It's not okay to stay afraid. That's why you're going to school. You're going to grow bigger than what was bigger than you. I want to encourage you to always think of goals like many of you have so courageously, with your families and working and getting yourself through school. That is better and bigger than most people would take on, quite frankly. Some of you have come from other countries. It is not easy. But you know how tough you really are and how good you are. We need to use that now. Don't back up your goal. Keep your goal where you want it and grow bigger than what was bigger than you. I'm going to show you how to do that. Remember, it's okay to be afraid. It's not okay to stay afraid.

So stay tuned. We have a lot to do.

UNIT 1
What's Holding Me Back?

Unit Overview

The question we must all ask ourselves is, "Am I seeing all there is to see?" Most of us don't realize that we don't see everything because of the way we were raised, where we were raised and how we were taught. The good news is that we can see more than we've seen in the past, and this will open up a new future for each of us.

Unit Objectives

By the end of this unit, I will:

- know that I have real potential.

- understand scotomas.

- realize that everybody has scotomas, we just don't know where they are.

- know that I am smart and capable, and that scotomas are caused by my past conditioning.

We behave and act not in accordance with the truth of our real potential, but according to the **truth** as we **believe** it to be.

finished files sheet "How many "f's do you see?
[look, read, turn over]

UNIT 1
What's Holding Me Back?

Key Concepts

scŏtō/mās

- Scotomas blind spots
- Conditioning
- Capable
- Smart
- Stuck : b/c way raised, cultures, teachers
- Potential : Be persistant must break thru scŏtō mās
- Subconscious
- Belief
- Truth

Notes

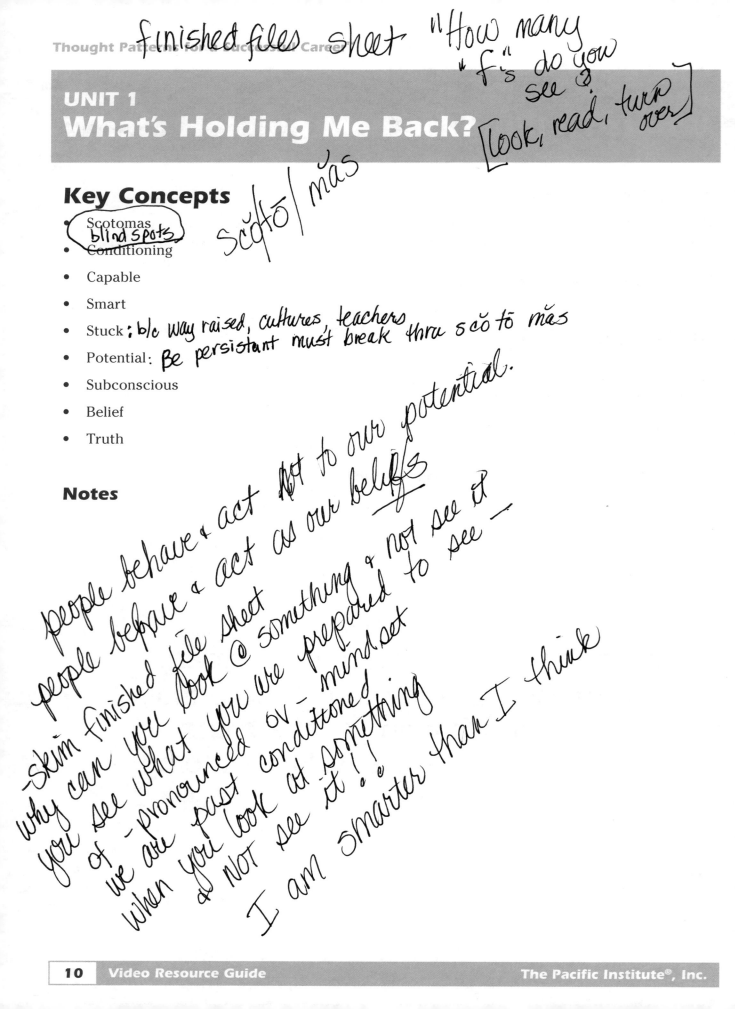

people behave & act Not to our potential.

people behave & act as our beliefs

-skim finished file sheet

why can you look @ something & not see it

you see what you are prepared to see —

of - pronounced 6v — mindset

we are past conditioned

when you look at something

& NOT see it !!

I am smarter than I think

UNIT 1
What's Holding Me Back?

Notes

UNIT 1
What's Holding Me Back?

Reflective Questions

- What are the benefits of knowing I have scotomas?

- What beliefs or thoughts do I have that might be limiting me in completing my education?

UNIT 1
What's Holding Me Back?

Reflective Questions

- Where am I stuck? Why? (The way I was raised, culture, parents or other?)

- If I could make one change in my life, what would it be?

UNIT 1
What's Holding Me Back?

Summary

Now, what I want to do is have you understand how smart you really are. Have you ever taken an IQ test or an aptitude test or anything like that? Do you know, I think that aptitude tests and IQ tests are one of the greatest injustices ever perpetrated upon people, because we don't know how much potential we really have. If you start thinking you're not smart at something or not good at something, do you know what happens? You behave like it. You act like it.

I'm going to give you a psychological principle or rule that I want you to remember for a long time: People behave and act not in accordance with the truth as it *might be*. We behave and act in accordance with the truth as we *believe it to be*. Those of you who have children, you want to help them see themselves as happy and smart and capable and worthwhile and wanted. If they see themselves as unwanted, they will unconsciously behave in a way that makes other kids not want to play with them. If I was your teacher and I didn't see you as smart, I would treat you like I see you. Make sense?

So, people behave and act not in accordance with the truth of our real potential. We behave and we act subconsciously – not in the mind consciously, but subconsciously – like we believe we are. Your beliefs are so powerful that they hold you back. I'm going to prove that to you as we go, and I'm going to show you how to improve your beliefs where you are under-living your real potential inside of you. My first proof was with the Finished Files card. How many F's did you see the first time through? Did you see all of the times the word "of" was used? This is where I want you to know why this happens, so you apply this to how smart you are and to your future. Why do you suppose you can look at something and not see it? You see what you're prepared to see. We all do.

Now, the reason you leave the Fs out in the word "of" is because when most of you were taught to read English, you were taught to read it phonetically. In other words, you sounded out your words. So, "of" is O V and not O F. The next thing you need to know is that you don't see with your eyes. You pick up light with your eyes, and then you translate the light in your brain based upon how you were taught or conditioned in the past. And, if your past conditioning doesn't match what you're looking at, you build a blind spot to it. That blind spot is called a scotoma, S C O T O M A. I want you to remember this forever. You just experienced a scotoma where you can look right at something and not see it. You are full of scotomas based upon your background: whether you came from White River or Tacoma, or if you came from Laos or California; you came from different religions, you came from different backgrounds. Because of the way you were raised, the way you were taught, you have recorded in your mind ideas about how you are and how the world is just as surely as you have conditioned yourself with the word "of" through reading phonically.

Now, you don't let yourself see information or hear information that doesn't match the way you've been conditioned. The problem with scotomas, or blind spots, is you don't know where

UNIT 1
What's Holding Me Back?

they are. You always think you're seeing the truth. You always think you're hearing the truth. Some of you will struggle in some courses, and you wonder, "Am I not smart? Do I not have the aptitude? Is there something wrong with me?" No! Chances are pretty good you're very smart, you're very capable, and you just have a blind spot, a scotoma. Everybody has them. Have you ever been in the class where two or three kids get the answer, but you don't? It's like, "Geez!" It may be you don't get it because you aren't capable, but more than likely you are capable and you just block out the information because of your past conditioning.

When I learned this years ago, I only saw three F's. I didn't get it right away. But what went through my mind was, "I wonder what else I'm leaving out? I'm smarter than I think." Because I used to think "I can't do that. I'm not good at that. I can't get that." Do you ever get that feeling? "I just can't get it," so we quit. We give up. Well, why try if you don't have the aptitude? Why try if you're not smart enough? Why try if this is too hard for me? It could be math or chemistry or some other subject. It could very well be that you're just blocking yourself by the way that you think. I'm going to show you how to break and bust scotomas. You are smarter and more capable by far than you even know that you are.

Everybody has scotomas. Now watch this (and I know teachers are going to watch this, too). Teachers sometimes teach their subject and their students don't get it, so we flunk the student and we keep the teacher. The teacher knows that there's six Fs but she or he isn't able to get the student to see the other, so they fix the blame on the student. You must start with the premise you're smart enough if the teacher's good enough. And teachers, you must start with the premise that your students are smart enough if you're good enough. See, the whole idea is, "I need to be able to explain it. I need to be able to break my scotomas." In my mind, when I found this, I said, "What else am I leaving out? What else can I find?" I let myself try things and do things.

I have a whole new appreciation for my capability. That's what I want you to feel inside. I want you to feel that you're very smart and you're very capable. And when you're stuck, all you need to do is find the solution to it. You're stuck not because you are born that way. You are stuck because of the way you were raised by your parents, by teachers you've had, and by others; and from the culture you came from, because cultures see differently. Make sense? You should feel, inside of yourself right now, very hopeful. When you're stuck, don't quit. Be persistent, because the answers exist, and you're smart enough to get them. It is just that inside of you, you must break through all of these scotomas. And as we go through this course, you're going to find how to do so.

So stay tuned. We have a lot of things to do.

UNIT 1
What's Holding Me Back?

UNIT 2
Who Am I Listening To?

Unit Overview

Most of us have spent our lives listening to others tell us "the way it is," and we believed them. What we didn't do was question if what they said was the truth or an opinion. We must learn to become skeptical listeners.

Unit Objectives

By the end of this unit, I will:

- be careful about who I listen to in the future.

- know that my past conditioning affects what I see.

- understand that I can look right at something and not see it.

- tell myself what I want, and not what I don't want.

You are very **capable** and very **smart.**

UNIT 2
Who Am I Listening To?

Key Concepts

- Potential
- Truth
- Conditioning
- Scotoma
- Mind-set
- Self-Talk
- Subconscious
- Skeptical
- Sanction
- Cognitive Dissonance
- Self-Fulfilling Prophecy
- Perception
- Goal
- Stuck

*rethink bad day – but day is good
discount brain like a computer
not fitting your picture*

Notes

UNIT 2
Who Am I Listening To?

Notes

Who are you taking in?

Parents wisdom - best interest to listen

Third grade teacher said girls aren't good at math

Belief systems imprinted in our head

- Rethink how do I change my thinking

- The truth versus "your" truth

- opinions of ourselves are the old story

* Need to work on internal self talk

* Do see the "g's" not in our world

  trained to read black

  need to retain thoughts.

Create a timeline - rushing but missing

brain can't see them

self talk "I'm not seeing —, I can see them

if I look carefully."

How many affirming

things do we say to ourselves?

UNIT 2
Who Am I Listening To?

Reflective Questions

- How is my self-talk affecting my performance in school?

- What others say about me can affect my perception of myself and my abilities. How can being a "skeptical listener" help me achieve more in school and life?

- Where have I been "conditioned" to think something about myself and how am I allowing it to affect my actions today?

UNIT 2
Who Am I Listening To?

Reflective Questions

- What kind of conversations do I listen to, and join in, at home or at school?

- What is my self-talk about attending school, my classes, my instructors, test taking, giving a presentation? How does my self-talk affect my behavior toward these things?

UNIT 2
Who Am I Listening To?

Summary

Potential lies asleep inside of each one of you. It's your job to wake it up – not the teacher's job, not somebody else's job; it's your job. You must have a goal for yourself, too, by the way. You need to have something you really want to strive for – a way of life, and what you want to do with it – otherwise the education is of no value. The other thing that's so important for you to recognize is you are smart, you are capable.

Oftentimes, through our histories, we develop opinions of ourselves, about what we can or cannot do, and then we behave like it's true. Once I decide something is true, I block out information that is different from what I think is true. Another way to block out the Fs, so to speak, is that when you get a strong opinion about, "This is hard. There's no way. I can't do that. This is how things are," you subconsciously filter information through your senses to match what you told yourself. Isn't that amazing? You can talk yourself into seeing or out of seeing what's right in front of you. I'm going to encourage you to be very careful about how you talk to yourself. We're going to call that "self-talk" as we get into that. It's how you speak to yourself in your own mind.

The other thing that's important is to stop believing people who tell you things that aren't true about you, or about business or about your future or about school. You need to become careful about – for those of you who have children – who is telling your children the truth. Because once you tell yourself, "This is the way it is," then you only see three Fs instead of six. So, who do you listen to? Who tells you how things are going to be? Before we get through, I want you to be very careful to not listen to people who will interfere with your future the way you want it. Opinions, I'm talking about. But, they tell you opinions like it's the truth. Listen carefully.

When we worked with the FLY card, I was trying to mess up your mind. I had you looking for a straw hat on its side and architectural drawings. I was getting you to look at the black spacing when the letters were in white. Well, sometimes people will do that intentionally. Sometimes, people do it accidentally because they think they know the truth. When you're looking at the wrong stuff, you don't see the right stuff.

Now, the other thing was that, most of the time when you're reading, you're reading black lettering on white paper. You're so used to doing that, conditioned to doing that, that when we see white lettering with black spacing, you build a scotoma to it. A scotoma is a sensory blocking out of what's right in front of you, and not because there's something wrong inside of you. There's something right inside of you. That's how your mind works. You get your mind set, and then you pick up information through your eyes and through your ears. You bounce that information off how your mind is set, and if it doesn't match how you've been taught or the way you've been raised, you don't see it.

You should be concluding, hopefully, that you're very capable and very smart, and that when you're stuck, it isn't because you don't get it; it's because of your background. Does that make

UNIT 2
Who Am I Listening To?

sense? If you feel that way, what would it make you do? Be more persistent, and try harder. You don't give up easily, and you don't come to the wrong idea. (I can't do this. I was born this way.) What an excuse for not trying! You must watch, not only what I tell you, but you must be careful of what you tell you. See, I'm telling you dumb stuff, but you tell you dumb stuff with your self-talk. "I can't do that. This is hard. I'm tired." Your subconscious just says, "Okay, whatever you say, I'll make it happen." Whatever you tell yourself, your subconscious has the need to make it happen.

You must control what we're going to call your self-talk – the way you speak to yourself in your own mind. I want you to become skeptical of people like me. I want you to become skeptical of the people you hang around. Don't they offer you opinions freely? Are they telling you the truth or is it just their opinion? Now, when you give sanction to it – when you agree with it – Bam! You can't see anything else or hear anything else.

Hey, do you ever expect a bad day and, sure enough, it turns out to be a bad day? You expect things to go wrong and, sure enough, they go wrong. How come? That's how your mind works. It's called the "cognitive dissonance" principle, which means that you can't hold two conflicting beliefs in your mind at the same time. So, if you tell yourself "No way," your subconscious won't let you see the way. If you say, "This is hard for me," it doesn't need to be, but your subconscious says, "If you say so, I'll make it hard." It's called the "sure enough" principle, the self-fulfilling prophecy. "This is going to be a rotten, stinking, no-good day." What will make you look crazy? A good day. So, instead of blocking out the Fs or the word FLY, guess what you do? You block out anything good. You can't make yourself look stupid. That's the way your mind works. So, stop telling yourself stuff that isn't true. Tell yourself what you do want, not what you don't want.

Have you ever said to yourself, "I'll go to that meeting" or "I'll go to that class, but I won't like it"? Watch, you're always right. Any of you ever lose your purse, your wallet or your keys? What do you tell yourself? "I lost my keys. I lost my wallet." Now, if what I'm telling you is true about how your mind works, and you told yourself you lost your wallet, your purse or your keys, your subconscious won't let you see them. Instead of Fs or the word FLY, you could be looking all over the house and not see them. Then, somebody in your family or around you will say, "There they are, right where you're looking. If it was a snake, it would have bit you." So how come you can look right here and not see it? Because you told yourself it was lost. Instead of Fs, instead of the word FLY, you build a scotoma to your keys. And how do you feel when you find them? Ooh, it makes you mad. What do you say? "Who moved them? I looked there and they weren't there." That's the way scotomas work, folks.

You must be careful about how you set yourself up for your day or for your career. How you talk to you affects your perception. Who you listen to affects your perception. You must become very critical of information when somebody tells you about a teacher or a class or a career. You must question, "Is that true?" Once they tell you it's true, you see it and think the person is smart. "Why, they told me it was going to be this way and it is that way." Why? Because you build a

UNIT 2
Who Am I Listening To?

scotoma to anything that is different than what they told you, if you believe it. Now, if they told you the truth, that's good. But if they told you stuff that's going to interfere with your future or your career, that's not so good.

High performance people are very skeptical – not negative, but skeptical – of information that is coming their way. Why? Because if you agree with somebody's opinion and it's wrong, you won't see the truth; and not just like the Fs, FLY, or the keys, but things that will interfere with you being as good as you are capable of being. I learned that a long time ago, and I changed my whole life. I'm very careful about who I listen to, and I want you to be also. There are a lot of people hanging around the halls or when you go home who are trying to tell you the truth.

UNIT 3
Lock-On / Lock-Out

Unit Overview

Each of us has tremendous potential, and no one can know its limits. For the most part, we are only limited by our beliefs, our truth; and sometimes, the absence of the truth will set us free.

Unit Objectives

By the end of this unit, I will:

- understand that I act according to the beliefs I hold about myself.

- learn that, as a human being, I cannot hold two opposing thoughts/beliefs at the same time.

- know that my job is to keep improving my beliefs.

- know that by locking on to my goals, I am locking out the things that would interfere.

The absence of the **truth** will set you **free.**

UNIT 3
Lock-On / Lock-Out

Key Concepts

- Belief

- Truth

- Reality

- Lock-on / Lock-out

- Perception

- Scotoma(s)

- Potential

- Collective Truth

- Conditioned

- Ah-ha

- Skeptical

- Goal

Notes

UNIT 3
Lock-On / Lock-Out

Notes

*Truth as you believe to be

Act, see, hear affects all your senses.

* Who described you?

You believe what people have told you

You must change so beliefs we hold are positive & what you believe

You MUST become your own authority.

Absence of truth will set you free!!

If beliefs are less than potential*

You must keep improving beliefs *

L.O. = Lock off

Humans have the ability to lock on to a goal.

Reflective Questions

- What are my academic strengths?

- What are my academic weaknesses?

- What beliefs have I "locked-on" to about myself that may hinder my academic performance or success in school?

UNIT 3
Lock-On / Lock-Out

Reflective Questions

- What positive beliefs have I "locked-on" to about myself that will help me achieve academic success?

- What factors outside of school may have an impact on completing my education (family, friends, transportation, work, children)?

UNIT 3
Lock-On / Lock-Out

Summary

Okay, let's just back up a little bit. The whole idea is for me to help you see how capable you are. This is what I do for people all over the world, in business, with presidents of countries, with the intelligence communities, like defense intelligence, armies, and so on. I'm teaching them the same thing I'm teaching you. You're just getting it earlier than most of them. As you apply this information to yourself, your life will get better. I promise you, it will get better and easier. So let's take the next step.

Remember when I said, earlier, that human beings behave and act not in accordance with the truth, but with the truth as they believe it to be; and that when you get a strong belief in your mind about something, you act like it. Also, remember that it affects how you see, how you hear; it affects all your senses. Then, you only let information get through that proves to you what it is that you believe.

When you were growing up, who described the kind of person you were? The kids on the playground, the big kids, Mother, grandmother, teachers, coaches; all kinds of people were trying to describe you as they saw you. Some were very hurtful. Some might have been very negative. Some of you came from backgrounds with people who weren't seeing the best in other people. The way they would describe you, you didn't want to believe it at first. But, if you give in to it, then you act like it.

We need to undo that, because you have enormous potential inside yourself, and it isn't your potential that's holding you back. For the most part, it's what you believe from what people have told you along the way and still are telling you. You must become your own authority. I'll show you how to do that. We also need to know that we must change some of the beliefs we have in our mind. I'll show you how to do that. The main thing is that we behave and act not in accordance with the truth, but what we believe.

Anybody believe in Santa Claus when you were little or have children that do? How'd you behave when you thought there was a Santa Claus? Pretty good. Okay. When you were a kid, were you ever afraid of the dark? Even though there's nothing there, if you think there's something there, how do you behave? You behave in accordance with the truth as you believe it. Make sense? What we want to do is to make sure that the beliefs we hold are going to serve us well. We're going to stop listening to people who are giving us beliefs that cause us to under-live our life. They may mean well, but they just tell you the truth from their view.

We have a company in Australia. One time while we were in Melbourne, Australia, there was this person by the name of Cliff Young who was getting all the media attention. What this guy did was enter in a race called a marathon. Now this was not just a marathon, it was a mega marathon; 600 miles between Sydney, Australia and Melbourne, Australia. The unique thing was he never ran against people who always ran in these races. He showed up to run against the best in the world in bib overalls and galoshes. No running gear, no Nike® shoes, just bib overalls and galoshes.

UNIT 3
Lock-On / Lock-Out

So they interviewed this guy, because he looked like he was some derelict that wandered in looking for a handout or food, like he was in the wrong food line. So they asked him, "What are you doing coming here running against the best in the world? How'd you get yourself in shape?" He said, well, on his ranch in Australia he doesn't have any horses, so all of his life he's been chasing his cows on foot. He has pigs, too, and had to chase his pigs. So he's been chasing his pigs and his cows, that's how he got in shape.

Now this guy, Cliff Young, not only did he enter the race against the best in the world, but he won the race. He beat the best in the world, the first time he ran, and he was 62 years of age. Now, not only did he win the race, but get this – he beat them by a day and a half. Now, these are the best in the world, and the guy outruns them by a day and a half! How come?

Here's why, and I want you to remember this as you apply it to yourself: All these people who were experts and the best, they would get together and they'd tell each other the truth. "The truth" was, if you are running 600 miles, you run 18 hours a day and you'd sleep six. Now, if I would tell you to run six hours and sleep 18, you'd probably believe that, wouldn't you? Now, this guy, living in the outback, never had anybody tell him the truth. He didn't know. It wasn't that he was faster; he didn't know that you were supposed to sleep. So the guy just kept running while the rest of them were sleeping. You know what they said? "He'll die. It's humanly impossible." He was too far ahead for anybody to tell him. So the guy just kept running, and beat them by a day and a half.

Now, the reason I want to bring that up to you is this: sometimes the absence of "the truth," not the truth will set you free. Sometimes the collective truth about people who are of your background, or people who are like you or your family or your family's history, hold that "truth," and then you act like it.

So, we behave and we act in accordance with the truth as we believe it. And if the beliefs we hold are less than what our potential is or what we're capable of doing, it doesn't matter. We behave like our belief. Your job is to keep improving what? Your beliefs. You must become very careful about the beliefs that you're going to accept from now on from people who are very interested in telling you their truth. "You know how you are. I've seen someone just like you before in class, and she wasn't smart either." People keep telling you all kinds of stuff and as soon as you accept it, you're stuck with it. We'll explore how to change that and how to fix that.

This is another piece you need to understand about the power of your beliefs, and we explored that with the "young lady/old lady" card. You can only consciously perceive one thing at a time, and what you experienced with the lady card is what is called "Lock-on, lock-out." If you lock-on to the young lady, you will lock-out the old lady. But if you saw the old lady first, your mind would have locked out the young lady. Does that make sense? So, when you lock-on to "I'm dumb at this," if the lock-on/lock-out is true, you lock out your ability to learn it.

UNIT 3
Lock-On / Lock-Out

Have you ever heard anybody say, "There's no way"? What do you think they lock out? The way. You follow how your mind works? When you lock-on to a self-image of how you are, when you lock-on to your own opinion of how you are, you lock-out being different. It affects your perception, and you act like it. So what have you locked on to about what you're going to be when you grow up, about your career, what you can do? What do you lock-on to about the people around you? What do you lock-on to? Remember, when you lock-on, you build a scotoma to the other information and you don't know you're doing it. If you lock-on to the wrong information, guess what you lock-out? The right information.

The problem with scotomas is you don't know you have them. You always think you're hearing the truth and seeing the truth. From here forward, I want you to be skeptical. But I also want you to recognize some of the stuff you believe about you and have locked-on to, because people have told you, may not be true. But you're behaving like it, and can't see anything else. The locking-on is good. You want to lock-on to your goal. You want to lock-on to your future. You want to lock-on to the kind of life you want and you want to lock-out all the things that would interfere with what you want. You don't have to try hard to lock-out. All you need to do is lock-on strong, and you automatically build scotomas to the stuff that would keep you from succeeding.

UNIT 4
My Brain's Filter System

Unit Overview

The human brain has a formation in the central cortex, the reticular activating system (RAS), which filters all the information that is bombarding our senses. It only lets through that which is important to us right now. We can put the RAS to work for us, by setting clear, concise goals, so that the right information gets through to us.

Unit Objectives

By the end of this unit, I will:

*   understand the reticular activating system.

*   know how to energize my RAS by clearly defining what I want.

*   learn that I am accountable for achieving the future I want.

*   be accountable.

The **goal comes first**
and then you see.
You don't see first.

UNIT 4
My Brain's Filter System

Key Concepts

- Sure Enough Principle
- Subconscious
- Reticular Activating System (RAS)
- Lock-on / Lock-out
- Goals / Goal-Setting
- Significant
- Awareness
- Accountability
- Beliefs
- Perception
- Scotomas

Notes

UNIT 4
My Brain's Filter System

Notes

We have a conscious brain:
everything comes into the brain.
If we were to process out loud.
Reticular Activating system for filtering
information for the brain.
"Drive a Honda" - see Hondas"
It's not important to me - didn't see it/remember it
Brain says what's important thats what you keep "brain stores"
Block out - accountabity blocks what you need to focus on.
Baby cry - your child you hear - your system tunes in.
We are all capable why do we struggle?
Perception = totally accountable to self
Take test = draw a blank = be responsible for self

UNIT 4
My Brain's Filter System

Reflective Questions

- Where have I discovered my perception of the truth was actually quite different from the real truth?

- What are my career goals? How can my RAS help me achieve them?

UNIT 4
My Brain's Filter System

Reflective Questions

- My RAS does a better job of providing clues when the goal is clear. Write some words to describe what you want your life to look like and be like when you graduate.

- I have a clear picture of the results I want from each class I am taking. (List each class and the results you want.)

UNIT 4
My Brain's Filter System

Summary

The main thing to keep remembering is we behave and we act in accordance with the truth as we believe it. The beliefs we hold, you see, affect our perception and much more. If we get a belief about what tomorrow is going to be like, sure enough. If you get a belief even about what the test is going to be like, sure enough. If you get a belief about, "I'll just flunk that. I'll blow the interview," you're going to see your subconscious wants to make that happen.

What I'm going to give you now is something that will help you forever, because, as with the blind spots and scotomas, it should be hopeful information. Did you know that there's so much information hitting your senses that the central cortex of your brain can't handle it all? There's too much information. There's too much light, too much sound, too much smell, too much feel. The information coming at you is so strong that if you need to be aware of all of it, you couldn't sit still.

For a moment, take your hand and run it lightly against the hair on the back of your hand. Do you feel that? Can you feel a little creepy and crawly there? Your whole body would feel like that all the time. All that information is going to your brain, so your brain would be overloaded except for one thing. What I'm going to give you now is going to show you how smart you are, how good classes are going to go, the way your future is going to go. What you're experiencing is the locking out of all information that is of no *personal value* to you *right now*.

Located from the base of your brain to the central cortex is a filter system. That filter system is called the Reticular Activating System. All you need to do is remember the initials RAS. Did you ever read a book and have nothing get through your thick head? Did you ever read it three times and have nothing get through? I'm going to tell you why: You didn't know what you were looking for. See, the reticular activating system filters out all information that you think isn't important. The only thing it lets get through, like the Fs or the word FLY or the old lady/young lady, is information that you have said is important. If it's not important to you, you could be immersed in it and never see it and never hear it.

Do you have children or know anybody who does? A mother could be sound asleep at night and if she has a baby one year or under right close by in the same room, or even the next room to her, she can sleep through the decibel level of an airplane going overhead. But if that baby wakes up in the middle of the night with the slightest cry, far lower than the aircraft's noise, the mother will wake up, just like that.

It's not the loudness of the information that gets through to your brain, it's the *importance* of the information that gets through. If it's not important, it doesn't get through. Remember that. What doesn't get through is called a scotoma – like the Fs, like the purse, like the word FLY, like the old lady. If it's not important, it doesn't get through. That's why, if you decide to buy an iPod® or you decide to buy some kind of a piece of equipment, and you're going to look through the newspaper, you say to yourself, "Ah, they're having a sale on it. What a coincidence!" Now,

UNIT 4
My Brain's Filter System

they're probably having a sale on that item and it's being advertised on television or on the radio or in the newspaper all the time, every day. But you won't see the ad until you want the iPod®. There's too much stuff hitting you, so your reticular activating system screens out the junk mail. It screens out everything that is not important to you, and the only thing it lets get through is what is important. Everything else is locked out. Instead of the old lady or the Fs or the word FLY, it locks out all the information that is nonessential, not important.

You're very smart and you're very capable, but the problem is, if you don't know what you're looking for in the book, if you don't set a goal, you'll read the book and nothing gets through. You must know what it is you're listening for in the lecture. You set a goal for the information, and then just like the baby's cry, it gets through. But if you go with no goal – no goal of a career to be a welder or no goal of a career for what you want – then the information isn't important to you, and it doesn't get through. You're not dumb, and it's not hard; it's just not important. You must know what you're looking for or it doesn't get through. That's how your brain works. Everything is filtered out because there's too much stuff bouncing in here for attention. You're built to block out information that is not significant.

So, who decides what's significant? You do. The goal you set opens up your awareness to information that helps you fill the goal. The goal comes first, and then you see; you don't see first. The goal comes first, and then you hear; you do not hear first. You are smart. You are capable. And I would say to you: Don't build your future based upon what you used to be good at. You could say, "Well, I was never good at math," or "I wasn't good at photography," or "I wasn't good at chemistry." Now it could be that you're stupid, maybe. But it could be, when you were going through school, you didn't care. It could be that that subject wasn't important. And if it wasn't important, it wouldn't matter; it would not have gotten through.

If you are at your age now and you're concluding, "Well, I wasn't good at that. I went through a class and couldn't get it," is it you couldn't get it because you weren't smart or you couldn't get it because it wasn't important? I don't know, but you know. So I would say to you, "Re-set your goals." Clearly define what it is you want in your life. Give yourself another chance, and you'll find yourself so aware that, like the baby's cry, the information will scream through. That is the way you're built. When you know how your mind works, which I'm going to keep showing you, your life gets better. You get "lucky." People say, "My, gosh, you just seem to fall into things. Things go well for you." Yep, because I know how to set goals. I'm going to show you how to set goals.

Now, those of you that might celebrate a holiday or a birthday, do you ever go shopping for something for somebody that you care about? What was my mistake? The mistake was I said, "I'm going to go get them *something* for their birthday. I'm going to go find *something* for Christmas." You know, you can spend all day looking and find nothing? How come? There's too much "something," so you see nothing. That's how your mind works. But if you say, "I'm going to get a wristwatch that's $50 or under and it's going to look like..." you'll see them all over the place. If you're going to get a bicycle for a child, you need to say, "It's going to be this size and this price,"

UNIT 4
My Brain's Filter System

and you'll see them all over the place. The goal comes first, and then you see. You do not see first. Seeing means hearing, too. The goal comes first, and then you perceive. You are smart, and you are capable; but most people haven't the slightest idea what they want in life. Oh, they have a slight idea – they're looking for "something."

So you need to know what you're looking for, folks. And I'm going to help you with that. It must be clear and specific; and when you do, it goes Zap! just like that. It's like "Ah-ha! I got it." You're going to be full of ah-ha's. That reticular activating system locks out everything that is not important to you. You are smart. You are capable. When I found this, I started setting goals for all kinds of stuff.

Now, I recommend that you try this: On your way home from school or wherever you happen to be, set a goal to find blue cars with yellow on them, with a license plate including the number 4 and the letter W. That's all. You can be going 60 miles an hour down the road and you're going to see them. That's how smart you are. You're just going to see them. Your subconscious is looking for stuff. Those of you who drive a car, set a goal to find a parking spot in the busiest part of downtown, someplace on the street. Watch how your system works. As you're driving down the street, you could be listening to the radio, talking to somebody, and your subconscious and your reticular activating system are searching for clues. You see heads in cars two blocks away, sitting on the side of the road. You see people approaching cars. You see red lights flashing and exhaust. There aren't even parking spots. You are that capable and that smart. Your reticular activating system is looking for clues to lead you to what you're looking for. You just need to know what you're looking for. That's how good you are.

If all this works, why doesn't the father wake up when the baby cries? Because he knows the mother is going to; he knows she will. Do you know what else shuts off your awareness? When you give up accountability. See, the father has given up accountability. But if the mother was gone, he'd wake up. No accountability, you shut off your awareness. "Teacher, teach me. I dare you." You are giving up accountability to the teacher. Hey, you need to learn, whether the teacher is good or not! You need to get your own job. You need to get your own life going. You must take charge of your own future.

Don't give up accountability. You put yourself to sleep, and shut off your awareness. You must become accountable. I'm going to show you how your mind really works now. We're going to put all this together and keep getting you more. Isn't this hopeful? Bigger goals. Bigger future. Brighter future.

UNIT 5
How My Mind Works

Unit Overview

As scientists unravel the mysteries of the human brain – the magnificent complexity of its structure – we have discovered the levels of the mind involved in the thought process. Our conscious, subconscious and creative subconscious work together to perceive the world around us, store our reality and make sure that each of us acts like the person we know ourselves to be.

Unit Objectives

By the end of this unit, I will:

* have a full understanding of the three parts involved in the thought process – conscious, subconscious and creative subconscious.

* know that if the outside world does not match my inner idea of who I am, I subconsciously make the outside match the inside picture.

* understand that I guide my life at my belief level, not my potential level.

We **self-regulate**
at our **belief** level.

UNIT 5
How My Mind Works

Key Concepts

- Conscious
- Subconscious
- Perception
- Truth
- Reality
- Sanity
- Creative Subconscious
- Behavior
- Self-Image
- Garbage in / Garbage out
- Beliefs
- Potential
- Self-Regulate
- Neurons
- Internal Standard

Notes

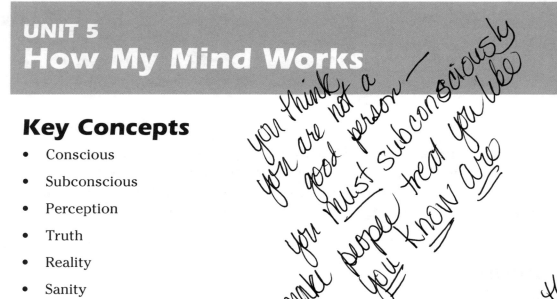

you think —
you are not a
good person —
you must subconsciously
make people treat you like
you know are —

into + misinformation
opinions/or your mind
that are not truth [cuts your potential]

they are.
called the truth I know where
* problem w/scotomas we don't know where
* stored info or truth "reality"

mind/brain works
senses = perception (before born)
→ stored on neuron of brain

creative
subconscious
→ Automatic → free flowing
you act you know u are
you think like you think you should

you hold you back !!
self regulating of
how you are

UNIT 5
How My Mind Works

Notes

The Thought Process

Perceives — Conscious — Evaluates

Associates — Decides

Subconscious

Creative Subconscious

Stores
Truths

**Stores
Habits
Attitudes**

Maintains
Sanity

Resolves
Conflict

Creates
Drive and
Energy

UNIT 5
How My Mind Works

Reflective Questions

- What are some beliefs I hold about myself?

- How did I come to form these beliefs about myself?

- What are my expectations of myself?

UNIT 5
How My Mind Works

Reflective Questions

- How did a great experience I have had on the job or in school affect my self-image?

- What are examples of the GI/GO concept that have affected my relationships at home? At school?

Summary

What I want to do is show you how your mind works, so you can motivate yourself. You can take charge of your whole life. You can see why you do well and why you don't do well, and you can fix it if you choose to. I'm going to give you a model, as best we know, of how our mind works. What do we mean by "the mind"? It's just how your brain works; that is what we mean when we say how the mind works. There's the conscious, then we're going to talk about the subconscious, and then the creative subconscious. I would say when you grasp this and use this, you'll have as much information as most people with a doctorate degree in psychology. The important thing is that you apply it to make your life go well.

One of the functions of the conscious process is called perception through your senses – sight, taste, touch, smell, hearing. Even before you were born, you started recording information on the subconscious level. So, you perceive through your senses and store all that information on the subconscious level. Every radio program, every experience, every book you've read, is recorded in the neuron structure of your brain. (We don't quite know how memory works yet, but we just know that there's some kind of a chemical change that takes place in the neurons of your brain.)

There is a chance that you left some Fs out along the way, maybe missed a little bit here. This stored information that each one of us has we call "the truth." You call it the truth. I call it the truth. But remember that some of you had three Fs, one had two, one had five, and another had six, and each one thought the other was crazy. That's the way life is. Everybody thinks, "I see the truth." "No, I see the truth." The problem with scotomas is you don't know where they are. There is another word for this subconscious stored information or truth, and we call it "reality." Put that in quotes, because we left some Fs out or we only saw the old lady, and didn't see the young.

Now, the problem, with all of this information that we're storing and perceiving, occurs when the creative subconscious comes into play. The creative subconscious has four jobs, and I'm going to give you one right now. One of the jobs of the creative subconscious is to maintain your idea of "the truth" or what we call "reality." Another word for this is "sanity." The creative subconscious is supposed to make you behave like you. It's supposed to make you act like yourself and not act crazy. Once you know how you are, something automatic takes over. This creative subconscious lets you behave like the person you know yourself to be, automatically. You don't need to think about it. You act like yourself free flowingly. Once you know how you are, you don't have to get up in the morning and remember how you are. Your creative subconscious takes over and lets you behave like you. Even if the information you think is true about you isn't true, it doesn't matter. You act like you know you are.

You behave like you think you are subconsciously, automatically. When you see yourself every day not behaving like you know you should, your subconscious corrects for the mistake. When you see yourself or your life going different than you know it should, this creative subconscious makes you behave or act so that you go back to being yourself.

UNIT 5
How My Mind Works

We had adopted some children, and among them were three boys. When they were five, six, and seven, they were taken away from their mother and fathers, whoever the fathers were. They were badly abused; were beat up, run over, shot at. Their impression of the world, by the time we got them, was the world beats me up and I'm not a good person – because it had. Now, we were going to be the best mother and father anybody could be. We didn't know much about this stuff in those days, so every time those kids did something good, we'd tell them, "Nice going." The nicer we were to them, the worse they behaved.

When you know you're not a good person and the world out here is treating you differently than you know you are, you must subconsciously make the people "out there" treat you like you know you are. The first day my six year old went to kindergarten, or the first grade, the sheriff brought him home arrested. And then things got worse. It wasn't going to get better. When we would compliment them on something that went well, they'd start a fire behind the couch or in the closet. I'd take the kid, slam him in a chair and say, "What did you start the fire for?" Guess what he said? "I don't know." "What do you mean you don't know? You just started the fire! Now get in your room 'til you can figure it out." See, he was setting us up to punish him. We were treating him nice, but it was so different from the way he knew his world to be, that it caused his behavior – not consciously but subconsciously – to make you or me act toward him like he knows the world.

You have an image of how you are inside of you. You know how you are, and you're checking and balancing your life based upon your idea of how good you are, what kind of a student you are, how smart you are. If you think of yourself as a C student and you get an A, you correct for the mistake. You'll flunk the next test or two – not consciously, but subconsciously. You can't get yourself to study, to get back-to-back A's. You can't. That's how your subconscious works. See, it doesn't just correct when your behavior is worse than you think it should be, you correct if it's better. You always are correcting the way your life goes based upon your subconscious idea of the way things are supposed to be for you.

Another way of looking at this self-image is this: You have an idea of what is good enough for you. Whatever your internal standard is, it's called a self-image. When you blow it, you correct up. In other words, if you're a C student and you fail test, somebody says, "Let's go out and party," you say "I can't. I've got to study and get an A." Why don't you study and get an A all the time? "Because I'm a C student. I can't do it." Your subconscious won't let you. You check and balance at your belief level. When we were treating our children nicer than they were, they would do things to make the world around them treat them like they knew they should be treated. Everybody does.

How did you get this belief in there in the first place? The founding father of the computer, Norbert Wiener, had a wonderful saying. He called it the "GI/GO" principle. You know what that means? Garbage in – Garbage out. When you put misinformation into your mind – your image of reality – don't expect the right answers to come out. I'll show you later how that works. Many of

UNIT 5
How My Mind Works

you are operating with beliefs about yourself, opinions about yourself, that aren't true. But if you have accepted them as true, then you guide your life, subconsciously, at your belief level, not your potential level. Your potential might be enormous, but you self-regulate how good you are, and what you do, at your idea of the way you are. How did you get that idea? I'll show you later. How do you change it? I'll show you later. See, you hold you back. I hold me back.

Watch someone who wins the lottery, somebody who knows they're poor and wins the lottery of millions of dollars. Do you know what they do with their money? They blow it. They get rid of it. And you say, "What did you spend your money or give it away like that for?" You know what they say? "I don't know." They don't know subconsciously, but they correct for the mistake of being wealthy. Someone who thinks they don't deserve a good marriage, if their marriage is going well, will unconsciously do something to cause their marriage to go wrong. See, you are self-regulating at your idea of how you are. You didn't necessarily put that in by intent. I do. And by the time you're through, I'm going to show you how to put in a new idea about how good you are. Would that be helpful? You bet it would. You would quit messing yourself up.

So, we need to raise your self-image, improve it to a new level closer to your potential. You'll always self-regulate, but at new levels; socially, in business, in money. Do you know anybody who can't save money and when they get money, they must correct for the mistake of having money in the bank. See, if you know you're always poor and you're getting money, it's a mistake. Your mind always corrects for mistakes, and it's the mistakes you believe about yourself, not your potential. We're going to fix that.

UNIT 6
Free-Flowing at a New Level

Unit Overview

As we go deeper into our understanding of the thought process, we see that we are constantly taking our perceptions of current reality and checking them against our past stored reality in our subconscious. We need to remember that this stored reality isn't just a memory of what has happened, but also our feelings about what has happened to us.

Unit Objectives

By the end of this unit, I will:

- understand the decision-making process of perception, association and evaluation, all leading to making a decision.

- know that my stored reality may not be "the truth" because of the emotions that are tied to my memories of a situation.

- have learned that stress comes when I try to behave differently than I know I am.

There is a **direct relationship** between the quality of **excellence** in your mind and the **way your life goes.**

UNIT 6
Free-Flowing at a New Level

Key Concepts

- Perception
- Conscious
- Association
- Evaluation
- Decision-Making
- Reality
- Garbage in / Garbage out
- Creative Subconscious
- Stress
- Potential
- Belief
- Truth
- Pressure

Notes

UNIT 6
Free-Flowing at a New Level

Notes

Decisions made not on what will happen rather what has happened.

The Thought Process

Info stored
↓
Emotions → Perceives involved →

Associates

Conscious

Evaluates

Decides

Helpful/Hurtful what is this leading me toward?

Subconscious

Creative Subconscious

Stores Truths

Stores Habits Attitudes

Maintains Sanity

Creates Drive and Energy

Resolves Conflict

Corrects up
Stress/pressure from trying to be better than you are

Accept reality of what people told you-you are
New truth

Subconsciously mess up life bc you believe you are not deserving

UNIT 6
Free-Flowing at a New Level

Reflective Questions

- How can changing my beliefs about my myself and my abilities actually change my performance or my success at school? In what way?

- What do I believe to be true about myself as a student, friend or co-worker?

- Why is it important to understand how the thought process forms my beliefs about myself and the world around me?

UNIT 6
Free-Flowing at a New Level

Reflective Questions

• How might I be letting others sabotage my opportunities?

• During the next week, I will list here 5 things I hear myself say or that I overhear others say that sabotage my success.

UNIT 6
Free-Flowing at a New Level

Summary

More about how your mind works. The more you know about this, the more confident you're going to be that you can make all the changes you want to make. You're going to quit messing up your own lives, and let yourselves do very well.

Remember, I talked about the conscious mind, through the perception of your senses, gathering information and then storing it on the subconscious. Now, once you have that information stored, another thing happens on the conscious level. You go into what's called association, and the third function is called evaluation, and the fourth function is called decision-making. Now, association just means, "Have I seen anything like this before?" You bounce what you're looking at off of your stored reality, but not only your stored reality of what it looks like, but how you feel about it. See, you have your emotions stored there, too. (That's going to be called an "attitude," and we're going to talk about those as we unfold.)

Once you associate, then you start evaluating what you're looking at. Evaluation is very simple. It just means, "What is this probably leading me toward? What is this that I'm perceiving probably leading me toward?" Now, when you evaluate, you also ask, "Is it going to be good or is it going to be bad? Is it going to be helpful or is it going to be hurtful?" You start judging based upon the information that you have stored. You are perceiving it; you're bouncing it off your stored reality; and you say, "Have I seen anything like this before?" Yes. "What's this probably leading me to; something that I want to seek or something that I want to avoid?"

So the decisions that you're making – about the career, the job, the family, relationships – almost all of us make based not upon what we can do, but we base it on what has happened to us in the past. Let's say you just tried something and it didn't work. You were made a fool of in front of a class. It was a stupid thing that happened, and it's stored in the subconscious. Now someone asks, "Will you get up in front of the class again?" So you say to yourself, "Have I seen anything like this before? Uh huh." You bounce that off of your stored reality, and you evaluate by asking, "What is this leading me to?" And you say, "Nothing good!" So, you decide not to try in this situation not because it may be safe, but because of the old situation. Many of our decisions aren't made based upon what *can* happen but what *has* happened to us.

Remember that GI/GO principle, garbage in/garbage out, and give yourself another chance. We must change some of this feedback. As I show you how to do that, you're going to let yourself do a lot of things that you aren't presently letting yourself do. I did this a long time ago. I'm still doing it.

Now, once we get this reality stored, remember the creative subconscious and how it works? It corrects for mistakes. When you perceive yourself falling beneath what's good enough for you, you subconsciously correct up. Well, why don't you just keep going to your full potential? Because when the outside that you're observing matches the inside in your mind of what is good enough, just like a light switch, you shut off.

UNIT 6
Free-Flowing at a New Level

Now, you not only correct when you're beneath your idea of how good you are, you correct if you see yourself doing better than you know you are. For example have you ever had company come and stay with you for a week or so? Did you fix your house up for company? A little bit? Okay. Now, why don't you live in a house that nice all the time? Do you follow? "Oh, well, it's too hard to keep it that nice. It would be too much." In fact, we might say it's unnecessary. Do you get the idea? You can, and you do, at times live better, do better than your idea of how good you are, but it's hard to keep it up. And isn't it nice when people leave, if you had company, so you can go back to being yourself?

So you always seem to be able to act nicer, try to come off smarter, try to do better than you know you are, but that's when pressure comes. Have you ever felt under pressure, or say, "I've been under a lot of stress"? Stress comes when you try hard to behave differently than you know you are. You know the goal that I'm going to have you set? Change how you know you are. No stress. I'll show you how to change your mind. Most of you are operating on garbage-in information, from teachers or coaches or parents or friends, who have described you as they saw you, and you fell for it. You've accepted their reality. It is how we are that allows us to free flow our behavior, but only at that level. Change it, and your potential changes. You let yourself do it.

If I would put one of you under hypnosis, I could go past the conscious level right to the subconscious with a new truth. Under hypnosis, I tell you that a pen weighs 500 pounds. Then I'd say, "Pick it up and take it back where you're seated and I will give you a thousand dollars." Worth a try, isn't it? If you are truly under hypnosis and believe it weighs 500 pounds and you know you can't lift 500 pounds with your arms, you won't be able to pick up the pen.

We need to measure how hard you're lifting, so we take and attach electrodes to your biceps, and connect them to an electronic measuring device. While it shows you are lifting up with 75 pounds of energy, the pen still stays down, why? Your creative subconscious must make sure you behave like the truth that you know about yourself. If you know you can't lift 500 pounds and you believe the pen weighs 500 pounds; and if we attach electrodes to your triceps, the muscles at the back of your arm, it would show that while you're lifting with 75 pounds of energy up, you're also pushing with 75 pounds of energy down. But you're pushing subconsciously. You don't know you're pushing. You have a scotoma to the push. What might you be aware of? How hard you're trying.

My point to you is, when you know you're only so good, even though you have the potential to be much better, you will subconsciously mess up your life at the level of how good you know yourself to be. Some of you, if you know something is going to be hard, you'll make it hard. Now, it may really be hard, but you'll make it hard. What happens to the person who says, "No Way"? If what I'm saying is true, what would your subconscious do? It will mess up the way.

We got one of my sons a tow truck business when he was about 23 years old, as he had just got out of the service. Now, when he was in grade school, the kids picked on him. When he was in junior high school, and he went to a different junior high, the kids picked on him. Then he went

UNIT 6
Free-Flowing at a New Level

to a new high school and, darn the bad luck, the kids picked on him. He went in the Army and the sergeant picked on him. He got out and he started in a fast food place, and the boss or the manager picked on him.

Now his idea when he was raised was, "The world beat me up" because his parents did. He'd been through all the stuff that a kid who's really badly abused would go through. So, we got him this tow truck business, and I hired this guy to teach him how to do it. He had been in the business about five months, and he came home and he said to me, "I quit." So I asked, "How come?" He said, "Bill's picking on me." (Bill is the guy I hired to help him run the business.) And I said, "Man, you can't quit. You own the business. You've got it. It's yours." Then I said, "If you don't change your inner idea of how you are, you'll get married and come back to me when you're 40 years old telling me your wife is beating you up, because you'll find one who will." Does that make sense?

You and I go out and create the world outside to match the world in our mind. So quit waiting for things to change on the outside. If you want to your life to go better, then change the world in your mind. There is a direct relationship between the quality and quantity of excellence inside and the way your life is going.

UNIT 7
Leaning in the Right Direction

Unit Overview

There is a great advantage to being able to rely on our habits. We don't need to stop and think about how to do many routine things. However, when those habits keep us stuck in a rut, under-living our potential, we need to see about changing them. In the same manner, our attitudes can limit our achievements. The good news is that habits and attitudes can be changed.

Unit Objectives

By the end of this unit, I will:

* understand that my subconscious holds my habits and attitudes.

* know that habits are good, if I have the right habits.

* understand that attitudes are neither good or bad; they just cause me to either lean toward or lean away from whatever is before me.

* know that by setting goals, I can uncover attitudes I may not know I have.

Habits are a learned behavior and can be unlearned.

UNIT 7
Leaning in the Right Direction

Key Concepts

- Subconscious
- Habits
- Conscious
- Visualization
- Affirmation
- Attitudes
- Emotion
- Creativity
- Ideas
- Perceive
- Creative Avoidance
- Goal-Setting
- Assimilation
- Potential

Attitudinal Scale →

Notes

UNIT 7
Leaning in the Right Direction

Notes

UNIT 7
Leaning in the Right Direction

Reflective Questions

- What are my attitudes about myself? How smart am I, how capable, and do I see myself being successful in life?

- How am I letting my past habits control my present and future?

UNIT 7
Leaning in the Right Direction

Reflective Questions

- What habits or attitudes do I have that have prevented me from being as successful as I know I could be?

- What are some habits or attitudes I would like to change so I can be more successful in life and in school?

UNIT 7
Leaning in the Right Direction

Summary

I want you to know that you weren't dealt a bad hand from the stars. You know some people say, "I inherited this bad life or it must have been in the stars." It's outside of me. Does that make sense? That's what I used to think. When you know how your mind works, you wonder, "Why does all this stuff happen to me?" What stuff? "Well, the stuff I don't want to have happen." Well, it could be that it's bad luck, but it could be what I'm talking about in this course. You decide.

If you really think that it has to do with what we know about how the mind works, then I'm going to show you how to improve it. Now, you're not going to improve to your potential level. You're going to improve it just a little bit, and a little bit more, and then a little bit more, and then a little bit more. Your life will get better month by month, and year by year. You're going to stop doing some of the stuff that makes you wonder, "Why did I do that?"

Now, I need to teach you more about the subconscious. Let me ask, what is two times two? Four? You got it. There was a time when you couldn't do that. But by repeating and repeating what we call your times tables, you turn it over to the subconscious. Was there a time when you couldn't tie your shoe? It took great focus and concentration to tie your shoe. Now, you don't know you're doing it; you just tie them. Your subconscious handles all of your habit patterns. You have emotional habits and piano playing habits, times table habits, and spelling habits. Habits allow you to do many things at the same time on the subconscious level. You start off consciously, putting in a pattern of doing something and through repetition and repetition you can let it go.

For many of you, the habits you have guiding your life aren't of the quality or quantity of excellence that will bring you the kind of life that you want. Let's say your mother wanted you to play the piano, but she didn't want to pay for the lessons. So, she got some guy like me to teach you how to play the piano. I don't know how, but I can get you playing with your fingers. You can get that down, but it wouldn't really be playing the piano.

You have habits, or patterns of flow, that come out so easily; they just aren't at the level that you're capable of. You could have learned that two times two is five just as easily, memorized it, and had it down as good as two times two is four. One thing you need to remember: Practice doesn't make perfect. Only practice of perfection makes perfect. It's good that you're going to these schools that you're going to, because you have great instructors teaching you about diesel mechanics, radio, court reporting, etc. If you're going to the wrong teachers, you can still get it down and flow it, but you aren't going to do well.

You need to understand that everything you do starts off on the conscious level, then you repeat and you repeat, and you turn it over to your subconscious and flow it. Once you get it into the subconscious, forget it. Don't try to get it to the conscious level. Did you ever ask yourself how to spell a certain word? What happens? You block it, don't you? When you have something in the subconscious, you don't want to bring it to the conscious level. You must let it flow.

UNIT 7
Leaning in the Right Direction

I used to teach driver training when I was a high school teacher. Drove me nuts! You'd get these kids, first time behind the wheel who couldn't get out of the parking lot. Their hands were frozen on the steering wheel, jerking the car, only going three miles an hour in the parking lot. But, by repeating and repeating and repeating it, they're flowing down the road with one hand on the steering wheel, the other around their girlfriend, listening to the radio, looking for the cops out of the back mirror. I mean, how could you do that in a month? Just repeat, repeat, repeat. Habits are good if you have the right habits.

The other thing that's in the subconscious are your attitudes. Has anybody ever told you that you had a bad attitude? Now, did anybody ever tell you what an attitude was? Probably not. Remember the stored emotional reality? That's your attitude. It's how you feel about certain kinds of food. Anybody not like liver? See, you can get attitudes about food. You can get attitudes about people, about colors of people. You can get attitudes about snakes. Anybody hate snakes? Attitudes are an emotional response.

The best definition of an attitude I ever got was from a pilot. Attitude, to an airline pilot, is the direction the wings are leaning in relationship to a fixed point like the horizon (the horizon being flat). So they talk about the attitude of the airplane based upon how the wings are fixed or leaning in relationship to the horizon. So, an attitude is just the direction in which you are leaning. Remember that, because you need to know your own attitudes to be successful.

You're said to have a positive attitude if you lean towards something. You are trying to seek the good that you see in the music, or the concert, or the class, the experience or the person. You see a positive emotion being fulfilled when you go to that concert or into that situation. It stimulates the creativity in your mind on how to get it. You get creative ideas on how to organize yourself to possess what it is that you want. If you have a positive attitude about something, you unconsciously get creative to possess it.

So, what does a negative attitude do? Well, when you perceive something and bounce it off your reality of "I've seen something like this before," and you have a distaste for it or a hurt feeling about it, or it makes you feel repulsive or ugly about it, you evaluate with "What is this leading me to?" and decide to negatively move away from it. Negative just means avoid or move away, it doesn't mean bad. Positive doesn't mean good. Positive, from here forward, means to seek. Negative just means to avoid.

Is there any work in school that you're avoiding? Is there anything that you're supposed to do or required to do that you're avoiding? You know what you might think? "I need to try harder." No. You need to change your attitude about it. If you need to change your attitude, you'll go after it. I'll show you how to change your attitude. When you start out to get employed, you may say, "I'm afraid of the interview." Watch, you'll spend all your time subconsciously trying to figure out how to avoid going where you don't want to go. If you are busy you may say you need time management. You don't need time management. Change your attitude. You don't need time man-

UNIT 7
Leaning in the Right Direction

agement to do the things you want to do; you need time management to do the things you *don't* want to do. Everybody is like that.

Most of you didn't volunteer for your attitudes. In fact, you probably don't even know how you got them. Attitudes are not positive or negative until you set a goal. When you do, your attitudes cause you to do the things that will help you achieve the goal or it causes you to engage in stuff that has nothing to do with the goal, called creative avoidance or procrastination.

If they're leading you away from it, you need to know. I want you to watch yourself. Don't try hard, but correct it at the root cause by changing your attitude. Changing attitudes is easy. I'm going to show you how to visualize. I'm going to teach you a process of internal goal-setting. I'm going to teach you a process of what is called affirmations. When you learn that, you can change your attitudes. I'm not going to tell you what attitudes to change. You must change your own.

I've had to change a lot of my attitudes in order to let myself do what I'm doing. At one time, certain kinds of people would intimidate me. Going places would scare me. I wouldn't tell you I was scared, I'd just say, "That's a dumb idea. That's stupid. Who wants to do that? I have other things to do." I would make up reasons why I didn't want to do something. Only I would know the real reason, just like you know. Once you find yourself not letting yourself do something that is essential for you, don't give up on your goal. You just change your attitude.

Habits and attitudes are a part of your subconscious. When you start a new career and a new future, some of your old attitudes aren't conducive to success in your life. Most of you didn't intentionally get them. You assimilated them from your mother, your father, your uncles, people around you wherever you lived. You inherited them, not through your genes, but through just observing, watching, and listening. What made them sick now makes you sick. What you don't like is because somebody around you didn't like it. Or you were embarrassed, made a fool of, ridiculed, made to feel stupid, made to feel "less than" under certain circumstances. "I'll never do that again," your subconscious says. Well, folks, let's get past that stuff and let's get on with your life.

UNIT 8
How My Beliefs are Formed

Unit Overview

Our thoughts accumulate to become beliefs, so it is important to control our thoughts. We do this by controlling our self-talk, that constant conversation that goes on in our minds. This self-talk is vitally important in forming our self-image, and can either build us up or tear us down. In fact, understanding the power of self-talk may be the most important thing we can ever learn.

Unit Objectives

By the end of this unit, I will:

•   know that self-talk is a three-dimensional form of thought: words trigger pictures, which then trigger emotions.

•   understand the importance of self-talk in my daily life.

•   realize that I need to clear away all the negative, destructive self-talk from my life.

Thoughts accumulate
to become **beliefs.**

UNIT 8
How My Beliefs are Formed

Key Concepts

- Beliefs

- First Nature

- Second Nature

- Self-Regulate

- Self-Talk

- Subconscious

- Truth

- Words-Pictures-Emotions

- Self-Image

- Sarcasm

- Sanction

- I x V = R

Notes

UNIT 8
How My Beliefs are Formed

Notes

A Belief doesn't have to be true
to be a belief -
How you describe your self becomes
your truth - whether it is true or not.

Self Talk 1) words
2) pictures
3) Emotion: how you feel about everything

Thoughts over and over
become beliefs

$$I \times V = R$$

Imagination × Vividness = Reality
(clear Picture   or
+   Subconscious
Emotion)   level

Self regulate de value w/in your mind

UNIT 8
How My Beliefs are Formed

Reflective Questions

- Where in my life did I believe in myself and it helped me to succeed?

- What am I dissatisfied with, and what would the new picture look like?

UNIT 8
How My Beliefs are Formed

Reflective Questions

- Where have I let my self-talk keep me from succeeding?

- What are some examples of positive self-talk that I have used to help me succeed?

UNIT 8
How My Beliefs are Formed

Summary

Have you ever heard the saying, "As a man thinketh in his heart, (or person nowadays,) so is he?" You know now that if you change the way you thinketh, you change the way you is-eth. Do you think you are born with beliefs, or do you think you develop them? You develop them. That's second nature. First nature is what you inherit through your genes, the heredity factor. Everything else is acquired, and you acquire beliefs.

So what? You self-regulate how good you are, how your life goes, at your belief level. Remember self-regulate, that check and balance at your belief level? So if you know that, how did you get your beliefs? Who gave you your beliefs? How are you getting them now? How are you going to change them? The most important thing I can teach anybody is what I'm going to teach right now: Control your self-talk or your self-talk will control you.

What is self-talk? Self-talk is that conversation that you're carrying on in your own mind right now. You speak to yourself three times faster than I'm talking to you. When I stop, you speed up six times faster. Now, that conversation you're having doesn't evaporate into thin air. Every thought you have is being recorded in the neuron structure of your brain. Again, we don't quite know how memory works. We think that there's a chemical change that takes place in the neurons. But, every thought you have is being recorded, whether it's good for you or not, whether it's true or not. You see, a belief doesn't need to be true to be a belief. So every thought you have, whether it's positive or negative, whether it's true or untrue, your subconscious accepts and records literally. "Literally" means no questions asked. It doesn't argue. It records what you tell it.

Now, you need to know that you don't record exactly what's happening at this very moment, or what happens at home, or what happens when you go out. You record light reflecting off of objects, and you tell yourself what you think is happening. What is being recorded isn't what is happening; it's your version of what is happening to everybody around you and to yourself. You don't record the event in your brain. You record light reflecting off of objects. And, how you describe to yourself what has happened, how you feel about it, becomes your truth.

Once you get the belief stuck, you act in accordance with the belief that you hold, whether it's true or not. And when you find yourself doing better than your belief, your subconscious makes you correct back to your belief. When you find yourself doing less than your belief, you'll correct up. Remember, you correct your behavior, your life, your social world, your grades – everything – is corrected at your belief level. Change your belief, and your life gets changed.

Remember, while I'm speaking to you, you speak to you three times as fast. When I stop, you speed up six times faster. That conversation you're carrying on in your own mind is either going to elevate your belief in yourself, keep it the same, or lower it. Now, it's been estimated that you and I have about 50,000 thoughts go through our mind a day. (I don't know who counted them. I didn't. There are a lot of them.) Every thought you have, if it is a destructive thought, lowers your

UNIT 8
How My Beliefs are Formed

opinion of yourself. If it is a thought about how stupid you are, you lower your opinion of yourself. When you speak to yourself negatively or destructively, you lower your opinion of yourself.

You speak to yourself with self-talk, in three dimensions: Words, or language, which trigger the second dimension, pictures. So, you record pictures in your mind, then you record the most powerful element, which is how you feel about everything. The language of the words is important, because you must understand the words in order to get a picture or an image in your mind. If you don't understand Spanish, Japanese or Russian, you won't get a picture. So words trigger the second dimension, which are images. And then, of course, feeling is the third dimension.

This three dimensional form of thought – words, pictures and feeling – is called self-talk. Now if I was to describe one of you, and I'd say, "That was really stupid of you. I've never seen you do much that was really good anyway, so it's pretty normal for you," do you think that would make a take in your image of reality and your self-image? It might or it might not. This is an important piece: An opinion of another describing you will not become a part of your self-image or your image of reality in your brain, until you agree with it. You must agree with the opinion of another before it becomes a part of your image of reality.

Now, you could have said, "Well, you don't look so smart yourself. You know, who are you to tell me that?" You could have said it quietly or out loud. It's only when you say, "Oh, do you think so? Yeah, I've been thinking that myself," that it becomes a part of your self-image. People could be negatively critical of you or give you opinions of you from their view and it doesn't become a part of you until you give sanction to it or agree with it. You need to become a disputer of the descriptions that other people have of you, unless you want it to be a part of you. Now, when you were growing up, you didn't know any better. You ran into teachers who shouldn't have been teaching. They may have said, "Well, I don't expect you to be good, Diana. I had your brother, and he couldn't spell either." People always described you from the time you were little, from their point of view, and when we don't know any better, we agree with them. You must stop agreeing with the opinions of others that won't fit who you want to be. You don't need to tell them out loud. Tell them in your mind, "Who are you to tell me that? See, I'm not going to buy into that." If you give sanction to and agree with it, it becomes a part of you.

Here's another piece. Did anybody ever embarrass you or tell you that you were stupid, and then you couldn't sleep that night because you thought about it? Or when you're driving home you thought about it? In fact, you might have thought about it all week. You ever have something like that happen to you? Now, you must know that every time you think about it, whether it's happening to you or not, your subconscious is recording like it's happening to you again. Wow! Thoughts accumulate to become beliefs; experiences don't need to. If your self-talk is running wild with you about things that you did when you were 7, 17 or 27, it's as good as if it's happening to you again. You don't need experiences over and over. All you need to do is think about them, over and over.

UNIT 8
How My Beliefs are Formed

There's a formula that I want you to remember, because we're going to use this for the good, and we're going to keep ourselves from doing it with the bad. I x V = R. "I" stands for imagination, "V" for vividness (and "vividness" means any time we get a clear picture with emotion) and have the picture repeated, it becomes reality on the subconscious level. We build our own beliefs with our own thoughts. We always have. Have you ever made a mistake and said to yourself, "How could I have been so stupid?" It would be all right if we stop there, but we go on to answer the question. "I'll tell you how you can be stupid, stupid. You were in the lowest reading group in the second grade, remember?" You go back and remember that, and it's like it's happening to you again. Stop it! When I found this information my self-talk was terrible. Some people do it for a day, some for a week. Some have been doing it for most of their lives. Can you see what you've done to your beliefs? In areas that you have negative, destructive self-talk, you have kept your belief quite low in relationship to the wonderful potential that you have inside of yourself; and you self-regulated at your belief level, not your potential level.

You must eliminate all the sarcasm, devaluation (making yourself less valuable), belittling (making yourself be littler) that goes on in your mind. You aren't going to be great at this to start with, but that's the goal. You must, when you're immersed in school or at home or where ever you are, recognize this coming your way. You don't need to tell them to shut up, all you need to do is not give sanction to it. Don't agree with it.

You're going to build your own self-image with your own thoughts. In the next session, I'm going to tell you more about self-talk and how you go about doing it. Right now, what I want you to do is to recognize no more negative, destructive self-talk going on in your mind. That is what you can control. You will control it and your life will get better. I promise you.

UNIT 9
Building My Self-Image

Unit Overview

The subconscious mind is a literal mechanism – it does what you tell it. If, with your self-talk, you are dwelling on the negative, that is what gets assimilated into your version of "reality" in the subconscious. Since thoughts accumulate to become beliefs, all of your beliefs become negative, and reaching your potential will not be possible. Now, if your self-talk dwells on the positive possibilities of life, what will happen to your beliefs and your behavior?

Unit Objectives

By the end of this unit, I will:

*   understand the power of self-talk to determine my beliefs and actions.

*   remember to give credit where credit is due, including to myself, for a job well done.

*   be mindful of how I teach the young people in my life, so that I am coaching them forward into positive achievements.

You build your
own self-image
with your **own thoughts.**

UNIT 9
Building My Self-Image

Key Concepts

- Self-Talk

- Assimilate

- Gestalt

- Humility

- Subconscious

- Sure Enough Principle

- Truth

- Self-Image

- High Performance People

- Affirm

- Belief

- Attitudinal Balance Scale

- Reality

- Potential

- Reiterate

Notes

UNIT 9
Building My Self-Image

Notes

Pay attention to your self talk —

Know that you can change your
self talk — Your old memory is "their
"Someone else's"
opinion

You MUST have your own opinion

Money earned
— to be happy
— just enough $30 – $40,000
to be successful

UNIT 9
Building My Self-Image

Reflective Questions

- What are ten things I have done well in my life?

- What are some self-talk statements I could start practicing to create a better self-image?

UNIT 9
Building My Self-Image

Reflective Questions

- What is the self-image I have about myself right now?

- What would I like my new self-image to be?

UNIT 9
Building My Self-Image

Summary

If some of you had a friend who talked to you the way you talk to you, would you go around with them? Maybe. But some of you would be up for murder. You wouldn't let people talk to you the way you talk to yourself. What's the self-talk like around the people you socialize with? What's the self-talk like with your family? What's the self-talk like in the classroom? You must become very conscious of it so you don't just subconsciously assimilate it and start acting like it. You must become disciplined. Discipline in your mind is being your own person, thinking your own thoughts and not letting the negative and the destructive around you build your image of the way things are.

Now, I used to be a football coach. In the old days, we would video or film our games. And you know what we would do? We would set our players down, after each game, and show them, over and over, everything they did wrong until they got it down good. Then we'd go out and practice. And they'd go out and do the same stupid thing I just showed them. What's the matter with them? See, the more I dwell on what I don't want to have happen, the more I assimilate it in my mind and the more I then need to act or behave like it.

You must stop telling yourself what you don't want and you need to learn to tell yourself what you do want. You're going to become very good at this. You're even going to learn to tell yourself how you choose to be before you ever are. That is the right way to speak to yourself, because if you keep describing yourself as you presently are, you'll be like this next year. I'll talk to you about Gestalt psychology, and about what creates growth inside yourself. When we know how the mind works, we're going to speak to ourselves differently.

Many of you still have children at home. How are you speaking to your children? Are you telling them what's wrong with them? Are you ridiculing? Are you putting them down, or are you telling them the good in them? Are you seeing the good? And are you telling the child what's good in them? That is the right way to grow your child, because as you keep giving them images of where they're wrong or stupid or unwanted, they will grow up acting like the people they know themselves to be. We're going to become very constructive parents. We don't want to be like the coaches, showing other people what they're doing wrong. We don't want to do that to ourselves either. You must tell yourself what you want to do right, and I'll coach you through that as we get into it.

I want to show you a little more about how your mind works, because most of you were raised to believe that it's wrong or bad, egotistical, to think well of yourself. Any of you grow up like that, where you're not supposed to brag about yourself or think well of yourself? Well, how are you supposed to think? "You're supposed to be humble and tell yourself what's wrong with yourself." Oh, that's good. Remember, your subconscious is a literal mechanism. When you tell yourself, "Ah, shucks, you're no good" it records, "Ah shucks, you're no good."

UNIT 9
Building My Self-Image

If you look up the definition of humility, all it means is truth. So be truthful when you do something well. If you believe in God, give credit to God. Give credit to your family. Give credit to your teacher. Give credit to your coach. Give credit to your teammate, or your friend. But very important, from here forward, you must give credit to yourself. If you had anything to do with it, outside you could say, "Thank you for saying that," but inside I want you to say to yourself, "Darn I'm good. Yes, I am good at that." This is important, because you build your own self-image with your own thoughts. When you push away that you can be good, then what you're doing is not letting yourself grow on the inside. You need to build your own self-image with your own thoughts.

If I were going to coach you, what I would have you do is write a list of 10 things you've done well in your life. They don't need to be great things, but things that you were proud of. Then I'd have you go back and remember them just like they are happening to you again. I'd have you take that thought, while you're thinking about it, and I'd have you go into something that's coming up in front of you (a job or a new class or a difficult circumstance). I want you to go back and remember how good you were, and I want you to color your future with it.

For those of you who have children, I'd have you sit by your child's bedside before they fall sleep and ask them what went well today. "What did you do that you're so proud of?" Have them reiterate it, which means repeat it, so they record it like it's happening to them again. Then when they have that emotion, you ask, "And what are you looking forward to tomorrow?" You're going to drop their forethought, or their imagination, into tomorrow, and you're going to color it with a positive emotion. That's how high performance people think naturally. You're going to develop your children that way. You're going to build your own self-image with your own thoughts. You're going to help your children reiterate, which means recall, the good things that they've done. You're going to help them, in their mind, hold that thought, and then you're going to drop them into tomorrow so they color tomorrow the way they expect it to be.

Remember the "sure enough" principle? Well, if you expect a good day, you unconsciously cause it also. This is what people who are doing extremely well think like naturally. That's all. We study how people who do well think. Most people don't know. I'm teaching you how you think, and it's up to each one of you to use it as you choose to use it. If you don't use it, it's your own deal. My job is to just teach you what I know; your job is to use it. You can get good at it with your family, good at it with your children, good at it with your friends. You must catch yourself in the act of doing things right and tell yourself, but quietly. If somebody says, "My but you've done something well," and you say, "Yeah, I really am good at that, aren't I?" they're going to say, "Yes, and you make me throw up, too." So you need to be quiet about yourself to others.

You need to learn to affirm your children and the people around you. You're going to catch them doing things good, and you're going to tell them. Be specific about it. What you're doing is uplifting their image of themselves, particularly if they trust you and believe you and care for you. (If you don't know them and they don't care, it won't make any difference what anybody says.)

UNIT 9
Building My Self-Image

Now, I use the attitudinal balance scale or a Dutch kid with the water buckets, to show you how a self-image is built. Remember we said that positive or a negative attitude is the direction in which you lean. Every time you had a positive thought about yourself as you're growing up, we'll put a positive weight in one bucket. But if it's a negative thought, we'll put a negative weight in the other bucket. If you grew up with a whole bunch of negative weights about yourself as an artist, the negative side is going to get pretty heavy and you're going to lean in the negative direction. Remember, thoughts accumulate to become a belief. But, if you grew up with people who complimented you and praised you about something, you'd put positive weights in your attitudinal balance scale, and you'd lean in a positive direction. In other words, "I can do that. It's easy for me. I'm good at this."

Now remember, when you're good at something, you seek it. When you believe you're not so good at something, you won't take art lessons. "Why take them? Why take art lessons? I can't draw. Why should I do that?" "Why should I take singing lessons? I can't sing." You act in accordance with the truth, and you allow yourself to seek the knowledge or the skill.

Let's suppose you have a kid who's three years old, doesn't know if they can draw or not, but he's got an older brother or sister. So the kid makes a drawing, and the sister says, "That's stupid." Now that's a five year old sister telling a three year old his drawing is stupid. How come? "Look, you didn't even color inside the lines." Now, that sister just handed this kid a negative weight to accept or reject, and put it on their attitudinal balance scale. So the kid knows sister is really an artist because she has her artwork on the refrigerator. She's an authority. So, "Sister says I can't draw." He puts a big old negative weight on his attitudinal balance scale, and every time he passes the refrigerator he remembers sister said, "I can't draw," and he leans in a more negative direction. Remember, thoughts accumulate to become beliefs.

Now, let's suppose he's four or so and he's colored another. He's going to go to his older brother who is eight, and hanging around with his friends. He comes up to his brother, who doesn't want him around, and says, "Look, look!" The brother says, "That's a stupid drawing. Man, you can't draw. Whoever saw a green man?" Now, the kid doesn't know the brother doesn't know what he's talking about, but he's an authority. So he accepts with his own self-talk, "Brother said I'm stupid and can't draw," and puts a negative weight on his attitudinal balance scale, and leans more in the negative direction. "I can't draw. Everybody says so."

He's five now, and coloring away. He spends all morning on this one, and decides he's going to have mother appraise it. He gets mother by the hand, "Come see, come see!" Mother walks into the room and yells, "What have you done? Get that off the wall right now!" All he did was paint on the wall, but his self-talk is saying, "Sure can't draw, can I?" In fact, he's probably thinking he's down right darn dangerous to draw sometimes, and that's the truth.

His idea about self has been handed by him to others, and accepted by himself. Now he's in kindergarten, and after a couple days the teacher says, "All right, class. We have something really

UNIT 9
Building My Self-Image

fun to do. We're going to pass out the crayons and we're all going to draw." That kid thinks, "Like hell we are. I can't draw. In fact, it's down right dangerous to draw sometimes." That kid has the potential but not the belief.

So when you're in the sixth grade, you're not going to enter the poster contest. When you get a chance to take an art elective in school, you're going to say, "Not me!" If you get a chance to go to a ball game or theater or go to an art show, you ain't going to the art show. You behave in accordance with the truth as you believe it. Every idea, which is called a self-image, that each of you have about yourself has been built this way. You built it with your own self-talk.

I'm going to show you that you need to put a whole quantity of positive weights on your own attitudinal balance scale in areas where you want to grow. You must change your belief about yourself, and you start with your self-talk. You must eliminate the negative, and you must accentuate the positive. If you sit around and wait for people in your life to tell you how good you are so you can agree with them, you aren't going to live long enough to use your potential. They ain't coming. You need to do it yourself, but quietly.

UNIT 9
Building My Self-Image

UNIT 10
My Future is Up to Me

Unit Overview

We have already discovered that human beings are picture oriented. What we dwell on in our minds tends to come about in our lives. So, it is important to dwell on what we do want, and use our self-talk to see ourselves into the future – the future we want.

Unit Objectives

By the end of this unit, I will:

• know the four levels of self-talk.

• understand that I move toward what I think about.

• use my self-talk to change my beliefs, working toward what I want.

We **move toward,** and **become like,** that which we think about.

Our present thoughts **determine** our future.

UNIT 10
My Future is Up to Me

Key Concepts

- Self-Talk

- Beliefs

- Attitudes

- Subconscious

- Teleological → *corrects itself = Goal, Idea*

- Past-Present-Future Time Frames

- Visualize

- Gestalt

- Energy

- Creativity

- Awareness

- Goal-Setting

- Four Levels of Self-Talk

  - Negative Resignation

  - "I should . . ."

  - "I quit."

  - "I intend to . . ."

Notes

UNIT 10
My Future is Up to Me

Notes

Negative Resignation - count on negative outcome

I should [but I won't
   recognizing problem who intent of
      changing

I quit

* I intended to - I am better than that -

Move foward, become like
      that which we think about
Our present thoughts determine our
      future.

You are drawn to what you dwell on -

Three timeframes - the strongest idea controls you
   past thinkers can't move on
visualize NEW dissatisfied w/OLD
think about future before it occurs -
   getout - change the order - visualize creates
      problem → awareness can happen.

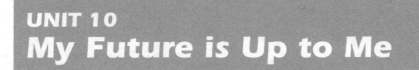

UNIT 10
My Future is Up to Me

Reflective Questions

• What is my self-talk like when I enter the classroom or the school?

• What past thoughts do I need to change to get a good picture of my future?

• How can I better handle negative talk I hear from others? What can I say to myself about it?

UNIT 10
My Future is Up to Me

Reflective Questions

- What do I want my future to look like after graduation?

- Knowing the importance of positive self-talk, what should I say to myself, quietly, when someone compliments me? Criticizes me?

UNIT 10
My Future is Up to Me

Summary

Here's an easy way to remember a little bit more about the power of your mind: Self-talk builds beliefs. Your beliefs control the attitude. The attitude controls the feeling. The feeling controls the action you'll take, and the action you take controls the results. So, don't get too hung up on the results. Go all the way back to the self-talk. Most people try to work on the results, and you should be working on the other end.

There are four levels of self-talk. I'm going to give you two now, and I want you to eliminate these two as best you can. One is negative resignation. Have you been around people who say, "I can't. It won't work"? They resign themselves to a negative outcome, and the subconscious just shuts right down.

Then the second level of self-talk only makes you feel guilty, and doesn't change you a bit. You know, "I should really stop smoking. I should really be nice. I should start studying." But your subconscious says, "But I won't." So "should" only recognizes the problem and has no intent of changing it. A better way would be the third way, which is, "I quit. I stop. No more." But that's still not good enough.

As we go under and over and through more of this material, you're going to see the fourth way is the way you're going to talk to yourself, and the way you're going to lead people: Tell yourself what you want to do in the future. "I'm better than that, and the next time I intend to…" You must give yourself a picture of what you're going to do to replace what it was you were doing. That is connected to how your mind works.

Now, let me show you another step. We know that human beings are teleological. You're like a guided missile. A guided missile seeks objects. They may seek the heat of a jet, or seek sound. They could seek metal. Human beings seek pictures or ideas. You, being a teleological mechanism, are different from a bullet or an arrow. If you shoot a bullet and the target moves, you can't correct. A teleological mechanism can correct itself in flight. What you really need is a target. What you really need is someplace to go. What you really need is what is called a goal or an idea. "I have an idea, an aspiration, a vision, a thought."

With your self-talk, you give yourself an idea of what you're seeking, otherwise you'll find your subconscious will seek the negative or it will seek the way it is. Here's something that you should write down, remember, and make a part of the way you think for awhile: We move toward and we become like that which we think about. We move physically and emotionally toward that which we think about. I'm going to add one more piece to that: Our present thoughts determine our future.

Let's come back to the first statement that we move toward and we become like that which we think about, because we think in pictures. Whatever the language is, the words give you a picture. You move toward whatever is in your mind, whether it's good for you or not. It doesn't matter. You seek the picture. This is the reason you must give yourself objects to seek that are what you desire in your life, not the objects you don't desire.

UNIT 10
My Future is Up to Me

Watch a little kid ride a bicycle for the first time, right as they get on the bike. They're not very good at steering the bicycle. As they're going down a path or down a road, they see a rock. Now, they don't want to hit the rock, but because they don't know better, they keep looking at the rock. Now, they don't want to hit the rock, but I'll bet you anything they'll run – Smacko! – right into the rock. Why? Your physiology is attached to what you're looking at. Do you know how you steer things? When you steer a car, your car is steered by what you're looking at. This little kid, not knowing, looks at the rock, what they don't want to hit, and they steer the bicycle right into the rock. Then they get mad at the rock! Now, why would they hit the rock? Because, you move towards what you think about. If you focus your mind on what you don't want, you're still going to run into it.

Now, when you get good on your bicycle and you see a rock, how might you think? You think the way you want to go, and your bicycle steers automatically. The same thing happens with a car. Formula One race drivers, the ones on the big speedways, are taught that if their car is going out of control and heading to the wall, they're suppose to look to the recovery point. Now, ordinarily you look where you're going, wouldn't you? However, if you look where you're going, you'll steer your car into the wall. So, the discipline is, even though you're heading to the wall, focus your attention on where you want to end up.

This rule is going to be so important and easy to remember about raising your children, raising yourself and how you're going to live your life, because if you dwell on what you don't want, you're moving yourself into it. You're drawn to what you dwell on. You move toward and you become like that what you think about.

Did you ever know anybody who was accident-prone? What do you think accident-prone people think about? Having accidents. They keep dwelling on what they don't want to have happen, and sure enough – Smacko! – they run into something. Now, what do you think the people around them, who know who they are, keep reminding them of? Watch, before you leave the house, "Be careful dear," your mom might say. "You know how you are." Almost forgot. "I'm glad you didn't forget. It's because I love you, I keep reminding you of your problem." So, the more you dwell on what you don't want to have happen, the more it will happen.

Control your self-talk or your self-talk controls you. Listen to the people around you and what they're talking about. Are you hanging around people who are always talking about what they don't want? In athletics, it's called a slump because they keep thinking about the mistake they just made, and they make it again the next time.

There are three time frames that human beings think in. You're aware of those, of course: the past, the present, and the future. You always seek the direction of the strongest picture. You always move in the direction of the strongest idea. So, when you're dwelling on how it used to be, you become unhappy with where you are, and you long to go back. There's another rule: As I visualize the new, which means think about, I become dissatisfied with the old. As I think about

UNIT 10
My Future is Up to Me

the new, I become dissatisfied with the old. That's how our mind works. That's why commercials work. As you visualize the new, you don't want to stay with the old.

If you are moving toward what you think about and you keep thinking about how things used to be, you're unhappy with where you are. You long to quit school and go back to the old. You long to get out of where you are, to go back to the old familiar. You must know how your mind works.

But what about people who only think present tense? (Present tense means in the now.) They will say, "Well, I'm not going to talk about the future. I'm talking about reality as it presently exists. I'm a realist." Well, if you keep telling yourself how something is and you move towards what you think about; if your present thoughts determine your future, and the only thing you talk about is the state of your emotion right now or your financial state or the way you're living; then what would tomorrow look like, if what I'm saying has any validity to it? What would tomorrow look like if you keep talking about today? Yep, same thing. Change doesn't occur if you're talking about what you're observing.

People who are really successful and changing and growing, if you study how they think and listen to their self-talk, think about the future before it happens. They are always thinking future, but get this, as though it's already done. They think about the future as though you already have the degree; you have already passed the class; that you already are the person you choose to be. They think about the future with their self-talk. They talk to themselves and they talk to others like they've already graduated, but they're only a year into school. They already have the job but they haven't even applied.

This is the way I'm going to encourage you to speak to yourself – to speak to yourself of the future before it ever occurs. What's going to happen inside your system, you're going to see, is you're causing yourself to be thrown out of order. We're going to call that Gestalt. You're going to find that you're always seeking order in your mind. Causing yourself to grow will mean you must deliberately throw your system out of order, correctly, by seeing yourself in the new job. Then, you will look around, and you don't have it. You have a problem, and that problem will create the energy you need and the creativity and the awareness you need to make the future happen. This is the key to setting goals or making changes – to think in the future in the present tense.

UNIT 11
I'm Worth It!

Unit Overview

Giving sanction, or agreeing with, what others say to us, about ourselves, is a risky business. What we are really agreeing with are the opinions of others, and they may not be "the truth." Then, we use our self-talk to reinforce a bad opinion, and before we know it, we tear down our sense of self-esteem. We need to remember our successes, and assimilate them fully, so that we escalate our self-worth, our self-esteem.

Unit Objectives

By the end of this unit, I will:

- understand that self-esteem is my estimate of my self-worth.

- build my own self-esteem with my own thoughts.

- take the time to assimilate my successes into my sense of self-esteem.

- be aware of those around me who may want to pull me back, and make a special effort to build up others around me.

Most people
pass through their **accomplishments**
too quickly and too lightly
to assimilate them.

UNIT 11
I'm Worth It!

Key Concepts

- Self-Talk
- Self-Esteem
- Subconscious
- Tension
- Respect
- Affirmation
- High-Performance People
- Conscious Level

Notes

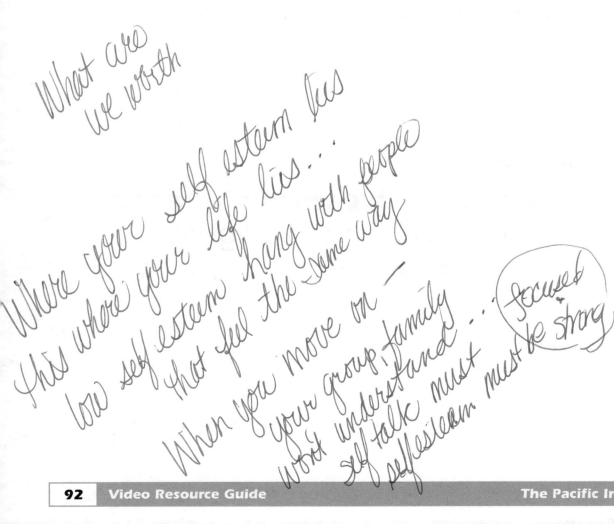

What are we worth

Where your self esteem lies

This where your life lies . . .

low self esteem hang with people that feel the same way

When you move on —

your group, family

won't understand . . .

self talk must [focused]

self esteem must be strong

UNIT 11
I'm Worth It!

Notes

UNIT 11
I'm Worth It!

Reflective Questions

- What are three academic skill areas where I have high self-esteem?

- What are some academic areas where my self-esteem could be improved?

UNIT 11
I'm Worth It!

Reflective Questions

• How can I help others develop their self-esteem?

• What are ten things that have gone well in my life and I am very proud of?

UNIT 11
I'm Worth It!

Summary

What has self-esteem got to do with anything? What do you suppose self-esteem actually means? Suppose you have a car and you want to go sell your car. You don't know what it is worth, so you walk outside and the first person you come to you say, "Tell me what my car is worth." They say, "Oh about $10." Well, it might be worth a lot more. But when you go around and ask anybody what it might be worth, you're in trouble.

Many of us go out and elicit from others what they think we are worth. Self-esteem is a self estimate of your own worth. Too often, we have had people tell us what we're worth. Maybe you went with somebody who was an abuser and put you down, or you know a sister or have a friend who has. Before long, because she thought she was in love with this person, she allowed this person to tell her what he thought she might be worth. You may have had parents who didn't know much better, who were always putting you in your place, or teachers who would always put you in your place. You grew up using your own self-talk, telling yourself what you thought you're worth.

Your appraisal of your own worth is so important, and here's why. You draw to yourself the kind of social and love relationships that you feel worthy of receiving. If a social or love relationship comes to you, that you think is too good for you, you will subconsciously destroy it or push it away. If you have low self-esteem, you will attract people who are similar to you. If you have a high self-worth you will attract people to you with high self-worth. It's going to be important to see why that's a good idea.

If you have low self-esteem and I say, "What kind of a job are you looking for?" Somebody with low self-esteem will say, "Anything." How much money do you think you should earn? "Oh, whatever they want to offer." But if you have a high self-esteem, you're not going to look for anything. You're going to look for a job that fits your idea of what you're worth. When they say, "How much do you want to earn?" if it's genuinely strong, authentic self-esteem, you will seek a job that will pay you not just anything, but what you feel you're worth.

I've asked guys who were really down and coming out of prisons, "Tell me what kind of a car you're going to get when you get out?" Do you know what their reply would be? I can almost write it out for you. "Just some wheels." Anything is okay. When your self-esteem is low, anything is okay. I don't want anything to be okay for you. I want you to decide that you're worthy inside of having good things come to you. You need to, in your own mind, build your own self-concept with your own self-talk. You can't sit around, as I said earlier, and wait for people to applaud you.

Now, this research comes out of Stanford University's highest level of psychological research. Most people pass through their accomplishments too quickly and too lightly to assimilate them. "Oh, it was nothing. I had nothing to do with that. Ah, shucks, it was nothing." Too quickly and too lightly. Now, remember your subconscious is a literal mechanism. When you say, "Ah, shucks, it was nothing," it records, "Ah, shucks, it was nothing." You must wallow in your suc-

UNIT 11
I'm Worth It!

cess, like a pig in slop, but you can't do it out loud. You must do it quietly. You must build your own self-esteem with your own thoughts. You must tell yourself when you're doing things right. You must tell yourself when you're doing something good. And those of you who do have children, and friends that you care about, I want you to look for good things in them. I want you to tell them how you feel about them and how good they are. And do it over and over so that you're constantly escalating, escalating, escalating.

There's another thing about this. When you have a low level of self-esteem and you're around people who you think are more important than you or wealthier than you in some way you'll be full of tension because you're faking like you belong there. You're trying hard to pretend like you belong. The pressure will get upon you, and you unconsciously want to get out of there as fast as you can and go back to being around people where you can naturally be yourself. What I want you to do is to raise, in your mind, not falsely, that you are an important and valuable person, and you are worthy of respect.

You must keep escalating your own self-concept, your own self-esteem, with your own self-talk. There is a process of written affirmations that I'm going to give you, so that you draw to yourself the kind of relationships, the kind of jobs, the kind of income and the kind of neighborhood that you deserve. If you don't, all you take is what was naturally assimilated accidentally by you – carelessly and by default – because you didn't know any better.

You are going to start escalating and raising your own internal idea of how good you are. But you need to be careful, because if you're hanging around people who have low self-esteem, guess what? They are intimidated by somebody who has high self-esteem. They won't tell you they are intimidated. But do you know how you can tell? They become the most devaluative, demeaning, fault-finding people to be around. They are critical, cutting, tearing and sarcastic. "Who are you to think you can go to college? Who are you to think you can get a job like that? Why don't you quit fooling yourself and get back where you belong?" They will try to grab hold of you and pull you down. Why? So that they look better. This is subconscious level stuff, not conscious level.

When you are around devaluative, demeaning, sarcastic, belittling people, they are low self-esteemed. They are trying to make themselves look better by putting you below them in their place. Husbands, who have low self-esteem, will be intimidated by a wife who is rising above the husband's opinion of himself. I've heard husbands say, "Who are you to think you can go out and get a job like that. You can't even organize the house. Why don't you get down where you belong? Who are you to think that you can do that?" Honest to goodness. You must recognize that some of you are caught up in that. You get caught up with people who are like that, and it's your choice to stay with it or outgrow it, stay with it and become like it. It is your mind that determines the quality of life out there. The kind of people, the kind of relationships, the kind of jobs, the way your world is going to go in your future, has a lot to do with the way you feel inside about yourself, and that is true.

UNIT 11
I'm Worth It!

When you study how high performance people think, notice this: Children of royalty are treated royally, because some day that kid will be king. What if you tore them down, beat them up, told them they were no good, and then said, "Go out and act like a king?" Can't do it. So you escalate, elevate; you raise the level of opinion. I know that in many worlds, it's just the opposite of that – run down, tear down and put down.

You must eliminate all the negative self-talk that goes on around you. Now, how do you eliminate it? You can't tell them to shut up. You don't need to accept it, but you can remove yourself from it, too. You must eliminate it if you have kids. You must stop it in your family, because those kids are going to be torn apart on the playground by bullies. Why would they bully? Because they're trying to put somebody beneath them, in their place. You will run into bullies in school, and in the workplace. Anybody who has a low self-concept is going to try to pull you down. Don't you let them. This is the essence of why people devalue and belittle and make fun of and tear apart others.

We work a lot inside of jails and penitentiaries, and the child molester inside of a maximum security penitentiary without protective custody will be killed within a week. They have been designated as the lowest form of life. Someone will kill this person and walk around like, "Look at the noble thing we've done. We've rid the earth of this person." Did they kill them for nobility? No, to look "better than." You don't have to kill with gas in their cell and a match to follow. You can kill anybody, any child's esteem, by tearing them apart. You can tear another spouse apart. You can tear a friend apart. No more.

Raise your self-image so you allow the people around you to have a high self-image. Employers will seek you because they like the way you take risks. They like the way you go after life. They like the way you challenge the world. High self-esteemed people will go after and fight Hell with a bucket of water. That is the way I want you to think.

UNIT 12
Make the Unfamiliar Familiar

Unit Overview

In our past, when we really didn't want to go somewhere or do something, we found excellent reasons for not going or doing. What we may not have realized is that we were coming face-to-face with our comfort zones. While some comfort zones are good for us, others hold us back; and it is time that we learn how to expand those limiting comfort zones and allow ourselves to grow.

Unit Objectives

By the end of this unit, I will:

*   understand that I am a self-regulating mechanism.

*   be aware of my reactions to situations, and know that these reactions are signals of comfort zone issues that may be holding me back.

*   know an easy process to help me make the unfamiliar familiar, releasing me from the restrictions of my limiting comfort zones.

Our **comfort zones** regulate our effectiveness.

UNIT 12
Make the Unfamiliar Familiar

Key Concepts

- Comfort Zones
- Self-Regulation
- Self-Image
- Potential
- Truth
- Tension
- Subconscious
- Visualize
- Imagination
- Self-Talk
- Feedback
- Anxiety
- Creativity

Notes

UNIT 12
Make the Unfamiliar Familiar

Notes

Comfort Zone

raise your comfort zone

self regulating

self image

→ Get Back
OR Change or modify regulating mech.
Recreate Old behavior

unknown
unfamiliar

*tension
uptight

As I visualize the new
I become dissatified with the old

UNIT 12
Make the Unfamiliar Familiar

Reflective Questions

- What situation caused me to feel out of my comfort zone? Why did this situation make me feel uncomfortable?

- What activities am I currently avoiding because they are out of my comfort zone?

UNIT 12
Make the Unfamiliar Familiar

Reflective Questions

- Do I resist change? Why?

- How can expanding my comfort zones help me be more successful at school? At work?

UNIT 12
Make the Unfamiliar Familiar

Summary

In the course overview, I talked about going into the wrong rest room. I was talking about being in or out of your "comfort zone." This is another way of talking about self-regulating your effectiveness.

Let's say there is a thermostat in a room that controls the temperature, you set the temperature so that it is at 70 degrees. Because it's operating electrically with an air conditioning unit and a heater, if the temperature rises above 70, an electrical impulse would be sent to the air conditioning unit to turn on and cool it off. If it drops below the set point, the heater comes on and raises it back up. It self-regulates with electrical feedback based upon where you have it set. If you set it at 80, and the temperature rises above 80, now it will turn the air conditioning unit on, but if it drops below 80, like to say 78, it turns the heater on. So, a self-regulating mechanism operates based on a set point.

The reason I give you that is because it's modeled after you in your mind. Your self-image of how good you are – of the kind of person you are, grades you get, relationships you deserve, your ideas about yourself – is the set point at which you self-regulate your effectiveness. We don't know how much potential we have, but the ceiling on the use of your potential is called your self-image. It is the truth that you know about yourself; it's your idea of how good you are. Now, you don't need to operate exactly like yourself morally, socially, academically or financially. As long as you stay relatively close to behaving like you know you are, instead of electrical feedback, you'll be free of tension, free of anxiety. You get uptight whenever you move away from the way you are "supposed to be." You start feeling anxious when you move away from the way you're "supposed to be."

Since you don't need to be just like yourself, as long as you have relatively closely stayed to yourself, you'll stay within what we're going to call a comfort zone. You're not just rigidly moral or rigidly honest or rigidly this way. However, if you get too far away from your standard of how you should behave, you're going to get uptight. Now, whenever you feel this tension, it stimulates inside of yourself creativity that tells you, first of all, "Get back where you belong." If you can't get back, you just re-create your old behavior, your old way, in a new place. The third way is modify or change the regulating mechanism.

What happens when you're out of your comfort zone? Socially, morally, academically, racially, as the anxiety increases, it blocks the input of information. Somebody could be speaking to you, and if you feel out of place, it doesn't get through to your brain. You block it, not because you're stupid, but because you're out of place. If you have the information, but if you feel out of place, anxiety interferes with your memory, so you can't remember. You can sit in the class talking to a friend about the subject, but you get up in front of the full class, and your mind goes blank. You get up in front of an assembly of the whole school, and your mind goes blank, not because the information isn't in there, but because when you're out of place, it squeezes off recall just like a

UNIT 12
Make the Unfamiliar Familiar

kink in the hose. So your subconscious says, "Don't do it again. You always make a fool of yourself. Don't go. Stay with the familiar. Don't go."

Another thing that happens when you're out of your comfort zone is your vocal cords lengthen and your voice changes. If you go to a used car dealer, and the guy was selling you a used car, it isn't what they say. The tone of voice will give them away if they're lying, because if you're lying your voice changes. It doesn't matter the words you're saying, it's the tone of voice that gives you away. When you're out of place, your voice changes.

When you're out of your comfort zone, the muscles in your upper body start to constrict, and they tighten down on your rib cage, which tightens down on your lungs. You'll hear people say, "I've been under pressure lately. I feel uptight about this." Now, you see, it is the difference, not whether it's bad or worse or better; it is the difference that makes you feel this way - the difference socially, environmentally, colors of people, people you think are better than you or worse than you.

When you feel out of place, it hits you. It hits everybody. When you're out of your comfort zone, your subconscious says, "Go back to where you belong." Now, you don't tell yourself to go back. Do you know what you say? "That's stupid. Who wants to be around those kind of people. Why should I want to do that? I like it where I am." That's your subconscious telling you to go back to the familiar, to go back where it's safe. Now, it might be that it's stupid. You must decide whether it is your comfort zone or whether it really is a dumb idea. You seek psychological and emotional safety naturally. Everybody does. You go back to where you already know how to do something. You go back to where things look right for you, where they look familiar to you.

Your job will be, as I teach you, to make the new familiar to you – to practice in your mind going safely into a new location, with people who are different, going into all kinds of situations. You're going to take yourself and your imagination correctly, with first person, present tense and positive imagery. "As I visualize the new, I become dissatisfied with the old."

If you don't do this and you force yourself to be up in front of the class, into a new situation, you're going to blow it. You're not going to remember. You'll be uptight and your subconscious will find all kinds of reasons to have you get out of here and go back to where people look like you, act like you, and are like you. You won't use your potential unless you really know how to expand all this.

A few more things happen when you're out of your comfort zone. Your stomach secretes more digestive juices than you need. Have you ever heard anybody say, "This job makes me sick?" It does, because your stomach is getting upset when you try hard to be different, go different, act different, than you unconsciously know you are. When you force yourself, your head's not only pounding and you're not getting information in or out; your voice is changing, your rib cage is caving, and you're puking up on the toilet all the time. Your talk is, "There is no way I'm going to

UNIT 12
Make the Unfamiliar Familiar

go," and then you're going to say, "This can't be right or I wouldn't feel this bad." Yes, it can. It's just your comfort zone, folks.

And that's not the end of it. Now your knees get shaky, so you lose balance. Your blood pressure goes up, moisture occurs immediately on the surface of your skin. I don't know if any of you have been attached to a lie detector, but that's how they work. You attach a lie detector to the surface of your skin, and when you deviate from the truth, you short the machine out, because you sweat immediately when you tell a lie. When you don't tell the truth, you immediately short the machine out. All of this hits and tells you, "What am I doing here? Go back where you belong!"

Now, your subconscious doesn't say, "Go back." You just find fault with the new to go back to the old. "My kids need me. I don't have the money. It isn't the right time." It comes up with reasons why you should not go.

Now, with what I'm going to teach you, you will learn how to raise your comfort zone. I'm going to teach you how to expand your comfort zone, and you're going to do it by visualizing processes, by using your imagination. That's why astronauts use simulators, why pilots practice in their mind, why Olympic athletes practice in their mind. That's what martial arts do in tai chi or kung fu – you practice in your mind.

UNIT 13
The Next Time . . .

Unit Overview

We now know how powerful our self-talk is, and how it has affected our thinking and behavior in the past. In fact, for many of us, our self-talk has been pretty negative. So far in this course, we have been working toward changing our self-talk from negative to positive, and now we go one step further by learning to give ourselves "next time" goals to create that new picture of ourselves in our subconscious.

Unit Objectives

By the end of this unit, I will:

- understand how my self-talk controls my performance reality.

- stop my negative self-talk about my performance and give myself new performance goals with the phrase, "The next time, I intend to . . ."

I'm better than that.
The next time,
I **intend** to . . .

UNIT 13
The Next Time . . .

Key Concepts

- Affirmations
- Subconscious
- Neuron
- Self-Image
- Assimilate
- Self-Talk (Words-Pictures-Feelings)
- Performance Reality
- Behavior
- Creative Subconscious
- Teleological
- Goals
- Belief
- Truth
- Conscious
- Potential

Notes

UNIT 13
The Next Time . . .

Notes

Self talk creates SELF IMAGE

1) WORDS:

2) PICTURES:

3) FEELING:

assimilate: making yourself fit
performance reality controlled by self talk

UNIT 13
The Next Time . . .

Reflective Questions

• If I let go and let the real me flow, how is it?

• What are some positive words I could use in my conversations that trigger a positive image in my mind?

UNIT 13
The Next Time . . .

Reflective Questions

- What are some negative words I should avoid when speaking because they trigger a negative picture in my mind?

- As I look forward to learning more about goals and my future, what are some important goals I have in each of these areas? Spiritual, Marriage/Relationships, Family, Physical Health, Mental Health, Personal, Social, Vocational/Job, Retirement, Recreation/Leisure time, Community Service.

UNIT 13
The Next Time . . .

Summary

This next piece is going to be very helpful in controlling what goes on in your mind. Remember, the key is to control how you speak to yourself, in your mind. Later on, I'm going to show you how to write out goals, which we'll call affirmations. By the way, I should tell you what an affirmation is: it's a statement of fact or a statement of belief. The Pledge of Allegiance to the flag is an affirmation. If you made a Girl Scout oath in your day, that was an affirmation. Prayer is an affirmation. An affirmation doesn't need to be positive, it can be negative. It's simply a statement of fact. Now, when I say "fact," it doesn't need to be a real fact. To you it's a fact. It's the truth to me. Remember, a belief doesn't need to be true to be a belief. Many of us are walking around with a lot of stuff in our mind that has nothing to do with "the truth;" it's just "our truth."

So, you're making all kinds of affirmations. If you said, "I'm tired. I can't seem to sleep," or "I can't seem to get myself past 3 o'clock in the afternoon," that's an affirmation. "I could never learn that," is an affirmation. Remember, your subconscious accepts literally — without question — what you say. In other words, even if it's not good for you, when you tell yourself, "I'm tired," your subconscious says, "Okay. You didn't need to be. But if you say so, so be it." "This is hard for me." "Well, it wasn't going to need to be, but if you said so, so be it." I want you to become very aware that how you speak to yourself, all the time, is what your subconscious is trying to carry out. So, be careful what you tell it to do. Some of you tell it some dumb stuff.

Here is how we start changing, now. What we've said up to this point is that you and I have what we call a self-image. Remember, a self-image is your opinion that is recorded in the neuron structure of your brain about how smart you are, what kind of a social person you are, what things you're afraid of, what things you like to do and what you don't like to do: in short, what you know about yourself. You have hundreds, if not thousands, of ideas about you can sing, can't sing; can draw, can't draw; can't cook, can cook. What kind of a driver am I? What kind of a skier am I?

What formed the ideas about yourself? You weren't born with them, you assimilated them, and what assimilates the idea about yourself, is your self-talk. Self-talk is that three dimensional form of thought: words, picture, and feeling. Your self-talk is going on all the time, and it either strengthens what you know about yourself or it lowers it. Your self-talk forms your self-image.

The reason why that is so important is because your self-image controls what we're going to call your "performance reality." Now, what does performance reality mean? See, your self-image controls how you act when you're not faking it, how you act when you let go and not consciously try to control your behavior. It's how I act when I allow my automatic pilot to take over. "But if I'm just myself, nobody will like me. If I'm myself, nobody will want to be around me. If I'm myself, nobody will hire me." See your self-image? So what do you do? You go someplace, and try to pretend like you're special. You override your self-image. If you let go and let the real you flow, how is it? That's the key.

UNIT 13
The Next Time . . .

Your performance reality is how you really behave when you're not trying to impress somebody. "As I think, I am." This is the control of your behavior. When you want to improve your performance, improve how you behave and how you feel, or what you'll let yourself do, don't work on your performance; work on your self-image.

What really shapes the self-image, and always has, is your self-talk – how you've talked to yourself. Now here's the problem: You're always judging yourself. "How did I do?" always goes on in your mind. Was it like me or not me? Let's say you blew a test or you got up in front of a group and screwed up giving a talk. Going in, you knew you would. You would say to yourself, with your self-talk, "Well, that's like me. I've always blown it. I always seem to screw up." What you do is observe how you're behaving and then, with your self-talk, you tell yourself how you are which just hardens your self-image. The next time you have to blow it again.

Now, what if you got up and gave a talk totally unlike yourself. It went well, and people would say, "Wonderful! You got an A. Nice going!" Do you know what your self-talk would be like, if you don't think you can do it? It goes in another vein. You'd say to yourself, "Well, I don't know what happened. That's really not like me. I always screw it up. I don't know what happened. I got lucky." You will not allow yourself to change your self-image, because when you do well you tell yourself it was luck or it was an accident. "I don't know what happened."

See, your self-image is so important. You must understand on that subconscious level, your creative subconscious is trying to keep you like you, even if like you is dumb, and you don't need to be; poor and you don't need to be; a screw up and you don't need to be. The creative subconscious' job is to make you act like your present self-image – not your potential, but like your present self-image.

You're always guiding your behavior on your present self-image. If you mess up and your self-image matches it, your self-talk will be, "There I go again. I always do this." Unfortunately, what makes it difficult to change when you do well, is because you say to yourself, "I don't know what happened. That's not like me. I usually fall down in places like that. I usually screw up. I'm always spilling things. I can never bake anything correctly. I never have been able to remember. I don't know why it happened." You reject good performance.

Here's what you're going to do from now on. When you observe how you're behaving and you don't want it to be that way, or you see your performance beneath the way you want it in the future, in your mind you're going to tell yourself, "I'm better than that. No more. That is not like me anymore."

Here's the key phrase that you're going to use whenever you observe something at school or home, or in any part of your life that you don't want to behave like that anymore: "That is not like me anymore. The next time I intend to..." and you will use that fourth stage of self-talk I was talking about. You're going to give yourself a picture of how you want to be the next time. It's all right to shut off your self-talk from being negative, but this key phrase needs to become a habit with you:

UNIT 13
The Next Time . . .

"The next time I intend to..." and you go on to tell yourself how you want to study, or how you want to converse, or how you want to handle the emotional situation with the relationship.

This is what all great athletes do. If they drop the ball and tell themselves, "There I go again," the next time they'll drop it. So what they need to say is, "I'm better than that. The next time I intend to look the ball right into my hands." "The next time I intend to..." is the key phrase that you must get into your mind. It's an easy one, because it shuts off all the negative, destructive self-talk. No more, "What's the matter with me anyway? How could I have been so stupid." Remember, if you don't control your self-talk, your self-talk controls you.

Now, this is also theologically sound, not just psychologically sound. If you do something that offends somebody or offends God, you ask forgiveness of God. If you look at the sacrament of penance, it is just, "Go and sin no more." Do it right the next time. It's not enough to say "No more," although you'll stop. You must give yourself a picture in your mind of the way you choose to be, the way you want your life to be, the way you want your behavior to be. See, you need to have something teleologically to seek. So, you shut off the negative and you give yourself the positive. That is the way high performance people work and operate in their mind.

What I want you to do for the next 24 hours is to play a game of no put down. What that means is I want you to eliminate all the, "What's the matter with me?" and "How could I have been so stupid?" No negative affirmations on yourself or anybody else for 24 hours. I know what you're thinking: This will be the quietest 24 hours I've ever spent. You might as well go home and go to bed. When you do something wrong, you say to yourself, "I'm better than that, that's not like me." When you do something right you need to say, "That is like me." You're going to say to yourself, "YES!" inside. Out loud you will affirm others; inside, quietly, you will affirm yourself strongly. 24 hours, no negative affirmations. The only thing you're going to do is accentuate the positive.

UNIT 14
Putting Life on a Want-To

Unit Overview

We have all felt, at one time or another, like we were being forced into doing something against our will. We may have done it, but we rebelled every step of the way. We felt pushed and we pushed back, and it used up a lot of energy while it made us feel unhappy. What if we put life on a "want to" basis, and used all that energy and creativity toward making a happy life for ourselves and those around us?

Unit Objectives

By the end of this unit, I will:

• understand fear-based "have to" restrictive motivation.

• understand value-based "want to" constructive motivation.

• know how to put my life on a want-to basis.

• take accountability for my decisions and accept the consequences.

Put your life on a
"want to" basis.

UNIT 14
Putting Life on a Want-To

Key Concepts

- Motivation

- Energy

- Self-Talk

- Restrictive Motivation

- Constructive Motivation

- Fear

- Have-to / Want-to / Choose to

- Push / Push Back

- Procrastination

- Subconscious

- Affirmation

- Creative Avoidance

- Goal

- Coercion

- Self-Esteem

- Accountable

- Compliant

- Mind-set

Notes

UNIT 14
Putting Life on a Want-To

Notes

Motivation
Restrictive (on fear)
Constructive (value
RESTRICTIVE MOTIVATION
Only one "have to" — have to die
* Everything is a choice w/consequences
* When pushed, you always push back

PROCRASTINATION
Creative AVOIDANCE
Slovenly work - only good enough NOT EXCELLENCE

Constructive motivation releases the energy
inside of you, its based on free will.
Focus on good —

I don't have to ... I choose to ... I intend to
Do what you want to do —
except consequences
I need to this ____
because ____

UNIT 14
Putting Life on a Want-To

Reflective Questions

• What are some have-to's that I have in my life?

• Now that I realize there are no have-to's in my life, what are some of the reasons I choose to do what I do?

UNIT 14
Putting Life on a Want-To

Reflective Questions

- Where have I let other people affect my self-esteem?

- Where do I give up accountability to someone else? Why?

UNIT 14
Putting Life on a Want-To

Summary

Do you ever have trouble getting yourself to do something? Let me give you an idea about something that I found a long time ago. This was so important for me, and it has to do with how I talk to myself in my mind. It has to do with the way I, almost, intimidate or bully myself. The other thing that I want to do is to make sure that from here and now, as best you can, you drive fear out of what you do and the way you live.

There are two kinds of motivation that I want to talk to you about. Motivation is the energy that you create inside yourself to get you to do your work or to live your life. It isn't some inspirational kind of a thing. It's the energy inside of you that either causes you to go after something or run away from it. These two kinds of motivation appear in your self-talk, but you'll also need to watch the people around you and how they try to motivate you. Sometimes the way others speak to you causes you to engage in behavior that is opposite of what they really want, or that you want.

The two kinds of motivation are restrictive motivation, which is based on fear; and constructive motivation, which is based primarily on the value you see in your mind of what it is that you want to do. Do you see the difference?

Most of you have been raised – by your families, or churches, or school, or teachers like I used to be – who use the fear one. This is totally not the way I want you to run your life or your family in the future. Those of you who are going to have businesses in the future, you're going to be much more successful as a leader when you go to constructive motivation.

Now, you can always tell when you're being restrictively motivated because it will have these two words attached to it, "Or else." Do it, or else something awful will happen to you, and let me tell you about the awful. It's "My way or the highway."

Think about all the things that you "have to" do for yourself in the morning. You have to get up and get the kids ready; you have to do your homework. What would be some other have to's? You have to put clothes on; feed the cat; eat breakfast; be on time; go to work. Okay, now stop. Here's the way I want you to be thinking: There is only one have-to in the world (although there maybe a few more). You have to die; everything else is a matter of choice. You don't have to take a shower, and you don't have to put your clothes on. You could just go to school without them. It is do what you want to do, but accept the consequences of your choices.

You must come to the realization that you are operating from free will. When you stop and think about it, there are very few have-to's in the whole world. But when you tell yourself you have to, something happens inside of you. When pushed, you push back. When you feel pushed, you always push back. When you push your children into something, they'll push back. Now how do you push back? You push back through procrastination. When you feel you are being coerced against your will into doing your work or into going to school or having to be on time, your subconscious causes you to slow down. Amazing! It doesn't make any difference, if I'm telling you that you have to or if you tell yourself you have to. Your subconscious does the same.

UNIT 14
Putting Life on a Want-To

I want you to become aware of how often you're telling yourself you have to do something. Remember, it's an affirmation and your subconscious accepts it literally; it's not arguing back. So when you say, "I have to do my homework," watch how tired you get. Watch how you put it off. Procrastination is caused whenever you feel coerced against your will. You're a person of dignity inside, even if you don't recognize it. When you feel you're being pushed or coerced against your will, whether by yourself or somebody else, you slow down because your subconscious says, "You say I have to, but if I had my way, I would rather be doing something else. But, I don't have my way. I'm being forced against my will." Your subconscious says, "Okay, but you've got to do this other thing, too."

Creative avoidance is caused when you tell yourself you "have to." Do you ever find yourself, when it comes time to doing homework, doing a lot of stuff you don't need to do? Your mind starts seeing things that have nothing to do with the goal, because when you try to force yourself into the work or the goal, your subconscious is trying to get you out of it.

Now, it doesn't matter whether I'm forcing you, or you're forcing you. When you tell yourself you "have to," your subconscious is trying to get out of it. Don't you think it would be good, from here forward, to eliminate have to? It really is. Otherwise, you get procrastination, creative avoidance, and the third one, slovenly work. "Slovenly" means only good enough to get by and never striving to excellence. That is how your mind works.

Those of you who have kids, tell them to, "Get in there and wash the dishes or else you can't go out and play!" Watch. You're coercing them against their will, and they'll say, "I've got to do my homework." They just thought homework when you told them to do the dishes. Then, they only wash the dishes not the pots and pans, and not the silverware. They're compliant, "You didn't say pots and pans. You didn't say forks. You just said dishes." Am I right? When you feel coerced against your will, that's what happens.

Constructive motivation releases the energy inside of you, and it's really based on free will. It's your idea; it's your choice. You do things because you want to, not because you have to. It is your idea, and you're willing to accept the consequences if you don't do them. You really don't have to, "But if I don't obey the law, it might cost me my freedom." Well, then it's your choice. Obey it or don't obey it; just shut up and accept the consequences. You don't have to go to school; you can quit. "I don't want to quit." What do you want to do? "I want to go to school because I want a better income and a better life." Well, then shut up and go to school. You don't have to go to school; you want to go to school. It is your idea. Watch the energy come from inside of yourself. Otherwise, it's like running with your shoes nailed to the floor or somebody holding onto your pockets. Remember that bicep/triceps principle, when you lift the pen and push at the same time? That's exactly what happens inside of each one of us when we tell ourselves we have to do something. It's a lie anyway. You really don't have to. You have a choice.

Those of you who have children, you don't even have to change their diapers. Leave them on; they eventually fall off. "I don't want to live that way." Well, shut up and change their diapers.

UNIT 14
Putting Life on a Want-To

You don't have to change them. You want to change them. Many churches would lead you to believe you have to be good or you're going to Hell. Now, that could be, but what they do is they paint a picture of Hell that scares you into being good. It's not, "I want to be good because I want to be good. I want to be good because I don't want to go to Hell." You spend your whole life outrunning the flames of Hell licking at your rear end. That's not the way you want to look at your life. You want to see the good, focus on the good, and then you're drawn to it.

The discipline isn't to discipline. The discipline is to see why you really want to do what you want to do. "I don't have to lose weight; I choose to lose weight." "I don't have to study; I choose to study." There's some work in here. It's, "Do what you want to do, but accept the consequences of your choices." Now you're free. Otherwise, you feel like a victim. "I'm being made to do this. I am not my own person." Remember when we talked about self-esteem? When you say you're not your own person, when you "have to" do something, you lower your self-esteem. This is very subtle stuff.

From now on, in your mind, you're going to eliminate the words "have to." Remember, your subconscious is a literal mechanism; it accepts what you tell it. Watch it over the day; watch over the week. Watch where you feel you have to do something. Watch your subconscious go to work on you. You will have more energy, and get more out of yourself. It's a very little but profound piece, and the most important piece that I can give you.

I want you to look at what the negative consequence might be, but I want you to dwell on the positive consequence of changing your life, of doing what you want to do, living free. People who live life on a have-to feel like victims. Being around somebody who feels like a victim is exhausting and ugly. What you must do is learn to live fully and accountably. It is your fault, and you're going to cause it. "For the most part, I am going to cause what I want. I'm going to cause the kind of marriage I want, the kind of job I want, the kind of life I want. I'm going to take charge inside." You'll be so far ahead of most people, because most people are stuck in this world. Eliminate all that "have to" stuff, but don't eliminate the consequence. The consequence is always there. Just make the right choice.

UNIT 15
Making the Pictures Match

Unit Overview

When the world outside doesn't match the picture of the world we hold in our minds, we have a problem. The creative subconscious goes to work to make the pictures match. We get lots of energy, and we get very creative. This is human nature. However, we can take hold of this process and use it to help us make the positive changes we want in our lives, using our power of visualization to reach our goals.

Unit Objectives

By the end of this unit, I will:

• understand that I am always working for order in my mind.

• learn that I can create my own energy by changing my internal picture.

• know that my subconscious doesn't care if I go back to my old picture or go to the new picture, it goes in the direction of the strongest picture.

• use visualization as I set my goals, to make the outside world match my new internal picture.

All **meaningful** and **lasting change**
starts first on the inside,
then works its way out.

UNIT 15
Making the Pictures Match

Key Concepts

- Affirmation Process
- Self-Talk
- Gestalt Psychology *— your truth - picture of reality*
- Neuron
- Conscious
- Subconscious
- Creative Subconscious
- Perception
- Out of Order / In to Order
- Anxiety
- Tension
- Energy
- Creativity
- Visualize
- Imagination
- Reality
- Potential
- Inner Standard
- Conflicts
- Goals / Goal-Setting
- Comfort Zone

UNIT 15
Making the Pictures Match

Notes

UNIT 15
Making the Pictures Match

Reflective Questions

- What are my goals after graduation?

- What goals have I set to make my vision of the future a reality?

UNIT 15
Making the Pictures Match

Reflective Questions

- What is good enough for me?

- Where am I not living up to my own expectations?

UNIT 15
Making the Pictures Match

Summary

In order for you to really understand why the affirmation process and the self-talk process really work, I'm going to give you insight into some deep psychology about how the mind works. Deep, but I'm a good teacher and you're a good student, so you're going to get it.

We're going to talk about what's called Gestalt psychology. According to Gestalt, every human being is working for order in their mind. Now, what does "order" mean? Do you ever say to yourself, "This doesn't taste right?" Do you ever say to yourself, "This doesn't look right?" Do you ever say to yourself, "This doesn't sound right?" "Order" means you have an idea of what is right stored in the neuron structure of your brain – the way your room should look, your car should look, your house might look, the way your life should look.

Remember the conscious and the subconscious and the creative subconscious? On the subconscious level, that reality you have stored here is really your idea of how things are supposed to be. Now, on the conscious level, through your perception (sight, taste, touch, smell, feel) you are bouncing what you are perceiving off of your stored reality and it darn well better match. If it doesn't match, you get mad and upset.

Have you ever walked into a room and the picture on the wall was crooked? Does it bother some of you? What do you do when you see the picture on the wall crooked? You fix it, back to the way it's supposed to be. That's Gestalt. You have an idea in your mind of the way it's supposed to be. Through your perception, you see it off-center or crooked, and you can't sit there. You must fix it back the way it's "supposed to be." That's Gestalt. You're always working to make the outside match the inside, even if the inside isn't very good, is less than your potential, even if the inside is crummy. It is the outside and the inside that you're always working to match up. Your job will be to change the inside picture to be better than it presently is. Your job will be to improve your idea of how things are supposed to be or what is good enough for you.

You see, you're always correcting in relationship to your idea, your internal standard of what is good enough for you. And, you always will, unless you change what is good enough. That's why you want to use the affirmation process. That's why you want to control your self-talk. That's why you're going to want to visualize a better environment, a better job, better relationships, better grades, a better you. Let me show you what happens.

Let's suppose I was born with my fingers knit together. Every morning when I wake up, I check my hands out, and they're put together. I'm going to feel okay. You feel okay when things sound all right, look all right, taste all right to you. No anxiety, no tension. One day, I wake up and, surprise, my fingers are apart. I see that. My sense is saying, "That's not right. That doesn't look right to me."

Now, that turns on anxiety and tension in the human system, when things don't sound all right or look all right. The anxiety or tension is also called energy. Energy to do what? To put it back to-

UNIT 15
Making the Pictures Match

gether. You need energy to fix the problem. You get energy to make it look the way it's supposed to look. The creative subconscious has the job of solving or resolving conflicts.

Now, what's a conflict? A conflict is when your idea of how the pictures look on the wall doesn't match what you're looking at. It's a conflict. That's where your energy comes to fix it. You can't stand it. It's not the way it's supposed to be. So energy is created when things aren't right for you, not when they are right. When things don't look all right, you get the energy. You don't need energy if they look all right.

Your job will be to change the picture on the inside, in your mind, so what is presently all right is no longer all right. In other words, if you're a C student ordinarily and you keep getting C grades, you get no energy except to get Cs. But if you change in your mind that you're a B student, and you get a C, the picture is crooked. "I have a problem here," and energy will be released inside of you to fix the problem. See how simple that is? Energy is created when these two pictures don't match.

The other thing that happens inside of you, when the pictures don't match, is creativity is released. Creativity happens when things don't look all right; you get ideas. What would you use the ideas for? To fix the problem. "I've got to figure out how to do this." Ideas come when you're out of order, not when you're in order. See how simple that is? Ideas for what you need come subconsciously. When something doesn't look right to you or isn't right to you, you get energy and ideas to fix the problem.

baby STEPS

Goal-setting and getting more out of yourself is deliberately causing a problem. The way to do this is by changing the picture in your mind, and you do that by using your imagination, correctly, to envision a better image of the way you want your life to go. You cause the problem inside by changing the picture. Let's say you're still living in that crummy old apartment, driving that junkie old car, and getting those C grades. Now if you change the picture to the kind of car you want and you go out and get into that crummy old car, you have a problem. You start creatively figuring out how you're going to get a better car. If you change in your mind about the location in which you live and improve it in your mind, where you're living becomes a problem. There is no problem if it looks all right to you or acceptable to you. "It's good enough for me." You must change what is good enough.

You change what is good enough in your mind first, and then you fix the outside. All meaningful and lasting change starts first on the inside and then works its way out. You need to visualize yourself in a better relationship, in the ideal job for you, with the kind of people you want around you. For the most part, most of you never intentionally put the picture in. For most of you, the picture was put in by chance, based upon where you lived, who you were around, who you hung out with, what your family was like. If it was affluent, you got an affluent picture. If it wasn't affluent, you don't have an affluent picture. If garbage in the street was okay, then garbage on the street's okay. If dents in my car were okay, then dents in the car is okay. But if you see your car the way you want it to be, with no dents, then a dent drives you crazy.

UNIT 15
Making the Pictures Match

Goal-setting is deliberately throwing your system out of order. You need to do it intentionally by envisioning yourself at the next level. It starts in your imagination, but the kind of imagination you need is first-person, present-tense imagery. I'll teach you more about that. Just looking at something doesn't change you. Just watching somebody live some way doesn't change you. You must see yourself doing it. That is the only kind of imagery that changes this image of reality. It doesn't do you any good to watch somebody living well or somebody getting good grades or somebody having the job you'd love to have. You must see yourself doing it. When you see yourself there, that's what alters the internal idea.

When you're out of order, what determines which way you're going to use your creativity? What determines which way you're going to use your energy? When you're out of order, your subconscious doesn't care if you go back to the crummy old apartment, the crummy car, or your old way. It simply doesn't care. All it wants to do is solve the problem. All it wants to do is to make the outside and the inside match. What determines which direction you're going to go is the strongest picture. What determines the direction you will use your creativity and your energy is the strongest picture. So, if your future, the way you want to be, isn't as strong as the old life that you lived, you'll always go back to your old way. You always go back to your idea of the way things are supposed to be.

Your goal, your process, is to use your imagination to make what you want more familiar to you in your mind than the way things are now. You must take yourself on a journey, in your mind, to stretch your comfort zone into different stores, different restaurants, different social settings; into the different places of the way you want your life to be. And you need to do it over and over, and over and over, until this picture is changed. Once the picture is changed, you may still be in the same, old circumstance. But now you have a problem, and you will straighten the mess up outside here to match the excellence inside. That's what goal-setting is really all about.

The process of affirmations and visualization is something I'm going to share with you next. You'll know that there is a way of guiding yourself and making sure you don't forget. The key is you must control your self-talk. You must make sure you don't tell yourself the old way is better.

UNIT 16
I Can See It!

Unit Overview

It is a fact of life – literally – human beings need goals. If we have no goals, we die. Since the survival instinct is so strong, if we have no new goals, we simply recreate our old ones and life doesn't change very much. We must dream big and give ourselves goals, causing tremendous energy and creativity inside ourselves to achieve these goals.

Unit Objectives

By the end of this unit, I will:

*   understand why I need to set goals.

*   know that I need new goals, so that I grow into the person I want to be.

*   dream bigger, because the bigger the dream, the more energy and creativity I release from inside me to accomplish my goals.

If you don't give yourself
a new goal,
you duplicate the one
you have in your mind.

UNIT 16
I Can See It!

Key Concepts

- Accountable

- Visualize

- Goals / Goal-Setting

- Comfort Zone

- Subconscious

- Current Reality

- Potential

- Efficacy

- Out of Order / In to Order

- I x V = R

- Self-Esteem

- Beliefs

- Neurons

- Discrepancy Production

- Discrepancy Reduction

Notes

UNIT 16
I Can See It!

Notes

neuron stores present Reality

w/o new goal you duplicate the one you've got

[OR] you become susceptible to the strongest suggestion

Efficacy – your idea to make things happen

Relationship between

UNIT 16
I Can See It!

Reflective Questions

- What is my vision for my income level and lifestyle?

- Where have I already achieved a goal and need to set a new one?

- Why am I going to school?

UNIT 16
I Can See It!

Reflective Questions

- What is my current reality in relation to why I am going to school?

- Who do I feel has power over me at home and away from home?

UNIT 16
I Can See It!

Summary

I'm leading you into how to make the changes inside yourself. As some of you said, "Now I'm accountable. I don't need to wait for the Fairy Godmother, I don't need to win the lottery." "Maybe I can make some of these changes myself, and I don't need to sit around and wait for the teacher to inspire me. I need to learn how to do it myself." It's going to be important to learn to write your goals out, the changes you want, and then create a process of visualizing them. In the morning and visualizing at night, at least two times a day, this speeds up your change. Otherwise, you'll do it only when you think about it, and that might be this week, or once last month. It takes a year or two to even change the picture. What if you wanted to change the picture in just weeks? You could. As soon as you change the picture, your whole system starts taking action.

The process of writing your goals out and visualizing them is a normal thing. It's just a matter of controlling the new pictures you're trying to put in. I would say you might want to make 10 or 15 changes, or goals, at a time. You're really going to get high on this stuff. You're going to raise your self-esteem. You're going to stretch your comfort zone. You're going change beliefs that are holding you back. You're going to grow socially. You're going to grow academically and grow into your career. Your whole life is going to get better because you're going to cause it, and you know how to do it.

Let's come back a little bit to see how important goals really are. Right now, you don't have an idea, I would guess, as to how important they are. Goals are so important that if you don't have a goal, you die. Death occurs without a goal. There are so many studies that have shown this. If you want to research it, look up Dr. Viktor Frankl. He started what was called "logo psychology." He was a Jewish psychiatrist who was interned inside of Nazi prison camps. He recognized that anybody who had a goal, even if it was revenge, had a better chance of surviving than those who gave up.

During the Korean War, the United States lost more prisoners of war than in any war in the history of America. 18 to 23 year old young men would crawl into a corner, captive in their barracks, pull a blanket over their head, and die within three days from no physical cause whatsoever. They quit living. The Korean and the Chinese communists were destroying any hope of the future. They were taking away goals.

You'll see this same thing with older people who have been married for so long. One dies, and the other one will give up and quit. Have you seen that happen? They just die, within weeks. You'll see people who will hold on for the special occasion. It could be a marriage of a child or could be a celebration of some kind. But as soon as the occasion passes, they die. People who retire with no goal, according to actuarial tables, will die within 16 months or so. It doesn't matter how old they are. They die because they don't have a goal.

Now, your subconscious knows that you need a goal. So here's the important thing: If you don't give yourself a new goal, you duplicate the one you have in your mind. You duplicate the way

UNIT 16
I Can See It!

you run your day, where you go, where you work. The way your life goes is pretty much just rolled over into each new day. If you don't give yourself a new goal, you re-create the one you have. In order to change your life, you need to change the picture, your present reality, in your subconscious.

Now, if you don't give yourself a goal, or you don't duplicate the one you have, you become extremely susceptible to the strongest suggestion from those you hang around. You become extremely accessible to somebody's strong voice. "Let's go have a beer." Why not? Got nothing else to do. Your subconscious needs something to do, and if you don't take charge of your own future by giving yourself the future that you choose to seek, all you do is drift. Now, you don't necessarily drift aimlessly. You aim at what somebody suggests, because you're not giving yourself any dominant suggestion. That's why it's important to decide what you want your life to be. Otherwise, all you're going to do is live out somebody else's idea. Change won't happen unless somebody outside of you influences you, or unless you decide you're going to do it yourself.

Now, how big a goal can you set? How large can the goal be? Not at all in relationship to how big your potential is. Your potential inside you is huge. But if you don't develop your inner strength, your dreams remain small. That inner strength or belief is called efficacy. Efficacy is your idea of your own ability to make things happen. It's your appraisal of your own strength of making things happen. There is a direct relationship to how big your dream is, how big your goal is, and how good you feel inside. You want always to be strengthening yourself inside. That's why you're going to school. You're getting stronger inside yourself with new knowledge, and new confidence.

The greater the efficacy, the bigger the dream. The dream is the container into which you release your energy and your ideas. Small dream gets you small ideas. Your subconscious only releases enough to fill the container; it doesn't release more than it needs. You only get enough energy and enough ideas to do what you said you want done. Your job is to create the container – not only the size of it, but what you want in it. Your subconscious, that is so powerful inside you, will get you to take action to fill it.

Now, you might be thinking, "I don't have the skills," or "I don't have the money," or "I don't have what I need." Goal-setting is what's called discrepancy production, or throwing your system out of order. It's natural as a human being to create order. The goal throws your system out of order and inside you must, if the goal is strong enough, create order. Now, a better way of saying this is the goal, or the aspiration, creates your appetite to gather what you need. That's why it's so important for you to get a clear picture of what you want in your life. It must be your idea, because it needs to be your energy. Otherwise, you can't figure out why you are doing anything. You'll see no reason for doing anything.

Look at your own kids. If they don't have an idea what they want, then the information out there is of no value. When I learned that, I set my own goals, and then I really become passionate about growing or studying or developing. And here is something so important to remember: All you need to do is to create a dream correctly and set it strongly, and you will grow into it. Look

UNIT 16
I Can See It!

at little kids who dream about being an astronaut or a nurse or a doctor. They set a dream, and grow into it. Set a dream and grow into it. This is the right way for you to live.

You don't need to set your goals based upon what you presently know. Don't set your goal based upon how smart you are or the knowledge you have right now. If you set your goal far beyond where you presently are, your subconscious is going to drive you to study, to read, to find people who can help you fulfill that passion that's inside of you. But, it must be your passion. It must be an inside drive, not an outside drive. And it must be stronger than the way you're living now. Remember, you always move to the dominant idea.

Now, are you going to wait for somebody outside of you to do it? Look around school, at people who sleep through class. (People will even sleep through this one.) They have no future in mind. Nobody needs to motivate me. I motivate myself. I change my life to the way I want it. When I'm stuck in my comfort zone, I set goals to expand it. Goal-setting is just taking yourself out of your comfort zone into new stores, a new neighborhood, a new life style. It is deliberately familiarizing yourself with the way you want your future to be.

You need to familiarize yourself. Goal-setting is the familiarization process, and all you need to do, in your mind, is visualize yourself safely, without fear, into the next level you choose to go. And when you do it over and over in your imagination, and do it correctly, your subconscious thinks you've already been there. Remember the formula I x V = R that I gave you a long time ago – *Imagination* times *Vividness* equals *Reality*. You record what you imagine correctly in your mind, and take yourself into the future the way you want to live. You must think and write your goals as though you've already done it, that you already are it.

It is the future in the present tense. Your goals are written as though you have what you desire now. You'll want to write that you've already graduated, that you already have the job that you're trying to seek, that you already have the social world that you want. Then as you picture it, if you do it right, your subconscious thinks you're there. When you look at your current reality you say, "But I'm *not* there." You have a problem, and you're supposed to.

UNIT 17
If It's to Be, It's Up to Me

Unit Overview

The best way for us to see our goals achieved is to write them down and visualize them happening. We need to "see" ourselves into a successful future before we ever get there. It's all about growing into our goals and dreams and we can speed up that process with effective visualization.

Unit Objectives

By the end of this unit, I will:

- learn that forethought is using my imagination to create the future before it happens.

- understand that I need to write down my goals and use visualization to see myself into the future I desire as though it is already accomplished.

- know that I must throw myself out of order, so that I cause energy and creativity to put myself back in to order at the new level.

As we correctly **visualize the new,** we become **dissatisfied** **with the old.**

UNIT 17
If It's to Be, It's Up to Me

Key Concepts

- Forethought

- Imagination

- Affirmation

- Goals

- Comfort Zone

- Self-Esteem

- Subconscious

- Creative Subconscious

- Visualize

- Potential

- Experiential Imagery

- Out of Order / In to Order

- Gestalt

- Energy

- Creativity

- Truth

- Mentor

- Reality

Notes

UNIT 17
If It's to Be, It's Up to Me

Notes

UNIT 17
If It's to Be, It's Up to Me

Reflective Questions

- How have I been using my forethought in the past? Has this helped me to achieve or hindered me?

- What is my ideal or perfect career? What am I presently doing to make my vision a reality?

UNIT 17
If It's to Be, It's Up to Me

Reflective Questions

- My present thoughts determine my future. What am I thinking about today that will have a positive impact on my future?

- Where do I find myself looking to others for approval?

UNIT 17
If It's to Be, It's Up to Me

Summary

Have you ever heard of forethought? It's very simple. It's imagination looking forward, which seems to be unique to human beings. (I don't know for sure if other animals can do it.) You use your imagination to see the way you want dinner to be. You might even see the way you want tomorrow to be, or use it to see the way you want your life to be.

Forethought is using your imagination to create the future before it happens, and you do it so easily. It's important to know that it's ordinary. If you looked in a room and saw a sign that says "Exit," it tells you something that you might need. If you're driving a car down the freeway and you see a sign, the sign alerts you ahead to turns or detours or things that you should know. Do you ever cook from a recipe in a cookbook? A recipe projects your mind into a future that you're making.

So writing your affirmations or your goals in affirmation form, is to project your imagination into the future in areas that are important to you, stretching your comfort zone, raising your self-esteem, the job, the career, whatever it is you want. There is nothing mysterious about it at all. But why write them out? Because your subconscious is going to try to make you go back to who you are. It will try to make you forget or find other things to get in the way.

You must take charge of the changes inside yourself, because you're working against your subconscious. Your creative subconscious is supposed to keep you the way you are now, and you're messing around with the way you are now. You're trying to throw yourself out of order. If you don't write down your affirmations, you'll probably forget them. That's why New Year's resolutions don't work so well. Do you ever try to make a New Year's resolution? Good intentions, but rarely get done. Writing affirmations or goals is a control tool to help you visualize correctly.

Now, how far from where I am, am I able to set a goal? In other words, is it possible to set a goal clear to your end of your potential? I don't think so. Well, what determines how big a goal I should set? Would that be helpful if you knew that? What I think will determine this for each of us, and I've seen this over many years, is you need to be able to take yourself into the future and be able to live the experience as though it's happening to you. Now, you may be able to see somebody else with the kind of career that you want, but you can't see yourself that way. You need to back it up to where you can see yourself that way.

Now, when I say, "see yourself," I don't mean like we're going to watch television. You see yourself as though you're actually participating in the event or in the situation. So do you see yourself now where you're seated? No, you probably see me and you see the surroundings. You would see as though it's actually happening to you, not like you're a spectator watching a game. You're part of the game. You need to become the player. It's called experiential imagery. You only see what you normally see, like you're looking through a camera. You don't see the picture of you. You might see your arms, but that's about all. Or you might see in a mirror a reflection, but you experience this as though it's happening to you. This is important.

UNIT 17
If It's to Be, It's Up to Me

Let's go back to the five year old going to school. When you have that five year old going to kindergarten, you might think in your mind that some day that kid will be in high school or college. What happens if you talk college to a five year old? They aren't going to get it, are they? "I can't imagine myself doing it," is what they'll say. You must imagine yourself doing it. If you take a three year old with brothers and sisters who are seven or eight and in school, and you say, "Do you go to school?" Watch. They'll say, "The big kids go to school. I'm just a little kid. I don't see myself in school. I can see my brothers and sisters in school. I cannot see me in school."

But what happens when he gets to be four or five and starts seeing himself in school? Kids play school in their mind. They might even go to school, sit in the chair and imagine how nice it's going to be. Now, as they visualize themselves or you help them visualize themselves, in school, something happens. The picture is changing of where they belong. They've taken themselves out of their present comfort zone, which is home, the yard, the dog, and stretched their comfort zone in their imagination. As we visualize the new, the next level, we become dissatisfied with where we are. As you visualize the new correctly, you become dissatisfied with where you are. That five year old is visualizing themselves into school, and you can't keep them home. They're out of order, by staying home. "I'm a big kid. I go to school." They'll get themselves up, make their own breakfast for the first time, or their own lunch, dress themselves, and be waiting for the bus at 8:00 in the morning – and school won't start until noon! You can't get them to come in the house, because "I'm a big kid now. I go to school."

As you visualize the new, you become dissatisfied with the old. The problem with most people is they don't visualize themselves into the new. There's no Gestalt, no energy and no creativity that takes them to the new. They're stuck where they are. They keep describing how things are all the time. "This is the way I live. This is the way I am. This is the way I feel." The more you do that, the more you harden the reality, the more you stay the same. If you want to take yourself from where you are into a better future, you must write your goals, visualize and talk to yourself about the way you want things to be in the future – as though they actually are. Now some people might say, "Well, aren't I lying to myself?" No. You take yourself in your imagination to the next situation as though you actually are. Then you look at where you are right now. You say to yourself, "I said I'm up here, but here I am. I said I have the degree, but I'm only in my first year. I said I have an A in the class, and here I am just starting it."

Remember, out of order, in to order. Out of order, in to order. By envisioning yourself into the future the way you want to be is throwing yourself out of order. What you must do is get yourself to see and recognize where you are now. It is the combination of the image in your mind and the feedback through your senses telling you you're not there that creates the gestalt. It creates the drive.

Anybody here not take a good picture? You say, "I'm just not photogenic." Me, too. When they take a picture and show it to me, it doesn't look like me. They say, "No, it looks exactly like you." I say, "No, I look too fat in that picture." They say, "Well, you are." I am, in my mind how I really want to be. I just won't step on the scale, because when I step on the scale that ruins my day.

UNIT 17
If It's to Be, It's Up to Me

You know how to keep from ruining my day? Don't step on the scale. It's the combination of the new goal in your mind and looking at the truth of how you are. You don't want to get stuck in the truth as you are, as the dominant idea is the new, and you're going to move to it. So, you write your goals out as though you already are.

Your goals must be written in a one sentence definition. One sentence. "I am," "I have," "It's easy for me," but you're talking about things you really don't have yet. You're talking about the person you really are not yet, and you describe yourself as though you already are. Now, every time you're going to read that, in the morning and at night, it takes your imagination correctly into the future as though you already are. Then you look in the mirror, step on the scale and say, "Whoops, I'm not what I say. I have a problem." No problem, no energy. No problem, no drive, no creativity. You must cause the problem.

Have you ever had a good mentor? What a good mentor has always done is see more in you than you saw in yourself. They saw what you could be before you ever were, and they described it so you caught the dream. They saw you as you could be before you were, and in your imagination you fell for it. That's what visualization does; that's what goals do. More than that, as the mentor took you into the future with the possibility, you caught it in your mind. But then, you knew it wasn't true at that moment. "I see it, but I'm not." But the more you saw and the more that became a part of your mind, the more you closed down the gestalt. You worked and you practiced, and you practiced and you practiced until you became it. That is what you do with your goals. You need to mentor yourself, otherwise you're hoping that some mentor will come along and turn you from a frog to a prince or a princess. You need to turn yourself from the frog to the princess or the prince.

Write your goals the same way that a mentor would, and drop yourself into the future as though you already are, then you grow into it. It's out of order, in to order. Out of order, in to order. Your goals must always be written in the first-person, present-tense, with what is called experiential imagery so you see yourself doing it, and it must be positive. "Positive" means describe yourself in your future the way you want to be: your positive future in the present tense.

Have you ever been around people who just talk about the good old days? They don't like where they are, but they want to go back. Have you ever been around people who just talk about how things are? They're just stuck, and tomorrow looks like today. But if you really listen to people who are very successful, they always talk about the future as though it already exists, and they seem to be progressing, don't they? This is the way you do it, folks.

UNIT 18
My Better Future

Unit Overview

It is normal for us to want to know "how" we are going to get where we want to go. But, we really don't need to know the "how" in order to set our goals. In fact, if we demand to know "how" first, we will usually back up our goals to match our current abilities, and we don't grow very much. The idea here is to see the end result.

Unit Objectives

By the end of this unit, I will:

•   understand that my mind is so powerful that I don't need to know "how" to grow in order to set and achieve my goals. I will invent the way.

•   know why it is important to see the end result.

•   know that I am good enough to invent my way to my goals.

The **goal comes first**
and then you see.
You don't see first.

UNIT 18
My Better Future

Key Concepts

- Goals
- Affirmation Process
- Visualize
- Comfort Zone
- End Result
- Subconscious
- Vision
- Current Reality
- Anxiety
- Tension
- RAS
- Lock-on / Lock-out
- Drive
- Energy

Notes

UNIT 18
My Better Future

Notes

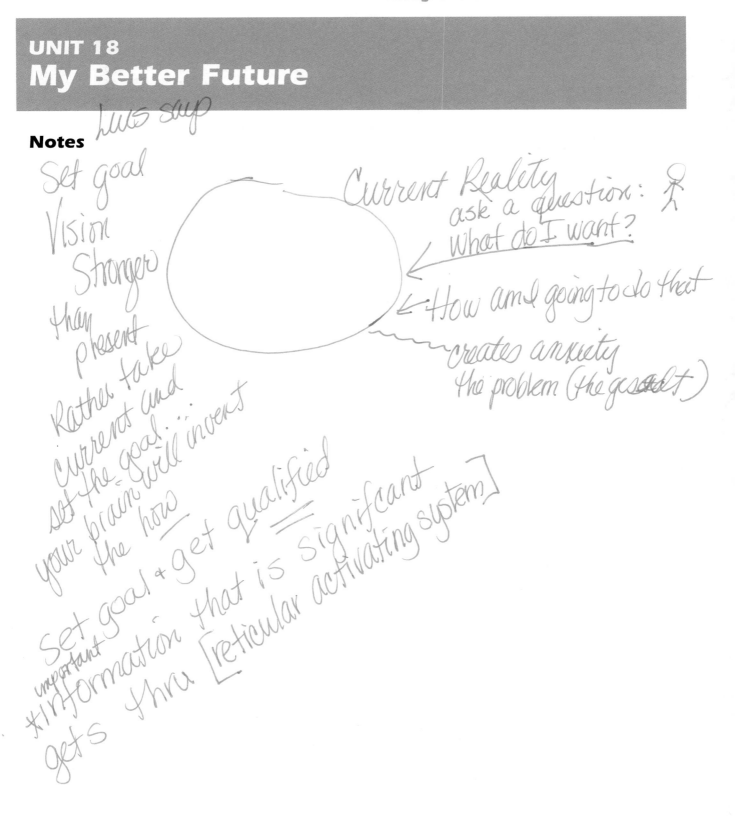

lets say

Set goal
Vision
    Stronger
than
    present
Rather take
    current and
    set the goal...
    your brain will invent
        the how

Current Reality
    ask a question:
    What do I want?

← How am I going to do that

    creates anxiety
    the problem (the gestalt)

Set goal + get qualified
important
*Information that is significant
gets thru [reticular activating system]

UNIT 18
My Better Future

Reflective Questions

• Describe in detail my vision of graduation day from school. What am I wearing? Who is there to watch me? Etc.

• What new goals do I need to set now, for my future after graduation?

UNIT 18
My Better Future

Reflective Questions

- Where has my current opinion of myself held me back?

- What are my three most important goals at this time?

UNIT 18
My Better Future

Summary

When I asked, "Is this making sense?" several of you answered, "I'm thinking it makes sense. I get the concepts. I see myself setting goals and using some of these skills, but I'm not consistent. I let myself get sidetracked or I'll start and just sort of stop. Then I beat myself up for stopping."

The affirmation process that you're going to use is not the goal. Your goals are the goal. Using this information isn't the goal, it's creating the life you want that is the goal. If you create a bigger life and a bigger goal for yourself, you'll need to apply this information to get there. Don't worry about being inconsistent right now. After 30 years, this becomes so normal for me, but you should have seen me 30 years ago. When I came out of high school teaching, the suits I was wearing were, well, let's just say I looked like a crumpled professor. So, Diane went out and bought a new polyester brown suit for me. Polyester – if you drop ashes on it, your pant leg melts.

Now, Gene Juarez and others were all getting together at the Washington Athletic Club, and they were teaching me about business, because I knew nothing about business. Gene complimented me on my new suit. I didn't want them to know it was new; I wanted them to think I always had a suit this nice. I couldn't understand how he knew it was new. Now, I went into the rest room. As I was combing my hair, I looked in the mirror, and guess what, still on my sleeve were the tags. I had been wearing this suit for a week! Those are some of the steps that I had to get myself past. I was learning all this stuff myself – visualizing, and trying to grow. I wasn't always where I am today.

There was a time I wouldn't go anyplace socially where there wasn't a football coach. That was how small my comfort zone was. I never flew in an airplane until I was 35 years old. I wouldn't go more than 155 or so miles from Seattle. I went to Wenatchee, which was about 150 miles from Seattle, and I would never stay in a hotel. I'd always go someplace where I knew somebody I could stay with. My comfort zone was that small! But as I keep applying this and visualizing and stretching, I keep growing.

You're going to get better at this to the degree you apply it. One good way of applying it is to go back and say, "How have I always used this anyway?" You have, you know. "Where did I use it to my betterment and where did I not use it and I messed up?" Then ask yourself, "Where do I see other people using this?" "How am I going to do this in the future?"

Now, what do you do, if you can see yourself doing something but you don't know which steps you need to take to be able to get there? You don't need to know the steps. You visualize the end result. Your mind is so powerful that if you can envision where you want to be, your subconscious seeks out new knowledge. It seeks out the way. You'll invent how to get where you want to go. You set the goal, and you grow into it. Don't think your goal can only be as big as you presently know the steps.

When you set a goal, you set a vision. It's an idea of what you want. And how do you get a vision? Very simply, you just ask yourself a question: "What do I want?" That's how you get a

UNIT 18
My Better Future

vision. What do I want from my family? What do I want from my life? What do I want from my job? What do I want for income? What do I want to wear? Now, the problem is, when people set a vision that's very far away from how things are right now, the next question that comes to mind is, "How am I going to do that?" "How am I going to get the money?" "How am I going to get the job?" "How am I going to get the house?" See, the "how" question comes up. I don't want you to start with "how." I want you to set the goal, which is making the vision stronger than the way you're living now, your current reality. Hold off on the "how" question for now.

If you get the idea of where you want to be and you see where you are right now, you create the anxiety or the tension. You create the anxiety and the tension in your system, and you cause the problem, or the gestalt. If the new picture is strong enough, I guarantee you'll take current reality and you will invent your way to the goal. You will invent your way to the goal. You don't need to know how to get the goal; you just need to know how to set the goal. Your subconscious is a genius. You'll figure it out. That's how your mind works. Now, if you already know how, go ahead. But don't let not knowing how keep you back. The people you're hanging around, when you're going to do this, will say, "Tell me, how are you going to do that?" If you don't know, they'll respond with, "What a stupid idea. Why don't you back it up to what you know how to do." That's what normal people do, but I don't want you to be normal. I want you to be way out.

Set the goal and you invent the how. Again, if you already know how, that's okay. But if you don't know how, never let it stop you from setting your goal. Your subconscious will invent the way. It has to close down the gap. But, if your vision is weaker than current reality, and the anxiety and tension is in your system, guess what you're going to do? Through excuse-making, reason-finding, and projecting the blame, you'll back your vision up to match where you are. Your subconscious has to make the two match. If you don't reach your goal, you rationalize to yourself that things were not right, and you go back to the way you were.

I never let being qualified stop me from setting a goal. I set the goal, and I get qualified. We've gone all over the world with this process. One time, we decided we wanted to help out in Northern Ireland, to resolve the conflict in Northern Ireland. "Who do you know?" Nobody. "Based upon who you know, it will take you awhile." See, I didn't need to know.

Remember the reticular activating system I talked about earlier, and how information gets through. What gets through? Information that is important. Another word for important is "significant." Now, what's getting through your awareness now is only information that's important to you now. You set a new goal, and new information gets through. See, the goal comes first, and you'll find books and courses, and people and opportunity. You'll find information that probably was all around you, but you didn't hear it or see it. Why? You didn't need it. No need, no get through. New need screams through like the baby's cry.

You always want to feel confident that you can set goals far beyond your present know-how. As you start to get near to your goal, if you want to, you can keep yourself going by setting a new

UNIT 18
My Better Future

goal. You don't need to wait to get there, you can set a new one and you go right through the old one. Remember, goal-setting through and not up to a point keeps you going. New goals. New drive. New energy. See how your mind works? Wonderful, isn't it?

Goal-setting doesn't have anything to do with time. It has to do with what you want, the end result. If you lock-on that it's going to take you two years to achieve your goal, you lock-out getting it done in one. You lock-out all kinds of ways of doing it. What is the shortest time frame you can possibly give yourself for a goal? *Now.* I want you to write your goals as though they already are with you, right now. You think as though you already have it. You're causing yourself a problem. You'll be driven.

Now, if you have things like you don't want to move for two years, then put down two years. For most of your changes and all of your goals, you need to write them as though they already are done. You will never be more energized in your life, because you tell yourself you have it, and you don't have it. See the drive? See the energy? It must be something that you want, because you're creating a fascination, a passion, a drive says, "I can hardly wait for tomorrow. That party is going to be something. I can hardly wait." Your goals are always going to be written with the tremendous value that you're trying to seek.

Your self-talk will go, "I want to. I choose to. I like it. I love it. I don't have to, it's my idea." That's the way I speak in my mind. Instead of "I have to" do something, I don't have to. I want to. I choose to. I like it. I love it. It's my idea. You write your goals the same way, and you'll attack life with the same anticipation of a child looking forward to a birthday.

UNIT 19
My Goals – My Vision – My Future

Unit Overview

We have learned about the importance of setting goals, and we have learned how to visualize what we want for our lives. Now it is time to learn how to write out our goals effectively, for the maximum positive impact on our futures.

Unit Objectives

By the end of this unit, I will:

- have learned the steps to writing effective affirmations.

- know that I must see my future as already having happened, which creates the energy to move into that future.

- visualize my goals as affirmations at least two times a day; more times, if I want to make the change quicker.

Read the words;
see the pictures;
and **feel** the emotions
welling up inside you.

UNIT 19
My Goals – My Vision – My Future

Key Concepts

- Goals

- Visualize

- Self-Talk (Four Levels)

- Accountable

- Subconscious

- Affirmation

- Words-Pictures-Feelings

- I x V = R

- Attitudinal Balance Scale

- Motivation

- Habit

- Familiarization

- Self-Determined

Notes

UNIT 19
My Goals – My Vision – My Future

Notes

See yourself as if changes have already happened

Step ahead 3-4 months –

Goals – [1 sentence]

WORDS – PICTURE (triggers in your mind — how you will feel

(Specific) X — X I feel b/c of

Vague (can't fail) I need to loose 'some' weight? Can't fail

Daydreaming / Alpha state before sleep = Read affirmation

Daily = Read affirmation X Picture X feel the Emotion

Picture must change and behavior will follow

I am completely self – determined, I need let
[I motivate myself]   others feel
I am my own person   the same.

I show I am 100% alive, by thinking
acting with great enthusiasm

I have a positive expectancy,
every setback is temporary.

UNIT 19
My Goals – My Vision – My Future

Reflective Questions

- "People can become successful as soon as they decide to be." —Harvey Mackay 1999. Where in my life have I decided to be successful?

- What pictures and emotions do I need to change in order to make my affirmations come true?

UNIT 19
My Goals – My Vision – My Future

Reflective Questions

- What are my general expectations for my life, now and in the next ten years?

- Review my affirmations. Am I able to read, picture and feel each one strong enough to make them come true?

UNIT 19
My Goals – My Vision – My Future

Summary

I'm going to show you a little more about how to write your goals. Wherever you happen to be this day, this month, step ahead in your mind. Pretend in your mind that it is three or four months from now. If this was October, you might think, "Now I'm into January." Take yourself and your imagination to January, and see yourself as though the changes you want have already taken place in you. If somebody says, "Tell me, how are you? Tell me about yourself," and you start to describe yourself as you are in January. "This is the way I am; this is what I do. This is what I have." Write that description down on a piece of paper, then take the description back with you to October. You already described yourself as you're going to be, but you described yourself as though you already were.

Lets say you have a terrible habit of getting mad at people and you want to change that. Here's what you do: You must step ahead about three or four months, see yourself when something occurs that used to make you mad. It happens, but now you remain calm, poised, and at ease. So you say, "How do you react when that happens? I remain calm and at ease whenever that person says stupid things to me." Then, you take it back to where you are, and as you read that, you're visualizing that situation occurring. What you're doing is changing the inside of you and your reaction when it does occur.

Let's suppose you don't have your degree but you're going to get it in January. You write, "I'm proud of the fact that I have the degree that will get me the job that I always wanted." Now you bring it back, and it's only October, and you visualize yourself graduating with that degree. You look around and it's only October. "I'd better study. I'd better read and learn. I see myself graduating, but I'm not there yet."

In order to be able to visualize them correctly, all of your goals need to be written out in one sentence. If you get paragraphs, it's too much to see. When you're setting goals, you want to be as clear as you can. Clear means to make it as exact and as specific as you can. If it's vague, it's hard to see. "I'm going to be a lot better." It's hard to get a picture of that. Remember, the description that you're making in your goals is to give you the second dimension, of pictures. (Remember, words trigger pictures, which cause emotion.)

The words that you're describing need to trigger the picture that you want as a part of your life, as a part of who you are. The words need to describe specifically the kind of behavior, the kind of job, the kind of social world, or what you want to do with your time. You want to describe it clearly. Many people keep it vague, because then they don't hold themselves accountable. "I'm going to lose some weight." You know how much "some" is? About a half a pound. Your subconscious says, "Okay, you lost some, but you need to lose much more." Oh, well, I didn't say much more, I just said some.

You want to be very clear and quite specific, because you're writing them out to control the second dimension, the picture. However, the most important part of an affirmation is the at-

UNIT 19
My Goals – My Vision – My Future

titude part or the feeling part, the third dimension. When you write your affirmation, put into it how you're going to feel when you have what you want. How is it going to make you feel? Write that into your affirmation. "I feel joyous." "I feel proud of the fact…" "I feel fulfilled because of…" That's going to draw you to what you want. You want to have something that draws you and attracts you.

Now that you have written your goals out as though you already are, you already have, comes the next job. You are going to read your affirmations at least two times a day. The best times are just before you fall asleep in your daydreaming state; and just upon awakening, when you're in the alpha state of consciousness. While daydreaming, your subconscious is most receptive to what you're giving it. We must trigger that I x V to = R. The way you do it is you take each of your affirmations – and you'll do no more than 10 or 15 to start with – and you read each affirmation. Read the words, which triggers the second dimension. You picture it happening, and then feel the emotion you want. That's all there is to it. Read, picture, and feel the emotion. And always, control your self-talk.

Don't go out and try hard to be what you're affirming. Remember you're changing the picture, and your behavior will automatically change. Change the inside, and the outside changes. Your job is to decide what to change, and then to change the inside. Your subconscious will automatically make you behave like the new person you know yourself to be. The picture must change first, and the behavior follows. So, at least two times a day you want to go through this. If you want to change faster, then do it three times a day or four times a day.

Each time you are making an affirmation, you are deliberately putting a positive weight on your attitudinal balance scale. As you do so over and over, you're changing the direction in which you lean. You're changing your inner idea of who you are. It's a deliberate process to change. It's a familiarizing process.

Now, I'm going to give you two or three affirmations. These are some affirmations I made when I was about at your stage. They are some very fundamental and basic ones.

One that I made, that was so important for me was so I'd be my own person. My world was "I have to do this" and "I have to do that." So I made an affirmation that, "I am completely self-determined, and I allow others the same privilege." What does that mean, self-determined? I motivate myself. I am my own person. In other words, my life was a bunch of have-to's, and I felt people were telling me what I had to do. So my being completely self-determined meant I am my own person and I'm making my own choices and I'm making my own life. It has nothing to do with luck. It has nothing to do with hoping the stars are right.

What I needed to do in my mind, when I needed to make decisions, I would see myself making different decisions. I am my own person, and nobody can make me do anything against my will. But if I choose not to, I will accept the consequences. This is the way my mind would go as I'm making that affirmation. Then I'd say that I need to let other people feel the same way, because I

UNIT 19
My Goals – My Vision – My Future

used to try to shape up everybody else around me: "You're not dressed right. You're not looking right. You're not doing right." Well, they're determined, too, so I quit shaping everybody else up. I'm not going to let you shape me, and I'm not going to shape you up. I am my own person.

The second affirmation I made was for energy, because I'd be running out of energy. Do you like to be around people who are vibrant, energetic, happy and enthusiastic? Yes. You're more employable and people like being around you, so I made an affirmation: "I show that I am 100 percent alive by thinking, acting, and speaking with great enthusiasm." Who am I going to be with in the morning? Who am I going to be with at lunch? Who am I going to be with in the afternoon? And I would practice being there, and I see and sense myself with energy, radiant energy, speaking thinking.

When you're around negative people who are trying to talk you out of your future and your dreams, here's another one I made, and I make it still today. "My inner spirit is so bright and so powerful that nobody can blow my light out. I'm like the birthday candle that won't go out." Got the picture? I would see where I might be where that might happen, and I visualize that nobody's going to take my future away. Nobody is going to blow my light out. You can cause the energy and the response in you.

Remember I said there were four levels of self-talk. This one only stops at the three, but it's a good one, and it is this: "I never devalue myself or others through destructive criticism." I don't run myself down. I don't tell myself I'm stupid. No, "What's the matter with me anyway?" It's easy to get caught in conversations that run somebody down. That used to be normal. I created a new normal. I don't do that anymore. And then I would say to myself, "or allow anybody to do so in my presence." Now I need to tell people to stop it, or change the subject. That was scary, but I did it.

So get started. Don't delay. You're too important.

Affirmation Workshop

Affirmation Workshop

In this session, you learn how to write affirmations and practice writing them. You will use the goal ideas you have worked on. An affirmation is a statement of fact or belief. When written correctly, an affirmation will trigger a picture in your mind of your goal already accomplished. Your affirmations are your tools to deliberately control your own forethought. As you have learned, this is how successful, high-performance people win so frequently. You can paint your own positive scenarios, change your picture on the inside first, and automatically gravitate toward your goals by using these tools. There are eleven basic guidelines for writing affirmations. Review them closely.

1. **Personal:** Affirmations are written with the word "I" in them. You can only affirm for yourself. The desired change will come about because of something you do, and it is your own inner picture that will change because of your affirmation.

2. **Positive:** Always describe what you want in your affirmation. Describe what you want to move toward, not what you want to move away from. What would it look like if it were fixed?

3. **Present Tense:** Affirmations are written as though they are happening right now. This requires using your imagination and becomes easier with practice.

4. **Indicate Achievement:** Eliminate words such as, "can, will, should, and want to" etc., from your affirmations. Include phrases such as, "I am, I do, or I have." It is important to give your subconscious a clear picture of the end result as though it is already accomplished.

5. **No Comparisons:** Comparing yourself to others is ineffective. The technique of affirming is a personal process. Your measurement of growth is based on yourself.

6. **Action Words:** Use terms that describe and trigger action pictures, such as "easily, quickly, thrive on, energetically, confidently," in your affirmations.

7. **Emotion Words:** These are of critical importance. The more positive emotion you feel when picturing your accomplished goal, the faster your affirmation will work for you.

8. **Accuracy:** If your goal is to exercise regularly, what kind of exercise? Is it jogging, walking, swimming, aerobics, or something else? How regularly? Three times a week? If so, on what days? What time of day and for how long? This is how accurate your affirmations must be. If written in general terms, the picture is too vague, and it gives you too many escape routes.

9. **Balance:** Set goals, and write affirmations in all areas of your life.

10. **Realistic:** After you have written your affirmation, close your eyes and picture it. Can you see yourself there? You need to be able to see it, visualize it, and imagine it.

11. **Confidential:** Share your affirmations with only those you are certain will support and help you achieve them. Most of your personal affirmations need not be shared.

Affirmation Workshop

Affirmation Preparation

What are some of my important goals for these areas?

- Personal

- Family

- Health/Physical

- Health/Mental

- Spiritual

- Social

- Career/Vocation

- Education

- Recreation/Leisure Time

- Community Service

Affirmation Workshop

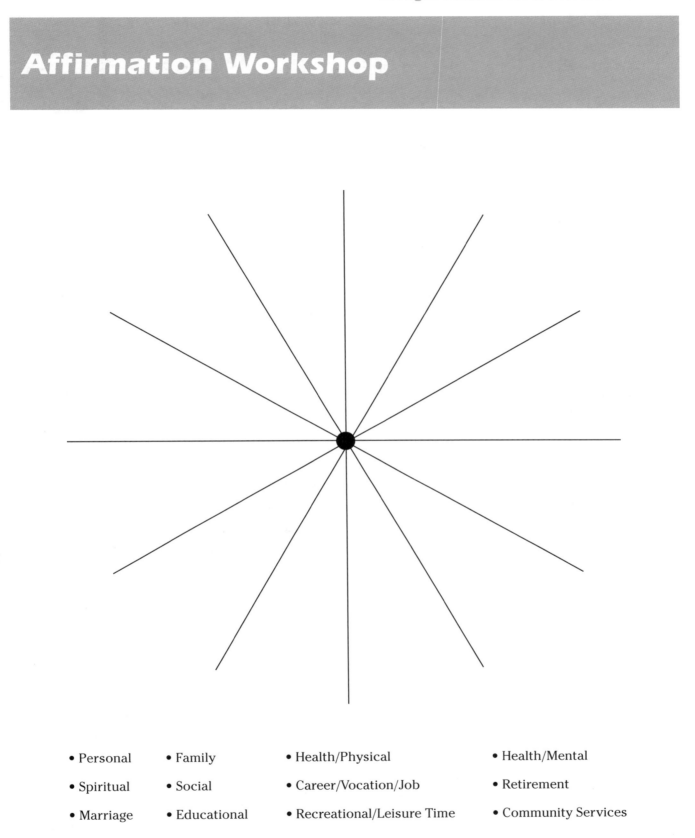

- Personal
- Spiritual
- Marriage

- Family
- Social
- Educational

- Health/Physical
- Career/Vocation/Job
- Recreational/Leisure Time

- Health/Mental
- Retirement
- Community Services

Affirmation Workshop

Sample Affirmations

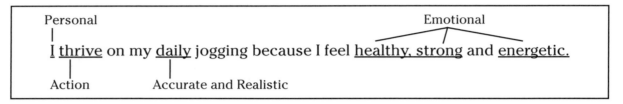

The following list has a variety of sample affirmations that may be helpful. Some may fit your career situation, others focus on your personal life, and some may overlap. If some of these affirmations work for you, please use them, but be sure to rewrite them so that they are you talking to you.

1. I like and respect myself because I know that I am a worthy, capable, and valuable person.

2. I enjoy my life and my relationships with other people.

3. I have an excellent, free-flowing memory with clear and easy recall.

4. It is easy and fun to write and imprint affirmations daily.

5. I enjoy making my affirmations daily because of the positive and quick results I get.

6. I have a positive expectancy of earning good grades, and I see all setbacks as temporary.

7. I have pride in my ability to find quality, affordable and dependable day care for my child/children.

8. I enthusiastically arrive at school on time and attend my classes daily with an open mind and a positive attitude.

9. I am very effective and efficient especially in stressful situations.

10. I have pride in my educational performance and positive expectations of my future.

11. I express myself well, and I know others respect my point of view.

12. I quietly do helpful and worthwhile things for others.

13. I look for ways of uplifting myself and others, and I do it with ease every day.

14. I am accountable for the results of my decisions and actions.

15. I reinforce my successes and positively correct for errors.

16. I am my own expert, and I accept only positive attitudes and opinions from others.

17. Because of the warmth and love I show my children, I teach them to show warmth and love to each other.

18. I develop feelings of self-respect and self-esteem in others and myself.

19. Because I sincerely care about myself and the quality of my life, I am financially responsible.

Affirmation Workshop

Sample Affirmations

20. My family and friends are benefiting from the successes that have come from my hard work and commitment to my education.

21. Taking tests is easy for me because I study and prepare for them well in advance.

22. Because of my careful, advance planning, I am well-rested for my exams.

23. I am healthy and energetic because I treat my body with the love and respect I deserve.

24. Because I am well organized and plan ahead, I have reliable transportation to school and back.

25. I am calm, relaxed, and clear-headed when I ask questions in class.

26. Giving presentations in front of my classmates is fun and uplifting.

27. I speak clearly and calmly and make positive contributions that benefit me and my classmates.

28. My classmates who are young and intelligent enrich my life. I value their contributions and learn many things from them.

29. I sincerely care about my instructors and am open-minded about what they teach me.

30. I am a successful professional and earn $____ per month. I live a comfortable and happy life.

Affirmation Workshop

Group Exercise

In groups of three or four, write an affirmation for each of the following situations as if you were the person with the challenge. Recognize that the person in current reality wants to change. The vision is what it looks like without the challenge. Refer to the checklist on page 171 and the samples on pages166 and 167.

Current Reality	Vision
Denise feels she is too old to learn anything new, but she wants to use computers.	See herself at a computer *family communication* → because it gives me joy. I enjoy the fact I am able to use a computer.
Affirmation: I ~~need~~ love to communicate w/ my family using my computer.	☹ 7:55 ☺
Melanie is often late for work. She feels guilty and knows her boss is beginning to notice.	
Affirmation: I am enthusiastic and proud I can start my day at 7:55.	
Juanita has ongoing transportation problems she would like to be able to solve.	
Affirmation: I am able to ~~joyful~~ to use my biking skills to get to where I need to be	
Maurice gets so nervous before making presentations that he "blows it" at meetings. He wants to do well.	
Affirmation: I can calmly give presentation I enjoy communication and am able to speak clearly w/ strong voice.	
Kurt has been concerned about his home loan. He feels very frustrated and worried.	
Affirmation: I efficiently pay my bills each month for my peace of mind	

Affirmation Workshop

Writing Affirmations

Now, individually, write three sample affirmations for yourself, following the same process with each. Refer to the list of helpful Action/Emotion Words on pages 173 through 175 and the Affirmation Checklist on page 171.

Current Reality (to move away from)	Vision (to include in your affirmation)
bad temper	calm, clear minded
lazy	energetic
procrastinate	accomplish immediately

Current Reality | **Vision**

reading time | *Sitting reading every day*

Affirmation:

I love for reading and relaxing with a book for fifteen minutes.

Current Reality | **Vision**

Affirmation:

Current Reality | **Vision**

Affirmation:

Affirmation Workshop

Writing Affirmations

_____

Current Reality   **Vision**
_____

Affirmation:
_____

_____

Current Reality   **Vision**
_____

Affirmation:
_____

_____

Current Reality   **Vision**
_____

Affirmation:
_____

_____

Current Reality   **Vision**
_____

Affirmation:
_____

Affirmation Workshop

Affirmation Checklist

☐ **Personal** – Include *I* or *me*.

☐ **Positive** – Describe what you want instead of what you don't want.

☐ **Present Tense** – Write like it's happening right now.

☐ **Indicate Achievement** – Use phrases such as *I have, I am* and *I do*. Do not include terms like *can, will, want to* and *should*.

☐ **No Comparisons** – Picture your own change and growth instead of comparing yourself to someone else.

☐ **Action Words** – Create pictures of yourself performing in an easy, anxiety-free manner.

☐ **Emotion Words** – Cause you to feel exactly how you want to feel when it is achieved. Refer to pages 173-175 for Affirmation Action/Emotion Words.

☐ **Accuracy** – Specific and detailed. Are there any escape routes?

☐ **Balance** – Coordinate well with goals you have in other areas of your life.

- Family
- Spiritual
- Health
- Financial
- Recreation
- Education
- Relationship
- Other
- Social
- Business
- Career

☐ **Realistic** - Can you see yourself achieving it?

☐ **Confidential** - With whom do you choose to share this affirmation? Who will really support and help you to achieve it? Most of your personal affirmations need not be shared.

Affirmation Workshop

Create Your Own Balance Wheel

On the Balance Wheel, list the areas of your life you would like to improve or change. For example: career, spiritual, family, physical and mental health, education, financial, etc. Refer to the ideas you have written in previous units.

On page 176, write an affirmation for each area listed on your Balance Wheel using the process of Vision, Current Reality, Affirmation. Refer to the Affirmation Checklist on page 171, and the Action/Emotion Words on pages 173-175. When you have completed this transfer them to 3x5 cards, and insert them into your affirmation folder.

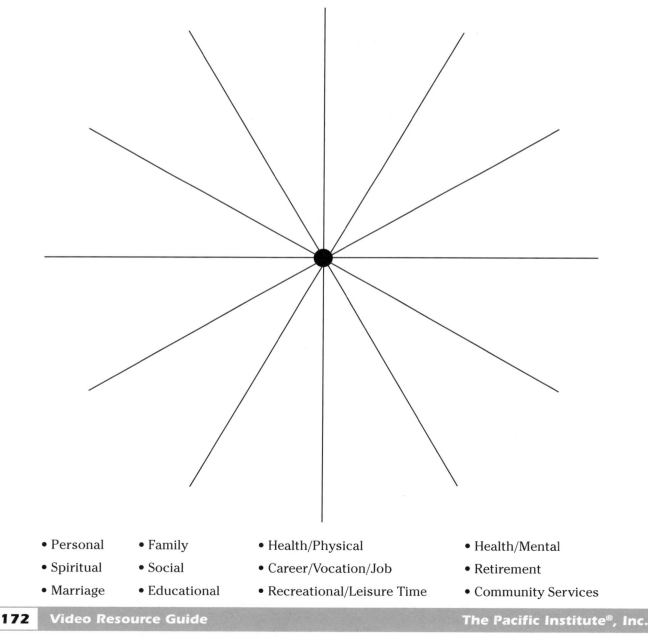

- Personal
- Spiritual
- Marriage
- Family
- Social
- Educational
- Health/Physical
- Career/Vocation/Job
- Recreational/Leisure Time
- Health/Mental
- Retirement
- Community Services

Affirmation Workshop

Action/Emotion Words

Accepted	Compassionate	Embrace	Genuine
Accomplish	Competent	Encouraging	Gifted
Achieve	Complete	Endearing	Giving
Acknowledge	Complimentary	Enduring	Glad
Active	Composed	Energetic	Glorious
Adaptable	Concise	Enjoyable	Good
Admire	Confident	Enlightened	Graceful
Adorable	Conscientious	Enterprising	Gracious
Adventurous	Considerate	Entertaining	Grammatical
Affectionate	Constructive	Enthused	Grand
Agreeable	Content	Enthusiastic	Great
Aggressive	Cooperative	Excellent	Growing
Alert	Courteous	Exceptional	Handy
Amazing	Creative	Exciting	Happy
Ambitious	Cultured	Expectant	Harmonious
Articulate	Curious	Expressive	Healthy
Aspiring	Dazzling	Faithful	Hearty
Assertive	Decisive	Famous	Helpful
Assured	Delightful	Fantastic	Honest
Attentive	Dependable	Fascinating	Honorable
Beautiful	Deserving	Fearless	Hospitable
Beloved	Determined	Feminine	Humble
Blessed	Devote	Fervent	Humorous
Blissful	Dignified	Festive	Idealistic
Brave	Diligent	Flexible	Illustrious
Bright	Diplomatic	Fluent	Immense
Brilliant	Disciplined	Forceful	Impartial
Calm	Dramatic	Forgiving	Impeccable
Capable	Dutiful	Fortunate	Important
Caring	Dynamic	Fresh	Impressive
Charming	Eager	Friendly	Independent
Cheerful	Easy	Frugal	Individualistic
Clean	Effective	Fulfilling	Industrious
Clear	Efficient	Fun	Influential
Clever	Effortless	Gallant	Ingenious
Colorful	Electric	Generous	Innovative
Comfortable	Elegant	Genial	Inspiring
Comic	Eloquent	Gentle	Inspirational

Affirmation Workshop

Action/Emotion Words

Instrumental	Myself	Punctual	Sensitive
Intellectual	Natural	Pure	Sentimental
Intelligent	Neighborly	Purposeful	Serene
Intense	Noble	Qualified	Sharing
Intentional	Nourishing	Quick	Significant
Intuitive	Obedient	Quiet	Simply
Inventive	Obliging	Quotable	Sincere
Jolly	Outstanding	Radiant	Skillful
Jovial	Passionate	Rapid	Smiling
Joyous	Patient	Rational	Smart
Jubilant	Patriotic	Realistic	Smooth
Just	Peaceful	Reasonable	Sociable
Kind	Perceptive	Receptive	Sophisticated
Knowing	Persevering	Refined	Sparkling
Knowledgeable	Personable	Refreshing	Special
Learned	Placid	Regal	Spectacular
Likeable	Pleasant	Relaxed	Speedy
Lively	Pleasing	Reliable	Spirited
Lovable	Pleasurable	Reputable	Spiritual
Lovely	Polite	Resourceful	Splendid
Loving	Positive	Respectable	Spontaneous
Loyal	Powerful	Respected	Sporting
Lucky	Practical	Respectful	Stable
Luminous	Praiseworthy	Responsible	Stalwart
Lyrical	Precise	Retentive	Steadfast
Magnetic	Prepared	Reverent	Steady
Magnificent	Presentable	Rich	Strong
Marvelous	Prestigious	Safe	Strengthen
Meaningful	Principled	Scholarly	Stylish
Mellow	Privileged	Secure	Stunning
Melodious	Productive	Seeing	Sturdy
Memorable	Professional	Seeking	Successful
Merry	Proficient	Selective	Super
Mighty	Progressive	Self-confident	Superb
Modest	Promising	Self-contained	Supportive
Moral	Prosperous	Self-reliant	Sure
Motivated	Proud	Sensational	Survivor
Musical	Prudent	Sensible	Swift

Affirmation Workshop

Action/Emotion Words

Sympathetic
Systematic
Tactful
Teachable
Tender
Terrific
Thankful
Thorough
Thrifty
Thriving
Timely
Tireless
Tolerant
Tranquil
Treasured
Thoughtful

Triumphant
True
Trusted
Trustworthy
Truthful
Understanding
Unforgettable
Universal
Uplifting
Useful
Valiant
Valuable
Venturesome
Vibrant
Victorious
Vigorous

Virtuous
Visible
Visionary
Visual
Vital
Vivacious
Vivid
Warm
Wealthy
Welcome
Well
Wholesome
Willing
Winner
Winning
Wonderful
Working

Worthwhile
Worthy
Young
Youthful
Zealously
Zestful

Words to Avoid Using

Better
But
Can
Could
Even if
Going to
Have to
Hope to
Less
Maybe
Might
More
Need to
Never

Not
Should
Some
Something
Try
Want to
Will
Wish
Would
Would like to

Affirmation Workshop

UNIT 20
If I Want It, I Can Create It

Unit Overview

By growing stronger on the inside, we allow ourselves to dream bigger and set bigger goals. In order to grow stronger on the inside, we need to escalate our self-efficacy – our belief in our own ability to make things happen in our lives. We look forward to success, and not fear of failure; and if we don't reach our goals, we are resilient. We pick ourselves up, and start again.

Unit Objectives

By the end of this unit, I will:

• have learned how to develop my sense of personal efficacy.

• look forward and see success.

• not be afraid of failure, as I know that I am resilient and persistent.

• dream big.

It's alright to be afraid;
it is not alright to **stay** afraid.

UNIT 20
If I Want It, I Can Create It

Key Concepts

- Efficacy · *confidence*
- Goal
- Anxiety
- Avoidant
- Negative Creativity
- Comfort Zone
- Forethought
- Belief
- Self-Talk
- Resiliency

Notes

scary movie

see it 2 I know the ending

No fear

Your Picture you must

see yourself passing test

You prepare

I see your notes inside yourself

You can see yourself passing

You are presistent

efficacious

It is not what you know

it is how you use

WHAT you KNOW

UNIT 20
If I Want It, I Can Create It

Notes

1st person - I

2nd person = self affirming
   You are

3rd person = The class

WIZards: people who uncondtionally tell us
   the truth

WIZARD of OZ: wizard was all powerful
You are brave - medal
You are smart - diploma   } one - time
You are heart - clock to tick   } affirmations

negative wizards

be cautious b/c it can become your truth
   of negtive

UNIT 20
If I Want It, I Can Create It

Reflective Questions

- What kind of adversity have I overcome? And how did it make me a stronger person?

- Where can I look forward and see success?

- I have high self-efficacy in these areas because . . .

UNIT 20
If I Want It, I Can Create It

Reflective Questions

- What gives real meaning to my life?

- Select a challenge. What attitudes, beliefs, comfort zones, self-talk, habits and goals do I want to adjust to overcome this challenge?

UNIT 20
If I Want It, I Can Create It

Summary

There are things I want to help you with. One is, I want you to grow strong on the inside. The stronger you are on the inside, the bigger the goals on the outside. That is one reason why you're going to school and why you're learning.

There is another reason why you're going to develop yourself. There's a direct relationship between how strong you feel in your mind, which is called efficacy, and what you accomplish. When people tell you, "You don't know how," you'll reply, "But I can learn it. I know I can know." Now that's self-efficacy, and let me come back and review it with you. If you set a goal, and if that goal is bigger than you, you ask the question, "Is this bigger than me?" What that means is, "Do I feel like I'm capable?" If the goal is big enough, it should cause a little anxiety inside of you.

Now, the problem is that if anxiety gets too strong in you, it triggers negative creativity. Remember, negative isn't bad, negative is just avoidant. Your subconscious starts figuring out why you shouldn't do it. And not only that, it will tell you you're biting off more than you can chew. "Let's adjust the goal back to what we know how to do. Let's be sensible about this. Let's be realistic about this." So you adjust your goal back to what you presently know how to do. No more. Anytime you set goals that are bigger than you, and most will be that way, you're going to get that feeling inside yourself. That's normal. But you're not going to give in to it. What you're going to do is grow bigger than what was bigger than you. It's all right to be afraid to start with, it's just not all right to stay afraid. This is the way you're going to run your life, and it's self-efficacy.

You need to learn how to handle the anxiety arousal. Suppose we have a platform or a beam as high as a table, and maybe twice as long as the room. I would be standing at one end, you would be at the other end. I'd say, "Walk across and I'll give you a thousand dollars. If you step off, you won't get it." You'd do it to get the thousand dollars. But what I'm going to do is raise the beam 50 stories up in the air. You're on one building and I'm on the other one. I'm going to say, "Come across and you get a thousand. Step off, and you don't get it."

Now, because of what's going on in your mind, your chance of coming across is very slight. You're dwelling on the fear of falling, the fear of failure. You're dwelling on death in this case, and it interferes because you're out of your comfort zone and you're going to tighten up. You lose your balance; you lose your coordination or your skills. The only difference is your mind afraid of falling, afraid of getting hurt. Now when you have high efficacy, you look forward and you must see success. To the degree you look forward and see yourself falling or failing, it interferes with your memory, and it interferes with the input of information. You don't use the skills that you have, and you do blow it – just like you thought you would.

So, when you have strong efficacy, here is the way you think: You look forward and you see success. You'll see obstacles, but now in your imagination, you're going to design how you're going to deal with the obstacles. "If this happens, I'll do this. If this happens, I'll do that. If this happens, I'll do this." You plan in your mind with your forethought. Now, people who are inefficacious – which

UNIT 20
If I Want It, I Can Create It

no longer is where you are – look forward and scare themselves to death. "What if this awful thing happens?" If you think like that, then you're going to fall off the edge. You don't even try. If you do try, you're too tense. You can't really be yourself because you're too uptight. The uptightness comes from the way you're thinking. You're letting your self-talk go crazy on you.

If you're low on efficacy, and if you do see obstacles that get in your way, you'll go forward toward the goal in hopes that the bad stuff doesn't happen. If the bad stuff does happen, you just quit; not because you don't have what it takes inside, but because you're not thinking right. Control your self-talk. Don't dwell on what you don't want; dwell on what you do want. That's why you need to write your goals out. Sometimes, when things are happening around you, it gets scary. If you go back to your goal, it will remind you. It will remind you to look forward to the way you're supposed to look and calm yourself down. Think about what you do want.

There was a lady who used to work for us. She came out of Colorado, where she had worked for the former governor. We were talking about this, one day. She had been the only child of old fashioned Catholic parents. They were very protective. So she'd say to her mom, "Mom, I'm going to the dance tonight." And mother would say, "How are you going to get there?" "Well, I'm going to drive the car." "Well, what time you coming home?" "I'll be home at 1:00." "Well, what happens if you're driving home and you get a flat tire? Something awful could happen." "Well, if I get a flat tire, I'll get out, get the jack and the wrench, and fix the tire." "But what if you're fixing the tire and somebody comes along and tries to attack you?" She said, "I'll hit them with the jack handle." "What if he's bigger than you?" And she said, "I'll run." "But what if he's faster than you?" She said, "You're right, I shouldn't go."

You see how somebody can talk themselves out of something with "what if"? Don't let your self-talk get that way. Remember, you're resilient and you live through it. You must control your anxiety. Don't let yourself get uptight when you're taking a test. How? See yourself successful, in your mind. See yourself as though the grade has already arrived. Have you ever watched a scary movie twice? Try it. Not so scary the second time, is it? How come? Because you know the ending; you already know how it came out. This is how you should be thinking. If you see yourself successful, then you don't get scared. It's when you see yourself 5, 10, 20, 30, 50 stories high and you're going to fall off the edge that it makes you get uptight.

Now, one more thing. Efficacy is job specific. You can be very good at something but not want to do what I'm doing. Then again, I could be good at what I'm doing and I couldn't do what you do. You don't need to be good at everything. What you're going to do is become very efficacious and competent in what you do. I have an airplane and my pilot knows how to fly it. He's very efficacious. But you wouldn't put him here instructing you. He can't do it. But I guarantee you, you don't want me flying you!

So, you're not just overall efficacious at everything. You need to be specifically, and that's why you want to get world class in your skills. That's why you want to get the knowledge inside of yourself for the careers you're going after. It is career specific, and take pride in it. There are some general

UNIT 20
If I Want It, I Can Create It

qualities and characteristics about being efficacious. One is you're very resilient. So you get yourself up when you get knocked down. The other is you're very persistent; nobody can blow your light out. Still another is you're able to control the anxiety that's inside of you. You see, it's not what you know, it's what you can use of what you know when you find yourself out of place.

That's why you want to keep developing yourself and your skills. You want to keep using the affirmation process, and wanting to learn, and learn, and learn. The better you are, the more financially rewarding it becomes. Instead of just saying, "I just hope they pay me," you become so valuable nobody can do without you. And you can do it. It's all inside of you.

UNIT 21
Rites of Passage

Unit Overview

While we have learned that in order to make a change in ourselves, we need to read our affirmations at least twice a day, for several weeks, there is something even more powerful at work in us. A vow – a one-time affirmation – made with great emotion can change your life forever. Rites of passage do the same, especially when sanctioned by a "who-said of the greatest magnitude." We are about to embark on our own rite of passage as we conclude this course.

Unit Objectives

By the end of this unit, I will:

• understand the power of one-time affirmations, or vows.

• have learned the influence rites of passage can have on the changes I want.

• be a positive wizard in the lives of my family, friends and co-workers.

A vow:
One statement of fact,
made with tremendous emotion, can
change you forever.

UNIT 21
Rites of Passage

Key Concepts

- Rites of Passage

- Affirmations

- Who-Said

- Vow

- Negative Wizards

- Positive Wizards

Notes

UNIT 21
Rites of Passage

Notes

UNIT 21
Rites of Passage

Reflective Questions

- Who are two positive wizards in my life? How have those individuals influenced me?

- Have I ever experienced a negative wizard? What impact did that person have on my life?

UNIT 21
Rites of Passage

Reflective Questions

- In what ways do I limit myself because I have listened to others tell me what was wrong with me?

- Examples of rite of passage situations in my life have been:

UNIT 21
Rites of Passage

Summary

Here's a way of putting everything we've talked about into one package. One time, when I was coming back from Australia, we stopped in Hawaii. I had been working with a group called the Alaliki, who are Native Hawaiian. They had asked if I would come to their graduation ceremony, because they were having a luau. My family was with me, and some friends were with me, so we said "Yes." Now, we weren't in a hurry to get there, because we knew the party would go on for a long time. But when I arrived, I found that what they really meant was, "Will you please give the commencement address?" I thought I was just coming for dinner! I needed to think of something to say. All of a sudden, in my mind, it just hit me. I was thankful for that, and I'm going to share that with you. It was rites of passage, one-time affirmations and the Wizard of Oz.

Now, I need to explain what all that stuff is. Well, first of all, what is a one-time affirmation? One time you say something to yourself and it's like that forever. Ordinarily, it's pretty hard to do. Do you ever say to yourself, "I'll never eat that junk?" Okay, that's a one-time affirmation. Ten years later you haven't even seen it and somebody serves it. All of a sudden, "Nope, I don't eat it." One-time affirmation. There is tremendous conviction and emotion involved. Ordinarily, it takes a lot of repeating, but under some circumstances it will work.

Now, what is a rite of passage? A right of passage could be a wedding ceremony, or a graduation ceremony. It could be a military ceremony. Usually, in a rite of passage, there is a ceremony. People dress differently and there is some specific occasion. In a rite of passage, there is somebody who you think is quite significant, who has the power given to them by the president, the state, the church or something like that. In a rite of passage, they will allow you to go from one state or one class to another class. It could be graduating to junior high school.

Now, the Wizard of Oz. For those Alaliki, the Native Hawaiian, very few of them ever graduated from the eighth grade. In their culture, they are oftentimes put down to the point where they feel not as smart. They're told they can't graduate, or that they don't need to go to school. It's the outside world telling them where they belong. But they were going through our curriculum, just like you have, and they are now ready to make a difference in their children and in themselves.

So, here is my version of the Wizard of Oz. Dorothy had the bad luck of her house being blown out of town. Darn the bad luck, it landed on the Wicked Witch and killed her. Dorothy saw the Wicked Witch's legs sticking out underneath the house, and she had on these beautiful red shoes. Dorothy knew she wasn't going to use them anymore, so she put the shoes on, which made the Wicked Witch's sister mad. The Wicked Witch's sister was going to get Dorothy, to get back the red shoes, so Dorothy has to get out of town. She didn't know how to get out of town and back to Kansas. So the good witch, Glinda, comes along and says the way you get out of town is to go to the Land of Oz. There is a wizard there, and the wizard can get you home. So Dorothy was off to see the Wizard, the wonderful Wizard of Oz. She was off to see the Wizard, because of the wonderful things he does.

UNIT 21
Rites of Passage

Now, Dorothy was a very up person. She fought off all those monkeys with wings and all the scary stuff that was coming after her and so on. But she also had difficulty, because she ran into a scarecrow without brains along the way, and a tin man without a heart, and a lion with no courage.

Well, they get to the Land of Oz, and I'm going to hold you at this point in the story. In the Land of Oz, Dorothy meets this Wizard who is the "who-said." He's got the power. So, let's go back to the idea of a rite of passage.

When you go through a ceremony like a wedding, you have a who-said like a minister or priest, a rabbi, or a judge. Keep in mind, you come in knowing you're single. This minister says, "Do you take this woman to be..." and with one affirmation or vow, you would affirm, "I do." Do you take this man to be? And with a one-time affirmation, one vow, "I do." And this who-said says, "By the power given to me by the holy church or by the state, I now pronounce you man and wife." Now think about this. You come in knowing you're single, and you go out knowing you're married. What changed? One statement, and you act like you're married forever. Isn't it amazing how your mind works? You go through a graduation ceremony. Before you know you can't do anything. All of a sudden they say, "I give you your degree." Yesterday I couldn't, now I can. One-time affirmations through a rite of passage.

So here's Dorothy with Toto, the tin man, the cowardly lion and the scarecrow. The Wizard says, "And what do you want?" The poor cowardly lion was afraid of everything. So the Wizard says, "I can understand why. Every brave person has a medal. I notice you're not wearing any medals. So by the power vested in me, the Great Wizard of Oz, I give you a medal. Now you have courage; go act like it." A one-time affirmation, through a rite of passage, just like getting married. And the lion goes out, "I'm brave, I'm brave," and starts to growl. It was always in him, but it took somebody else telling him to bring it out.

The tin man didn't have a heart. The Wizard said, "Well, because of all the good things you've done," he gave him a clock so he could hear it tick. "Now you have a heart. Go act like it." A one-time affirmation, through a rite of passage, caused the person to behave differently.

The scarecrow, his head was full of stuffing; his mind was full of nothing. And the Wizard said, "I can understand why. Every smart person has a diploma, and I notice you don't have a diploma. So by the power vested in me, the great Wizard of Oz, I give you your diploma. Now you have brains. Go act like it."

Now, it was always inside of them, but it took somebody affirming them or telling them they had what they already had, and then they act like it. See, a one-time affirmation through a rite of passage.

As I spoke to the Alaliki people, I told them that many of them were not like Dorothy, the tin man, and the scarecrow, and the cowardly lion. "You've come across negative wizards, along the way, who told you that you didn't have brains, or you didn't have heart, or you didn't have courage.

UNIT 21
Rites of Passage

And because they were big kids – or teachers or parents or uncles or aunts or neighbors – you fell for their description of you; then you acted out the way they described you." See, you've come across, many of you, people who try to take away your brains or take away your heart, and then you behave like they have described you. I was trying to encourage them to recognize that they have given sanction to people in their life and in their history who are holding them back; they may still be doing so. That's how powerful belief is.

One time, I went back and wrote down 75 to a hundred-and-some people in my lifetime who tried to tell me as they saw me, and it wasn't at all what I wanted to be. There are always negative wizards in your world. You must recognize never to give them sanction. Teach your children that they must remain in control of their own personhood, because when they allow others to affirm who they are, they act like it.

Do you ever get a song stuck in your head and you can't get it out? Remember the song in the Wizard of Oz? Put this through your mind, and instead of "I'm off to *see* the wizard," just change a couple of words: "I'm off to *be* the Wizard, the wonderful Wizard of Oz. I'm off to *be* the wizard because of the wonderful things *I* does."

When you see your children, the people at work, your spouse, or your friends, you're going to see the goodness in them. You're always going to be affirming them. You're going to tell them what's right with them. You're going to eliminate the negative, the destructive stuff that goes on. Also, within yourself, you're not going to allow people outside of you to do that to you. No more.

Now, you may doubt yourself. So in my final act, by the power vested in me, given to me by me, I now declare each one of you an Associate Wizard. Go act like it.

AUDIO ASSIMILATION JOURNAL
Table of Contents

Audio Assimilation Journal

Affirmation Imprinting Reminders

1. **Read** the words. Close your eyes and visualize the image that these words trigger.

2. **Picture** vividly. The picture you get by visualization is vitally important. Create an experiential picture, not an observed picture. It is one that you are actually experiencing yourself.

   Remember **I x V = R (Imagination x Vividness = Reality).** The clearer the picture, the more effective it is. The picture in your mind should not be hazy: it should be specific, down to the finest details you can imagine. Clarity and detail are two qualities that we seek. So as you read the words, you imagine the event in vivid detail and see the accomplishment of your goal.

3. **Feel** the emotion, as if the event is happening right now. You can use the borrowing technique flick-back / flick-up to help you gain a positive emotion. Simply borrow from a past positive experience and bring the good feeling into your present affirmation. In summary:

   - Use Experiential Imagery.

   - Take no more than 20 seconds to imprint each affirmation.

   - Affirm twice a day. (The best times are just before you fall asleep at night and upon awakening in the morning.)

   - Give yourself feedback.

   - Record your affirmations if you wish.

   - Affirm that your word to yourself is good.

Remember:

Just reading the affirmation = **good** impact on the subconscious

Reading and picturing = **better** impact on the subconscious

Reading, picturing and feeling = **best** impact on the subconscious

Audio Session 1 — Overview

A Message from Lou

Hi. This is Lou Tice, and I thought I'd share with you a few thoughts that might make your first day, or your first week, or your first month, or your first experience here in your new venture more successful.

You have so many things that might cause you to be what we call "out of your comfort zone." You're going to learn more about that, but you could be overwhelmed with all kinds of different circumstances, different situations – even more on your plate, if you will, than you've ever had before. If you're not careful, your mind can cause you to quit by creating more difficult circumstances than really exist. Actually, I might even call that "obstacle illusions," where you could talk yourself out of a better and greater future. So, take a moment and listen to this audio, and I'd suggest you listen to this two or three times during the day.

Have you ever had, those of you who might celebrate a birthday or a special event, a religious holiday – it could be a Christmas, a Hanukkah – something that you really look forward to? Have you ever noticed that if you spend the time (it could be a month, or it could be even more than a month) planning in your mind the way you want that event to go or that day to be, that you see what you're going to have for dinner; or you see the decorating of the environment in which you're living; and you see the people who will be with you. You might even see or feel how good it's going to be on that day. Well, I know that when you do those kinds of things, it almost turns out exactly like you planned it.

Well, that's the way your mind works. But, the problem is, most people don't use their mind to create their first day of school, or their first week of school, or their first month of school, to turn out the same way. They just kind of let things happen to them. Then, they're surprised because there are so many new things that are unfamiliar that it interferes with their thinking. Then, it stimulates negative creativity in your mind that tells you, "Quit. Go back. Go back to where you feel safe, to where you feel comfortable." Do you know that if you can take in your imagination and just make yourself safe in those situations that appear to be new or unusual or even scary, if you can practice in your mind the way you want that day to go, it will be like that special holiday or that special day for you.

So here is the way I would do it if I were beginning something that strange. Now that I know what I know after all these years, this is exactly what I do. Well, before I fall asleep, I tell myself how I want to sleep. I don't know if you can do this, but can you tell yourself exactly what time you want to wake up and then wake up at that exact time? You could if you trusted yourself. Anybody can do it. But then not only tell yourself what time you want to wake up, but you must tell yourself how you want to sleep and how you want to feel when you do wake up.

That is controlling how you think and the power inside yourself. So what you want to do is to tell yourself that you want to be fully rested and that you want to wake up happy, looking forward to a great day today and that you want to expect some really great things happening today. "It's

Audio Session 1 — Overview

going to be a wonderful day." This is the way you want to talk to yourself, because if you don't and you tell yourself, "Oh, I'm afraid, things won't go well. I don't know what to do," your subconscious will create either picture for you. It does what you tell it to do.

So, if I were you, I'd be very smart and I'd tell myself what I do want instead of what I don't want. You tell yourself that you're going to get up and you're going to have a great early morning. Then you want to talk to yourself about the way your day will look, how you're going to get there, how easy it's going to be, the new and the adventure and the wonderful things that you're going to experience. I want you to see how your morning goes, and I would like for you to plan yourself through your morning as clear and as in detail as you can. I'd practice going to school in my mind. I would practice going to school in the afternoon, if it was in the afternoon, or in the evening if it was the evening. But you practice the first part of your day and then you practice the second part of your day. Then you practice the third part of your day. "Practice" only means the same as if it was a special holiday; you just take yourself through it in your mind. You see the people, and you create the mood that you want. You tell yourself how you want to feel – a positive expectancy.

I would like to have you just go back and remember the good things in your life, the joyous things in your life, and then I'd like to have you color tomorrow exactly the way you felt when things went well for you. This is exactly the way most people, who are very successful, think. You're going to run into all kinds of obstacles, like maybe you'll be late for a class or maybe there will be something happen during the day, that if you weren't going to have your mind set on the end results that you want, you'd let these little tiny obstacles cause you to quit. But because you're going to use what we call your forethought, which is your imagination, to anticipate things that might happen, you're going to create how you're going to get around it – how you're going to do this, how you're going to do that. In other words, "If this happens, what would you do?" And you say, "Well, if this happens I'll go here," and you do so in your mind. "Well, if that doesn't work, what else would you do?" I'd have two or three or four ways of getting through something that I think might be difficult to handle.

See, what you're doing is thinking in a very positive, constructive way. You're looking at things that might be normal blocks or setbacks, and you're going to create in your mind a plan to go around, to go through, to get what you want. I know you've done that in many places in your life. If you were ever attracted to somebody that you really wanted to be with and there were all kinds of obstacles in the way, I know that your subconscious would be so creative at helping you get yourself with that person, to be in that person's presence. Well, that's the way you want to see your classes. That's the way you want to see school. That's the way you want to see life. That's the way you want to see the outcome. You must hold to the image as far out as you can. If it is only the first month, you've got to know that you've have so many people who want you to succeed. Your teachers want you to succeed. Many people in your world want you to succeed. You've got to want to, and be so determined to succeed, that nothing will get in your way.

Audio Session 1 — Overview

I want you to tell yourself that your spirit is so strong, your intent and your goal is so important, that you're like a birthday candle – the one that won't go out when people blow it. Have you ever seen that? You try to blow a candle and the light won't go out? Well, that's you, your inner spirit, and your desire to succeed for whatever the reasons are that you have in your mind of your better future. You are so strong and you are so bright inside that nobody and nothing can blow your light out. That's the way you talk to yourself – you have such a positive expectancy in your mind, that nothing, nothing is going to keep you from going to school and being successful and having the future and the career for yourself, for your family. You know why you're going to school, and if you don't, you better figure it out. It's so essential.

Well, these are just a few things. You'll get much more as you get into the process. The potential is so great inside of you that the only thing that can stop you would be you, and you know how, by controlling how you're talking in your mind. You see the future you want. It's a can-do. "I can do it. I choose to do it. I want to do it. It's my idea; and nothing – nothing – will get in my way."

Well, I look forward to seeing you some day in person, and if not, I know that through your faculty and through the video curriculum, you're going to get every tool that we have that will help you be successful. Your success means a lot to us. So if you don't really think that you have the confidence yet, you've got to know that I know you can do it. I don't know if you *will* do it. I know you *can* do it. And I know that many of the teachers and the faculty and the people in your school believe and know that you can do it. So, you need to ride on our beliefs until you get a strong belief. That's all you need to do.

I wish you well. I know you'll do well, but you must then think not only about what I'm telling you before you go to sleep, but when you wake up, and at lunchtime and before you go home. Listen over and over to this, and let this dwell in your mind – the success and happiness and joy and abundance that you deserve. And you've got to go after it and get it. It's all in your mind. You can do it.

Lou Tice

Overview

Now that you have completed the core program, you are ready to begin thoroughly understanding and assimilating these basic principles you have learned, and make them a part of your daily life. The intent is simple and straightforward: to have fun, to successfully understand the concepts and principles, and use them to improve your life.

Step 1: Listen to the audio session for the day.

Step 2: Main Concepts

After listening to the audio session for the day, write the most important ideas and insights you have gained from this session.

Step 3: Choice of Activities

Choose an activity, or decide your own application of the day's information.

Step 4: Affirmations

Write your own Affirmations using your ideas gained from this session, your review of related information and notes, as well as affirmation ideas from the Video Resource Guide portion of this textbook.

• Refer to the Action/Emotion Word List on pages 173 through 175 for appropriate words.

• Review the Affirmation Checklist on page 171 to be sure you are writing them effectively.

It may be helpful to write down the current reality first, and then describe what it would be like when it is fixed. Use this as the basis to write your affirmations.

Transfer your completed affirmations to 3 x 5 cards and place them in your Affirmation Folder.

My Affirmations

Review of related information and your notes and affirmation ideas, from our Video Resource Guide.

Step 5: Assimilation

Refer to the Affirmation Imprinting Reminders on page 194 as you go through your affirmations.

• I get a clear and vivid picture in my mind, and I feel the wonderful emotion and mood of already achieving my goal.

• I dwell on this feeling of achievement, which gives life to my affirmations.

• I do this for each affirmation. I set aside time at least twice daily to imprint them.

Step 6: Journal

Use this journal page to capture ongoing insights you have related to the information in this day's session. You may wish to date your ideas as you record them over time. These insights will be helpful in your ongoing affirmation writing.

DAY 1
Getting Started

Key Concepts

Affirmation; Alpha State; Assimilation; Emotion; Forethought; Goal; Pygmalion; Self-Image.

Forethought is unique to human beings.

Main Concepts

The most important ideas and insights I have gained from this session are:

Choice Of Activities

One occasion from the past when I was particularly successful was:

During that period, how frequently did I look forward to it with vivid visualization and with positive emotional anticipation?

DAY 1
Getting Started

How did it materialize?

Thinking ahead, what is my plan for the next 3 hours? For tomorrow?

With what emotion will I flavor my weekend?

DAY 1
Getting Started

Affirmations

Write your own Getting Started Affirmations using your ideas gained from this session, your review of related information and notes, as well as affirmation ideas from your Video Resource Guide.

- Refer to the Action/Emotion Word List on pages 173 through 175 for appropriate words.

- Review the Affirmation Checklist on page 171 to be sure you are writing them effectively.

It may be helpful to write down the current reality first, and then describe what it would be like when it is fixed. Use this as the basis to write your affirmations. Transfer your completed affirmations to 3 x 5 cards and place them in your Affirmation Folder.

My Affirmations

Read
▼
Picture
▼
Feel

Assimilation

Refer to the Affirmation Imprinting Reminders on page 194 as you go through your affirmations.

I get a clear and vivid picture in my mind and I feel the wonderful emotion and mood of already achieving my goal. I dwell on this feeling of achievement, which gives life to my affirmations. I do this for each affirmation. I set aside time at least twice daily to imprint them.

DAY 1
Getting Started

Journal

DAY 1
Getting Started

Audio Summary

Well, I know what you're thinking. "I think I'll wait until tomorrow to do my affirmations. Today I'm so busy." Well, let's talk about that for a moment.

One of the things that happens is you were so engrossed in those days of intense learning that that consumed your whole time, didn't it? Remember, once you arrive at a goal that you set, what do we do? We flatten out. And if the goal was to go to the seminar and not through the seminar, here we are, flattening out. Oh, maybe not flattened completely, because the F card and the old lady or the young lady was fun. But I know what you want to do now. You want to go out and just teach the whole seminar, don't you? You're just going to teach them off the F card or you're going to show them the old lady, show them the young lady, but that's not what it's all about. It is where your enthusiasm is right now, but we need to take it past that one point of either flattening out or "What can I do to go out and shape up my spouse, or my children, or somebody at work. I know all these people that really need it, but I don't know that I do."

So don't wait; we're going to start right now. I'm your coach. My job now is to take you past the video burst. We're really going to get serious now about assimilating what it was that we learned. I'm not going to start at the beginning like we did with the first unit in the video. That's not the way to do it. The way to do it is to start like on the fourth day. If you went through three days of video burst, you don't need to start at the beginning. Where you need to start is with the new knowledge that you have, and how you are going to apply it and how you are going to use it.

So if you were sitting with me right now, the first thing I think I'd talk to you about is using your forethought correctly, because that's so simple and it's so easy. So, let's just talk about using our forethought. Now, forethought really is what? Using your imagination, which is unique to a human being, to look forward. To look forward to what? Well, let's not make this too mysterious. Let's just look forward to breakfast. Let's look forward to dinner. What are you going to have for breakfast? What are you going to have for lunch? What are you going to have for dinner? What are you going to do in the morning? What are you going to do in the afternoon? What are you going to do this evening? That's forethought. What are you going to do at work, if it's a work day. What are we going to do? Who's going to be around us? What are our plans? That's forethought.

You know, another thing about forethought – it's so simple if you stop and think about it – forethought is like writing a grocery list. You write a grocery list, and what it does is it triggers your thought forward, forethought, triggers it forward. It lets you imagine yourself going to the store, but you even go past the store, don't you? What you do if you're cooking or preparing a meal, is you go past the cooking and you go right to the preparation. No, you might even go past the preparation and go all the way to enjoying the meal and seeing the people around you enjoy the meal. Well, that's forethought. Nothing mysterious. So forethought isn't something that we need to relearn or something that we need to start with. This is something we've been doing all the time.

DAY 1
Getting Started

Do you know another example of forethought? As you drive to work or you drive home or you're driving someplace today, look for the road signs. You might see a sign that says "Danger" with a swervy little line or something like that. Well, what that is doing is triggering your thought forward so that you can imagine what's coming up. That's forethought.

Now, can we make road signs for ourselves? Yes, they are the affirmation process. But even more so, if you never write an affirmation (which is a mistake), and let's just suppose you don't write an affirmation, the only thing you're going to get out of this whole course is to every day plan the next day. When should you do it? Well, the best time to do it would be when you're in the alpha state of consciousness. That's just before you fall asleep. Just before you fall asleep, if you could plan the next day for yourself, not only do you look through the day, but you mentally rehearse it. You practice in your mind, with your forethought, the way you want your morning to go, the way you want your afternoon to go, the way you want your evening to go. That's forethought. That's a practice of forethought.

Now, you not only take yourself through it with logic, but you take yourself through it with emotion. How do you want to feel? What's the emotion you're going to flavor it with? Let's flavor the day with emotion. Now, remember we spoke a little bit about in the past about the Pygmalion principle. What you're going to do is you're going to Pygmalion your day. You're going to sculpt your day. You're going to create your day with your thought. Now, you've done that many times when you've had a special occasion or a special day. It could have been a special religious holiday, or it could have been a birthday or something like that. What you've done is you've taken your time, as we mentioned, and you carefully thought your way through the whole day, the gifts you're going to give. You've thought yourself through who's going to be there. You've decorated the whole environment in your mind. You've put in fun, joyous emotion, the happiness, the joy, whatever it was that you wanted to flavor it with, and you saw the dinner and how you're going to plan the dinner around and so on. All that is just the use of your forethought.

But you didn't start that very day. You didn't even start the evening before. What you did, if I think right, was you started several days before, several weeks before. And in doing so, as you rehearsed it over and over in your mind, you said, "Well, no, I think I'd rather have it this way or I think I'd rather have it that way." And as you did, as you built that, and did it over and over in your mind, with enough time involved, it almost matched perfectly, didn't it? Almost matched perfectly.

Well, that's the power of forethought. That's also why we're going to write our affirmations, because our affirmations will control the forethought about the party or about the day. But what we're going to do instead of doing it on that special religious day or that special day, we're going to do it every day. We don't want to just do it the night before. What I'd like for you to do, if you're going to use your forethought, is to start thinking about not only the first day, but what are you going to do, say, towards the end of the week? What are we going to do one week away? Can we use our forethought to plan one week away, and then back it up and plan the day before, the day before that, and the day before that, and the day before that?

DAY 1
Getting Started

So what can we do? Eventually what you're going to see yourself doing is plan out maybe two weeks in advance. Not only are you going to plan out two weeks, you're going to plan out three and four; and then what you're going to learn to do is to plan a month ahead, and you might even think a year ahead. The more we can use our forethought to look forward and see the way we would like our business to be – the way we'd like our family to be, the relationships to be, our life to be, our health to be – the further out we can do this, the greater the likelihood that we can cause it. It's going to take some time for us, if we think big enough, and we start thinking magis enough, outrageous enough, we're going to need to grow into that dream. We're going to need to grow into what it is that we want to be. The most important thing is looking forward, thinking forward, seeing what it is that we want, and mentally taking ourselves through it. This needs to become a habit – this is a new habit.

So this is the first lesson. I want you now to just take your time. If you can only think forward for the next three hours, do so. But if you can take yourself six, do so. If you can take yourself 24, do so. It's using very practical things that you're doing today or you're looking forward to today, and then let's see what we can do about tomorrow. So I'll see you soon.

DAY 1
Getting Started

DAY 2
Forethought

Key Concepts

Adventure; Affirmation; Efficacious Mood; Goal; Imagination; Negative, Forethought; Positive Forethought; Scotoma; Visualization.

Efficacious people look forward and see success.

Main Concepts

The most important ideas and insights I have gained from this session are:

Choice Of Activities

One situation I am looking forward to is:

I look forward and visualize clearly all the details, and feel the positive emotion of achievement of the end result.

DAY 2
Forethought

One way to achieve:

Second way to achieve:

Third way to achieve:

I use my forethought in a very positive way, to look forward to the following event within the next week and see two alternative plans to achieve this result:

●

●

DAY 2
Forethought

Affirmations

Write your own Forethought Affirmations using your ideas gained from this session, your review of related information and notes, as well as affirmation ideas from your Video Resource Guide.

*   Refer to the Action/Emotion Word List on pages 173 through 175 for appropriate words.

*   Review the Affirmation Checklist on page 171 to be sure you are writing them effectively.

It may be helpful to write down the current reality first, and then describe what it would be like when it is fixed. Use this as the basis to write your affirmations. Transfer your completed affirmations to 3 x 5 cards and place them in your Affirmation Folder.

My Affirmations

Read
▼
Picture
▼
Feel

Assimilation

Refer to the Affirmation Imprinting Reminders on page 194 as you go through your affirmations.

I get a clear and vivid picture in my mind and I feel the wonderful emotion and mood of already achieving my goal. I dwell on this feeling of achievement, which gives life to my affirmations. I do this for each affirmation. I set aside time at least twice daily to imprint them.

DAY 2
Forethought

Journal

DAY 2
Forethought

Audio Summary

Some of the questions that you might have in regards to the use of forethought: Will I lose my flexibility? I mean if I just keep planning my day, do I then not have any spontaneity? No, not at all would this interfere with spontaneity or flexibility. In fact, what you might do, in using your forethought, is create several scenarios. You cannot necessarily control all the things that are going to happen around you at work or what might happen to you as you drive down the road in traffic. So, what you need to do is use your forethought to look for alternatives, to look for ways of overcoming a blocked traffic pattern. Well, not just a blocked traffic pattern, but it might be some problem that it jumps out at you at work. How will you deal with that? It might be a problem with a child. It might be a problem with a family member. It might be that you get some serious news about an illness or something that you have no control over. Well, how are you going to deal with that? Not only how are you going to deal with it, but how are you going to help others with their forethought?

Remember, now, you can look forward two ways, can't we? Highly efficacious people look forward, and they see success. It doesn't mean that they see it smooth and perfect. They may see, what would I do should my child, who's two, have a serious accident? What would we do if we had a fire in our home in the middle of the night? What would we do should I hear the news that my father was ill and my mother was seriously ill? How would I handle that? That's forethought.

So forethought doesn't mean that you build scotomas to the bad or the negative or the awful that will go on. Forethought means, how are you going to control your mood? How are you going to control your actions and your behavior? Are you going to throw yourself into a panic? Are you going to lose your ability to think effectively? Is your anxiety going to go so high that you're out of control and you lose your memory or your recall or you don't hear people around you? Or, if you use your forethought without dwelling on the awful things that might occur, you can see them as obstacles; you see them as setbacks; you see them as difficulties. They're in everyone's life. But if we're going to really use our forethought correctly and develop our efficacy, what we do is we see the situation and then we create a plan to deal with it, to handle it.

What we also want to do is not just work for the alternative going around to the left or going to the right, or going over or going under it. We need also to program in the flavor of the mood that we need. The second lesson is, as you look forward, you might see what would block you from achieving the goal at work or the goal on the way to work, the goal home, or when you call and invite somebody over and they say no. You can see those things as you look forward that might turn out to be challenges or problems. Well, don't stop there.

Now, remember, once you arrive at a goal that you set, you flatten out. So you not only use it to goal-set through, but here you're going to use it to look at one, two, three, four ways to reach your objective or your goal. Now, we're using simple and small things to think about right now, because we're going to extend this into very outrageous goal-setting. The important thing now is

DAY 2
Forethought

to develop the habit, develop the skill of using your forethought correctly.

So now as we look forward and we see all these obstacles in our way, you ask, "How am I going to get past this? If this occurs, I'll do this. If this occurs, I'll do that. If this occurs, I'll do this. Nothing is going to stop me." Now, if we don't think that way, what is the other way? Well, the other way is to look forward, and while we still see the desired outcome in our mind with our forethought, we also, if we're not careful, is scare ourselves. We could look forward and say, "Well, if I apply for the job and not get it, look at how disappointed I'll be." Or, "If we invest our money and lose it, oh, my gosh." "Why, if we merge the company and it doesn't work out . . ."

So, you see, using your forethought and coming up with scary end results, scary situations, what do you suppose that's going to do to you? Is it going to cause you to seek it out or cause you to go forward almost cautiously? You will go forward not boldly, not energetically, not enthusiastically, but go forward as if it comes out all right the next step, I'll take another step. And if that one is good, I'll take another step.

Well, that's not the way to go forward, is it? You must go forward boldly and confidently, because you need to inspire others around you to go confidently and boldly. If they see you hesitantly or tip-toeingly or fearfully moving forward, you can't then collect the people around you, the team you need, in order to bring them forward. The first time an obstacle occurs, I know what you do; you'll quit, you'll abort your effort.

What we want to do now is to learn to look through the day. We're going to see challenges that might jump up, but what we're going to do is have another way to go. We won't have just one way to reach the goal. We're going to have many ways to reach the goal. Today, it's very important, particularly in your businesses; because in your businesses, there are so many things that happen that cause you to abort your plan. You start off with a goal, and somebody says this is how we're going to reach it; and then sure enough, something happens and somebody – might be somebody in authority over you, changes the plan. There it goes.

Well, in order to reach an objective or a goal today, what we need to learn is the goal we're going to lock onto – the goal, the end result – is what we're going to really focus on, as well as the way we're going to get there. We may start out this way, and we're blocked. We're going to need to back up and go to the right. We're going to need to back up and go to the left, need to go over or jump it. We cannot really put all of our faith and trust in the plan. We're going to invent the plan, remember? We're going to create the way, remember? So it isn't a matter of us getting disappointed and stopping because we're blocked.

What we're going to do is hold our trust on the end result or the goal. We're going to invent the way and create the way, but we need to do our forethought work the night before, the day before. We must look through the weeks. We need to see and fiercely lock on. Now we're going to be around a lot of people who are inefficacious, who are going to be intimidated. How is that self-talk going to influence you? How are you going to influence them? That's a part of your

DAY 2
Forethought

forethought. See, as you're going forward, some of these monumental and big goals that you're setting for yourself are no easy task. There's going to be a lot of difficulty, a lot of land mines, a lot of things that are going to get in the way. You're going to have a lot of people who are going to try to talk you out of it because they aren't as tough as you, aren't becoming as resilient as you.

So using your forethought now is extremely important – at work, at home, with your family. It doesn't mean that we're not going to look forward and see the obstacle. We're going to look forward and see the obstacle, but we're not going to stop there, remember? What we're going to do is we're going to develop our plan. Now, do that with just your morning. Do it with the evening. Practice on the way to work. Practice in traffic. Practice and see. Nothing is going to stop you. Don't make it too big today. Just make it easy, make it easy. This is just rehearsal, rehearsal for the big time.

Everything we're doing now is similar to using the affirmation process, and we haven't even got you focused on your written affirmations, although I expect you to be doing this. What we're doing now is just talking about forethought control, the use of your imagination, a wonderful gift at looking forward and planning the way you want things to be. It doesn't mean that we're not going to be knocked down and hurt and damaged and emotionally, but it means that we're not going to stay there. We're going to get up and go past it. What I want you to do now is to look through the day, look through the week; if you can, look through the month. Just plan something special. See you soon.

DAY 2
Forethought

DAY 3
Half-Step Method

Key Concepts

Affirmation; Current Reality; Forethought; Goal; Half-Step Method; LO/LO; Reflective Thinking; Vision.

The life that is not reflected upon is not worth living.

Main Concepts

The most important ideas and insights I have gained from this session are:

Choice Of Activities

A small project I am thinking about doing or something I would like to change is:

DAY 3
Half-Step Method

And my half-step method to completing the project is:

Step 1: Aware of situation and how I feel about it:

Step 2: Examine in depth:

Step 3: Explore "what if?":

Step 4: Experiment:

Step 5: Decision: Move Forward? Abandon? Need more information?

Step 6: Commitment:

Step 7: Let go:

DAY 3
Half-Step Method

Affirmations

Write your own Half-Step Method Affirmations using your ideas gained from this session, your review of related information and notes, as well as affirmation ideas from your Video Resource Guide.

- Refer to the Action/Emotion Word List on pages 173 through 175 for appropriate words.

- Review the Affirmation Checklist on page 171 to be sure you are writing them effectively.

It may be helpful to write down the current reality first, and then describe what it would be like when it is fixed. Use this as the basis to write your affirmations. Transfer your completed affirmations to 3 x 5 cards and place them in your Affirmation Folder.

My Affirmations

Read
▼
Picture
▼
Feel

Assimilation

Refer to the Affirmation Imprinting Reminders on page 194 as you go through your affirmations.

I get a clear and vivid picture in my mind and I feel the wonderful emotion and mood of already achieving my goal. I dwell on this feeling of achievement, which gives life to my affirmations. I do this for each affirmation. I set aside time at least twice daily to imprint them.

DAY 3
Half-Step Method

Journal

DAY 3
Half-Step Method

Audio Summary

If you are, why are you hesitant in getting started on your affirmation process? Why are you hesitant in setting goals for yourself? Well, maybe one of the reasons might be that if you do get there and you do achieve it, what happens if it's not what I want? Perhaps I wanted to be a teacher, and I get there, and I say, "Ah, this isn't what I wanted." Or maybe you say to yourself, what if I choose to open my own business and I get there, and it's not what I want? What if I go to medical school and find out it's not what I wanted? What if?

Okay, there's a half-step method that I'd like to have you explore, and you want to keep doing this, not once, but do it a lot of ways. Every time you're starting to make a change in your life, use this half-step method. One of the problems is if you don't commit – like the old lady, young lady – you know that if you lock-on, you lock-out, don't you? You know now all about that lock-on/lock-out stuff. "I might not want to get started on this affirmation process just in case I'm locking onto the wrong thing, right?" Okay. Now, keeping your options open causes paralysis, doesn't it? There's no movement. So, let's go back to the half-step method.

One of the things you need to do with your reflective thinking process – and remember that reflective thinking is keeping a diary, keeping your thoughts, doing this every morning – is write out one page, two page, three pages a day. Just let your thoughts come. Let your ideas come. That's an essential. That's something that we can't skip. In fact, you'll enjoy this, I think, as you do it. Keep it private.

But now what you're doing, as you're doing your reflective thinking, I want you to reflect on the first step in this seven step process, and that is to really become aware of the parts of your life that are incomplete. Become aware of the parts of your life that are kind of dull, the parts of your life where things aren't going well for you, the parts of the life where you've had this nagging toothache or headache, or this knot in your stomach about it. It's like, "I just feel dull. I feel despair when I'm in this environment. I feel unhappy when I'm around these people. I feel like I'm under living my life. I feel like there must be more."

Most people do not take the time to find out what is it that they don't like about the last weekend? What is it I don't like about my job? What is it I don't like about the friends I have? What is it I don't like about the house I live in? What is it that I don't like about the way I've spent my last year? Well, you need to do some serious work if you're going to get some serious growth. This is very powerful information. It will move you in that direction, and so you ought to be a little concerned about what it's going to be like when you get there. If you don't really do a good job of choosing, you're going to end up wherever "there" is, saying, "Holy cow, this isn't what I wanted at all." So you need to do that awareness work.

Then the next step is where you need to do some real good examining and become aware – really get into the depth of examining. What is it about the friends, what is it about the job, what is it about the way my life is going, what is it about the way I spent last year? Really get into the

DAY 3
Half-Step Method

examining of it. Take it past that superficial level and go into some depth. It might take you a day or three days or five days to go back over what you wrote and look at it. Take it another step, go back to the next layer, and the next layer and the next layer.

So if you were afraid to look in-depth at your marriage or your relationship, or what it is about you don't like, how are we going to fix it? How are we going correct it? You must be courageous enough to do this. So, the second step is to examine.

Now, the third step is to explore. Explore, very simply, is using your forethought, your imagination. "I wonder what it would be like to not work at all. I wonder what it would be like to be wealthy. I wonder what it would be like to be poor. I wonder what it would be like to..." and you go on and you let your imagination take you in the exploration. See how you feel; see in your imagination what it might look like. It doesn't mean you need to do it, but some people won't even let themselves think about that, and it's because of the fear feedback. Maybe I shouldn't even let myself think about that." No, right now it's healthy. Let yourself wonder, way past the present reality. I'm not asking you to actually do it; just let yourself wonder.

Now let's go to the next step. We're going to experiment a little. Experimenting very simply is, "How are we going to try it just a little bit." Maybe what you'll do is make a visit. You might take a trip. You might take a vacation someplace that's unique or different. Maybe you just go out and bum around a little bit. Let's say, you decide, in your wondering, that you wanted to live on a farm. "Ah, that's what I wanted. I'd love to live in the country, live on a farm and have animals. What a wonderful life that would be." But now you find that it's cold and you need to get up and milk the cows. "Oh, I don't want to get up." But the cows aren't going to wait, and they smell bad. They have manure on their tail and they slap you in the face when you're trying to milk them. Then they kick the bucket, step on your foot and knock you into the manure. And you say to yourself, "Oh, I wish I hadn't bought the farm." Well, don't buy it. Go live on one for a week. That's experimenting. You might say, "I love it," and you might say, "I don't love it, and I'm sure glad I didn't pay all that money and didn't commit myself to it."

What you're doing is gathering information that you didn't have before. This is a process of leading you to the next step of making a decision. Now we have enough information to make a decision – a decision to buy or to change what it was that I thought I wanted. Decisions can be to move forward, to abandon the thought, or the decision can be, "I need more information." See, you can't jump from awareness to decision-making, so don't get down on yourself. You haven't taken the time. You can't go from experimentation to decision-making either. I mean it takes some time to be able to make the decision, so don't be in a hurry. That's all right.

But now the next step, after decision-making, is to make a commitment. Now you can't go from awareness to commitment. A lot of people do. They're aware they don't like their marriage. They examine it and dump the marriage, and commit to somebody they just met. That one didn't work out either. Or, they don't like the boss so they quit the job. Out they go, and they don't even have another one.

DAY 3
Half-Step Method

It takes some time and some work. Now we can make a commitment. But don't worry about committing yet. You haven't done enough exploring. In those areas where you're hesitant and holding back and unable to make decisions to move forward boldly, you have some more work to do. Now that you made the commitment, you can let go. We can let go of where we're living. We can let go of what we're doing. We can let go of the old friends.

And, by the way, this letting go process may not be a conscious decision. You'll just find yourself spending less time with the friends than you used to spend, or doing the things that you used to do. And, it isn't a matter of, "Oh, I've got to decide to let go." It's a natural process. You just start filling your life with those things that you now want to do, and you squeeze out those things that you don't want to do. You'll find that true of friends, the way you're spending your money and everything else you're spending.

It's a good idea to do some serious thinking, because this affirmation process, and this whole course on how to be effective and cause your future, really works. If you're going to apply it, let's apply it to those things that we spend a lot of time thinking about and really know that this is what we want. In doing so, by the way, it will make that fierce, fierce lock-on to that future, that family, that job, that commitment. It comes from doing all this examining. Keep using your forethought correctly, just for today, for the week, for the month.

DAY 3
Half-Step Method

DAY 4
The Next Time

Key Concepts

Attitude; Negative Self-Talk; Positive Self-Talk; Pygmalion; RAS; Sanction; Second Nature; Self-Esteem.

People are selective information gatherers.

Main Concepts

The most important ideas and insights I have gained from this session are:

Choice Of Activities

The last occasion at home when I corrected someone incorrectly was:

How would I use the three stages or steps to constructively handle the situation?

• Step 1

• Step 2

• Step 3

DAY 4
The Next Time

One thing I do well is:

When I do it well my self-talk is:

and I feel:

One thing I do not do well is:

When I do it well my self-talk says:

and I feel:

When I don't do it well, my self-talk is:

and I feel:

I am focusing on the following ways to handle the talk of others towards me:

DAY 4
The Next Time

Affirmations

Write your own Next Time Affirmations using your ideas gained from this session, your review of related information and notes, as well as affirmation ideas from your Video Resource Guide.

* Refer to the Action/Emotion Word List on pages 173 through 175 for appropriate words.

* Review the Affirmation Checklist on page 171 to be sure you are writing them effectively.

It may be helpful to write down the current reality first, and then describe what it would be like when it is fixed. Use this as the basis to write your affirmations. Transfer your completed affirmations to 3 x 5 cards and place them in your Affirmation Folder.

My Affirmations

Assimilation

Refer to the Affirmation Imprinting Reminders on page 194 as you go through your affirmations.

I get a clear and vivid picture in my mind and I feel the wonderful emotion and mood of already achieving my goal. I dwell on this feeling of achievement, which gives life to my affirmations. I do this for each affirmation. I set aside time at least twice daily to imprint them.

DAY 4
The Next Time

Journal

DAY 4
The Next Time

Audio Summary

Well, how's your day going? Some of the things you might have noticed is how negative the world is. You've noticed it in the newspaper. You've noticed it on television. You've noticed it in your family. You've noticed it at work. Isn't it amazing how negative people are? "Negative" in that they become very critical of others, very demeaning. You have probably noticed a great deal of sarcasm, too. You've noticed people talking about what's wrong with the world instead of what's right with the world.

It's always been there; it's just that your reticular activating system is picking it up. You're hearing things because you have a whole new awareness and you didn't even know it. You need to be careful you don't have the tendency to want to shape them up. They don't really know what they're doing, but don't you get caught up in it. You can see where you were getting caught up in the past. You'd go into wherever you have coffee at work, and it is complain, ain't it awful, and what about this. Do you know what that does to your perception if you give sanction to it? Well, you know that your self-talk affects your perception, because once you get an opinion about the way someone is or this situation is, you become a selective perceiver. So these people are really seeing what it is that they're preparing themselves to see.

Let's take a look, if you have children, at how you can help your children through this. When you hear your children with negative self-talk, make a positive suggestion. Take them right past it. Don't argue with them. Just make a positive affirmation, a positive suggestion to them. When your spouse is making a negative, ain't it awful, things aren't going right comment, what you need to do is not argue or teach the course. What you do is you just be a very positive wizard, a positive Pygmalion, and you make a statement about seeing something in a different way, and you affirm them right past it. "I see it as," or "There's a lot of opportunity here," or "Have you ever thought about," and just change the subject. Switch them past it. Bring up something positive. Bring up something good. Lead them past that.

You do the same at work. You do the same socially. What you're going to do, probably, is find yourself not socializing or hanging around those kinds of people. However, there are some situations that you can't ignore, where those people who you love and are committed to, are in that negative state. It could be a parent. Oftentimes, you get a parent who comes over and, if you have children, that parent may be the one who is negatively affirming your children. Are you going to shape up that parent? I might have a private talk with that person, if I were you. Now that you know the power of negative affirmations on the people that you care about, what you're going to need to do is not embarrass them in front of someone. You know, "I found some new information, and I know you really don't mean to, but what if," and you go on to name the child, "What if they really believe or think that they are the way you're describing them? What if they never change and what if they just stay that way? My goodness. What would their life be like?"

DAY 4
The Next Time

What do you suppose it would be like? Let's just try an experiment. When we see the behavior we don't like in that person, what if we tell them, "I see you as being," and you go on to describe the way you'd like to see them. Instead of telling them, "There you go again. You've been doing it for all your life, you'll never change," what you might say, in some way, maybe even firmly, is, "Stop it. You're too good for that," and you go on to describe the way you positively see them or want them to be.

Remember, the more we affirm the behavior in a person that we don't want, the more they become like it. Now, what I want you to do is become very aware of people who are affirming you when you don't even know it. "That's like you" kind of affirmations are coming your way that really don't fit the way you would like to be. You want to listen for them at work; you want to listen for them at home; you want to listen for them when you're out socially. You're going to hear people telling you and describing you as they see you; and you've given sanction to it unknowingly, and it's negative or it's limiting. Have you ever noticed how hard it is to overcome somebody who has an opinion of how you really are? And you try. Growing now with the affirmation process you're using and applying to your life, you're also living around people who want to keep you as you are, even though the way you are isn't a happy way and isn't fully utilizing your full potential as a person. Yet they know how you are, and they keep telling you, "Why don't you," or "Here's how I see you." Sometimes you need to change your friends. You can't change your family, and I wouldn't recommend that. But what you need to do is not give sanction to those people who are affirming you.

This piece is so essential. Remember what you need to say when they affirm you as "You've always been this way." You could say to yourself, "Well, up until now I might have been, but no longer." And you go on to describe yourself as you are in the future, but in the present tense. Remember you are going to think future in the present tense. You're going to talk to yourself about the way you intend to be as though you already are. You can't get into arguments with people all the time because they see you as you are. But in your own mind, you're just going to say, "That's not like me. That is not like me."

When you do make mistakes – and sometimes your self-talk is more brutal on you than the people you're working with or the people you're living with – remember the whole key is to say to yourself in some way, "No more, that's not like me," and use the phrase, "The next time I intend to." The next time I intend to go this way in the traffic pattern. The next time I intend to say this. The next time I intend to. The next time I intend to be better prepared. The next time I intend to control my temper. The next time I intend to. "The next time, the next time, the next time, the next time, the next time," is what I want you to use.

This whole week, if there were three words that are going to stick in your mind like a song, it is going to be "the next time." And then I want you to add, "I intend to." That's going to control your forethought to be positive instead of repeating the mistake or the pattern, the habit, the behavior or the action. It is going to control your forethought, remember. It's going to push your

DAY 4
The Next Time

forethought forward with a positive change, with the way you would really do it the next time. Now, remember, we're trying to make this second nature to ourselves, automatic. So it doesn't need to be great big things in life; it can be little things in life. This just becomes the way we think every day. This is natural. This is the way you speak to the people around you. How would you do it right, or how would you do it better, or what would you do the next time.

DAY 4
The Next Time

DAY 5
Second Nature

Key Concepts

Affirmation; Assimilation; Attitude; Belief; Forethought; Goal; First Nature; Second Nature; Habit; I x V = R; Potential; Pygmalion; Self-Image.

I enjoy making my affirmations daily.

Main Concepts

The most important ideas and insights I have gained from this session are:

Choice Of Activities

Stepping ahead five months, I see one concrete fun goal for myself which is:

The benefit(s) its achievement would bring me is (are):

DAY 5
Second Nature

My feeling(s) of achievement would be:

One aspect of my life, and my second nature, where I definitely know that I have potential that I'm not using is:

The benefit(s) I would get from increasing the use of that potential is (are):

The attitudes I have about myself that might be hindering me are:

My feelings of satisfaction in the achievement of this increase would be:

DAY 5
Second Nature

Affirmations

Write your own Second Nature Affirmations using your ideas gained from this session, your review of related information and notes, as well as affirmation ideas from your Video Resource Guide.

• Refer to the Action/Emotion Word List on pages 173 through 175 for appropriate words.

• Review the Affirmation Checklist on page 171 to be sure you are writing them effectively.

It may be helpful to write down the current reality first, and then describe what it would be like when it is fixed. Use this as the basis to write your affirmations. Transfer your completed affirmations to 3 x 5 cards and place them in your Affirmation Folder.

My Affirmations

Read
▼
Picture
▼
Feel

Assimilation

Refer to the Affirmation Imprinting Reminders on page 194 as you go through your affirmations.

I get a clear and vivid picture in my mind and I feel the wonderful emotion and mood of already achieving my goal. I dwell on this feeling of achievement, which gives life to my affirmations. I do this for each affirmation. I set aside time at least twice daily to imprint them.

DAY 5
Second Nature

Journal

DAY 5
Second Nature

Audio Summary

We've gone a couple of days now, and we haven't insisted that you do your affirmations. Negligence on my part; negligence on yours; but only if you're not making them. So I'll make the assumption that you are. Those days of the video burst inspired you to do your work and you're writing your affirmations and making your affirmations.

Well, let's talk about affirmations and which ones we should make to start with. Well, let's talk about first nature and second nature. First nature has a lot to do with what you inherited through your parents, right? Your coloring, height, etc., and everything else that goes along with what your genes provide you. We don't know about temperament and musical ability and a lot of those things that perhaps are part of what you inherit.

Let's talk about second nature, the way you run your day. That's the way you run your week. That's the way you run your job. That's the way you run your life. Pretty much all of it is second nature. Second nature is what you have assimilated habitually, attitudinally; it's knowledge and skill, and has been assimilated to where it free flows pretty much automatically. Well, how's your day going? How's your work going? How's your life going? How are your finances going? You'll hear people say, "Well, this is just the way I was born. It's because I'm ..." Well, some of it is, some of it isn't. I don't know which is, and I don't know that you do. But let's act as though most of it is second nature. It was acquired or learned or assimilated, and if that was so, then why don't we use the affirmation process that we learned in the video burst to see if we can improve our second nature?

Where do we want to improve our second nature? Where do we want to free flow? What if we didn't need to try hard to make more money, we just made more money? But what good would it do us to make more money if we don't invest our money or save our money? I know people who would increase their income, maybe double it, but spend a little bit more. Then they'd make more and spend more, make more and spend more. Maybe we need to look at not just making more money, but look at what we want to do with the money. Let's look at our habits and what our second nature is when it comes to dealing with money. What are your beliefs about money?

Now, let's not just talk money. The money is the fuel, isn't it, that causes you to send your kids to school or allows you to live in the style or with the freedom or creature comforts that you wish for or you want. It allows you to build the industry, the business. Maybe, you even have an attitude about making money that needs to be examined, and perhaps changed, in order to release the potential inside yourself.

Oftentimes, I think a lot of people really do want to attack that one issue or that one problem. So I would recommend that as a fun place to start. That's an interesting place to start. It's a nice emotional place to start, because a lot of other things really do connect to whether I have enough money to take the trip or buy the car, or to pay the bills, or give to the church or give to charity. So money is important, and your attitude toward it, your beliefs toward it, have a great

DAY 5
Second Nature

to deal to do with the way your world goes. I wonder if the beliefs you hold on the inside are what you create on the outside. That's what we've been talking about.

The affirmations that you want to make about changing the quality of your environment, or the way your work goes or your life goes, might have a lot to do with your attitude towards wealth, money and finance. I would encourage you to start right there. Don't try to start with something way out so far out that you can't imagine it. Let's just practice for a couple of months and see what happens. Make some affirmations that aren't so far out right now, because we're really trying to learn this information. We're trying to make this information second nature to us.

Now, what are some other areas that you want to examine? One of the ways of doing it is to look and say to yourself, "Where do I have some potential that I'm not using?" – potential in relationships, potential in being a more loving human being, a more responsive human being, a more appreciative human being. What value would that be to you at work, at home, in your community? What changes would transpire if you changed instead of waiting for the other person to change? "I wonder if I changed the way I appreciate people, whether they would be different around me. I wonder if I looked at them with love instead of disdain and disrespect, I wonder how they would be around me. I wonder if I was more thoughtful, I wonder how they would be around me." In a sense, what you're going to do is Pygmalion the people outside of you by changing you on the inside. Not conscious level, "I think I'll do it today because it's a good idea." Remember the affirmations that we're going to use. What they're there for is to cause this to be second nature, automatic, free flow. It's learned, it's assimilated, it's part of me, but I wasn't born this way.

Really, what I'm saying is you look at every area that you feel is important for you, and step ahead three or four months – maybe five months – and say, "I think that what I would like to do is to be," and then you go on to describe that person. Then you back it up and you make the affirmations that would cause you to become, in a second nature way, that which you have the potential to be, that you can see the profitability in being.

It isn't my job to tell you what affirmations to make. I am here to inspire you to build a new second nature; and not just once, but we want to do this in three years, in five years, in ten years. This is an ongoing process, because it's pretty hard for you to see yourself perfect. What you're doing is striving toward not necessarily perfection, but just improvement. You're going to see, in your reflection or in your daily encounters with other human beings, all kinds of opportunities to improve your second nature through the affirmation process – to unleash this beautiful potential inside of each one of you. Remember now, this isn't a conscious level thing. It's conscious level as we write it out. It's conscious level while we're affirming it. But the reason to affirm it over and over with the formula I x V = R – imagination times vividness becomes reality – is really just another way of using your forethought, isn't it? You mentally rehearse as though you are. You mentally rehearse as though you are, over and over.

Now how often you want to make the affirmations each day has a lot to do with how fast you want this assimilated and habituated, so that you free flow in your second nature. You can do it

DAY 5
Second Nature

once a week, if you want. I don't care if you do once a month, but once a month might take you about two years to change your second nature. If you do it a couple of times a day and do it with emotion and clarity and really using your forethought in a focused way, you might be able to recognize this new second nature within just a month or two. You're worth it, and it's worth it. So pick out something that would be easy and fun in order for you to make the change. Work on maybe 10 or 12 changes, just to see if it works.

DAY 5
Second Nature

Wondering About Affirmations

Key Concepts

Act in Accordance with the Truth; Affirmation; Assimilation; Belief; Comfort Zone; Forethought; Potential; Reality; Second Nature; Standard.

We act not in accordance with the truth, but the truth as we believe it to be.

Main Concepts

The most important ideas and insights I have gained from this session are:

Choice Of Activities

I use my forethought to visualize the following examples of a better standard closer to my potential in the areas of:

Income:

Alternative, additional or future ways of earning a living:

Relationships with spouse, child, colleague:

DAY 6
Wondering About Affirmations

One aspect of my life to which I have become accustomed is:

It is good enough for me?

I can improve it by:

A missed opportunity, which could have made a marked difference in my life, is:

I missed it because:

If a similar opportunity occurred now, I would take advantage of it by:

One belief (about myself, a relationship, work or money), which is seriously holding me back, is:

The basis, in reality, for that belief is:

That belief might be based on erroneous opinion and imagination because:

One event of my life in which I was extremely successful and the best for me was:

My affirmation to change, so that the very best I could imagine becomes a new standard, would look like:

And the good feelings of achievement would be:

DAY 6
Wondering About Affirmations

Affirmations

Write your own Wondering About Affirmations using your ideas gained from this session, your review of related information and notes, as well as affirmation ideas from your Video Resource Guide.

- Refer to the Action/Emotion Word List on pages 173 through 175 for appropriate words.

- Review the Affirmation Checklist on page 171 to be sure you are writing them effectively.

It may be helpful to write down the current reality first, and then describe what it would be like when it is fixed. Use this as the basis to write your affirmations. Transfer your completed affirmations to 3 x 5 cards and place them in your Affirmation Folder.

My Affirmations

Assimilation

Refer to the Affirmation Imprinting Reminders on page 194 as you go through your affirmations.

I get a clear and vivid picture in my mind and I feel the wonderful emotion and mood of already achieving my goal. I dwell on this feeling of achievement, which gives life to my affirmations. I do this for each affirmation. I set aside time at least twice daily to imprint them.

DAY 6
Wondering About Affirmations

Journal

DAY 6
Wondering About Affirmations

Audio Summary

Let's take a look at the affirmation process in more depth. I want you to wonder if you could raise your expectations, which we call a standard, through the affirmation process, like raising the bar that you're going to jump over. I want you to wonder if the affirmation process could cause you to expect a higher income. "I wonder if it could cause me to expect people to treat me better, or me to treat people better. I wonder if it could cause me to expect to live or work in a better environment." I wonder, in every area in which you're now working or performing, whether it be the arts or music, whether it be athletics, or no matter what it is, if you can use the affirmation process to change your internal standards, raise your comfort zone, broaden your comfort zone. Because what you're receiving in an automatic second nature way is controlled by your level of expectation on the inside.

Very simply, use the affirmation process to expect a little more of yourself. Now, you might really take off too big a bite. Remember, what we're doing is making this information not Lou Tice's information, but my information. "This isn't the way Lou Tice thinks, this is the way I think. This isn't the way Lou Tice does it. This is the way I do it." I just want you to wonder – which is a part of using your forethought, part of that exploring, part of that experimenting in your mind, taking yourself into the future – if you raised your expectation about communications, what would happen? "I wonder what this quality movement is all about – improving the quality of my work life, my home life, my spiritual life, my social life." I just want you to wonder, "Where I could improve the quality," which is an internal standard, by using the affirmation process.

So up the standard on yourself just a little bit. Don't take off the big bite yet; just see if you can bump it up a little bit. Then if it works, in two or three months do it again. If that works, do it again, do it again, do it again, do it again, do it again, do it again. We are acting in accordance with the truth as we believe it; that's the whole premise of the curriculum. We behave not in accordance with the truth as it really is, but what we do believe it to be. If it's not the truth, it doesn't make any difference; we're limited by it. We're limited by our beliefs.

Ask yourself, "What was the most outrageous, best day I had last year? What was the best workday I had? What was the best I ever performed athletically? What was the best? What was so special? What was, when I look back, once in a lifetime?" And you look at all those areas of your life where throughout last year – or your lifetime, if you want – where you were absolutely, outrageously different than you ever have been, better than you ever have been. Then you say to yourself, "I wonder what it would be like if this would happen all the time. I wonder what it would be like if that was the standard." Well, that's the whole idea of it.

You look at where it was at any part of your life where you want improvement. Those of you who golf, go back. If you had a favorite course that you play, and over the last few years go back and add up the best you ever did on each one of the 18 holes. That would be perhaps an outrageous score at the end, wouldn't it? Well, that's your potential. You've actually done it on different

DAY 6
Wondering About Affirmations

days. What you need to do is to put it all together, and you need to expect it, and change that internal standard.

Well, do the same with every part of your work world. Do the same with every part of your social world. Do the same with everything that you have ever done around your family. What is the best you've done? Now, that's where your affirmations come in. We don't really need to go out and try to invent something we want to do new in the future. Maybe what we've been doing has really been fun and exciting and worthwhile, but not often enough, only once or twice. What we want to do is use the affirmation process to visualize ourselves doing it regularly, automatically.

In a sense, this is just the way I am. I know what you're thinking, "If I use up all my specials, my life will be dull." What happens then is you have new peaks, new specials, and then you make that an affirmation process. You keep raising your internal standards, and you keep acting like the person and being like the person you know yourself to be. We're just using this affirmation process to improve "how I'm supposed to be." Does that make sense? See how simple that is? Don't make it hard. Don't make it complicated. Make it easy.

DAY 7
Habits

Key Concepts

Current Reality; Flexibility; Forethought; Goal; Habit; Serendipitous; Superstition.

Is this habit necessary?

Main Concepts

The most important ideas and insights I have gained from this session are:

Choice Of Activities

Daily/weekly routines or habits I could spend less time on, or cut out completely, because they hinder my new goals, are:

DAY 7
Habits

My superstitious habits, that I would like to change, are:

I would like to change these habits because:

DAY 7
Habits

Affirmations

Write your own Habits Affirmations using your ideas gained from this session, your review of related information and notes, as well as affirmation ideas from your Video Resource Guide.

- Refer to the Action/Emotion Word List on pages 173 through 175 for appropriate words.

- Review the Affirmation Checklist on page 171 to be sure you are writing them effectively.

It may be helpful to write down the current reality first, and then describe what it would be like when it is fixed. Use this as the basis to write your affirmations. Transfer your completed affirmations to 3 x 5 cards and place them in your Affirmation Folder.

My Affirmations

Read
▼
Picture
▼
Feel

Assimilation

Refer to the Affirmation Imprinting Reminders on page 194 as you go through your affirmations.

I get a clear and vivid picture in my mind and I feel the wonderful emotion and mood of already achieving my goal. I dwell on this feeling of achievement, which gives life to my affirmations. I do this for each affirmation. I set aside time at least twice daily to imprint them.

DAY 7
Habits

Journal

DAY 7
Habits

Audio Summary

In your own mind you ought to be thinking bigger, having a greater sense of wonderment, aspiring to new things. This will occur on an ongoing basis. One of the things we need to discuss is that once you get an idea about what you want to do – say, at work or do with your family or even something new with you – there doesn't seem to be enough time in the day in order to accomplish what it is you want to accomplish. You're trying to figure out, "Should I stay up more? Do I get up earlier? How am I going to get more time?" Well, you're not going to get more time.

What we need to be able to do is change some habits or routines. Some of the things that we're doing we won't be able to accomplish because you're too busy doing the things you're presently doing. "Well, we always see the Nisses on Thursday night." Well, see them every other Thursday. "Well, Monday is my bowling night." Well, go bowling once a month instead of once a week. You don't need to necessarily let go of these things. It's all right if you do. You don't need to sit down and consciously plan. But as you start visualizing the new end results, a part of your creativity should be to reorganize your day. Some of you are so locked into your day, you're so firm in your routine, that you don't allow yourself to let go of what you do in the morning or what you do in the evening or what you do on the weekend.

You need to become a little more serendipitous now. You need to allow yourself to reorganize your time for you, and let yourself drop some of the things that you have been doing in order to allow yourself to enlarge your life. Some flexibility is needed. Sometimes you can deliberately pattern in a new habit. Sometimes you just let it happen, just let it flow in.

When I was coaching in high school, there was a wonderful person by the name of Joe. (I won't use his last name.) He was the baseball coach, and he was so predictable. I would know that at lunchtime, when I would be sitting in the locker room in the office, he would come in with two cups of soup – one for him, one for me. He would come with crackers in his right pocket. He would kick the door two times because he had soup in both hands, expecting me to get up and open the door. He would come in, and he would set his down and then walk over and set mine down, take the crackers out. This would happen every day for months and months and months. He was so routined. One time when I was coaching and he was one of my assistants, I made the mistake of stopping at Zesto's for a milkshake before I went to the game. He was in the car with me. Now, before every game for two years we needed to stop at Zesto's for a milkshake and it had to be the same flavor. It's called superstition. It's called so locked into a routine that you almost feel guilty or uneasy if you don't follow the same pattern or same routine.

Many of you are that way. You don't have the flexibility to change what you think you might. But that wasn't so bad. Remember about forethought? If we missed the milkshake, guess what he would think? "We're going to lose." How come? "We didn't get a milkshake." What's practice all week got to do with it then? Why don't we just stop at Zesto's for a milkshake and skip practice all week? Can you imagine what you do to yourself, some of you?

DAY 7
Habits

Another thing that I did, which was just to drive him crazy, I would walk to one end zone before a game and I'd pick up chalk and put it in my right pocket off the field. Then I'd go to the other end zone and pick up chalk and put it in my right pocket. And he would always ask me before, "Have you got your chalk?" Have you got your chalk. Like if I didn't get the chalk, we were going to lose? Yeah. That wasn't so bad, but if I didn't get the chalk or if I told him I didn't have it, he would get this feeling, "I don't feel right about the game." And he'd communicate, "I don't feel right about the game" to the kids, the players. Something's wrong. The coach doesn't feel right.

Can you imagine how you get so grooved and so into your routines, almost superstitious about them, that you don't allow yourself a new pattern? You don't allow yourself the inventiveness and the creativity to flow, and you need to have a new pattern in order to accomplish new goals. You are already busy, already doing, filling your day. And if these new goals are coming about – the new, bigger aspirations, or just different ones – it means you can't just jam more into your day. You're going to need to let go. So check yourself for flexibility, look at where you're almost superstitious, look at where you get that inner feeling that, "I'm not doing something right, something's not there."

I can remember when we first started in this business, Diane and I didn't travel much. She was going to go to Colorado, when I was working with the University of Colorado football team for the first time. I came home, and the airplane was going to leave in a couple of hours. (This was before we needed to go through all those security checks.) So I walked into the kitchen, and here was Diane – we still had all of our children – scrubbing the kitchen floor. Now, we're going to catch an airplane to Colorado in two hours, and the airport is about 20 minutes away. And I said, "Diane, what are you doing?" She said, "What's it look like? I'm scrubbing the floor." But what I really meant was, "Aren't you going?" She said, "Yes." "Well, what are you scrubbing the floor for?" "Oh," she said, "I don't feel like a mother unless I scrub the floor." Well, how do you argue with that? You don't. But you don't go to Colorado either. I mean you need to get somebody else to scrub the floor.

You must look inside yourself and ask, "Where are those emotional tugs?" Where are those things that don't let you be what you're capable of being or do what you're capable of doing? What is it to be a mother? What is it to be a father? What is it to be who you are? See, don't be so invested in who you are presently in order to restrict you from becoming who you are going to be in your new you, your new life that you're creating for yourself. Some of those habits, some of those processes, some of those ways, we need to examine. "Maybe there is a better way, and I need to be able to be an option thinker and a creative thinker." We're going to talk about option thinking and creative thinking in some of our next segments, so see you in a little while.

DAY 8
Comfort Zones

Key Concepts

Affirmation; Attitude; Comfort Zone; Creative Subconscious; Flick-Back/Flick-Up; Forethought; Goal; Habit; Self-Talk; Subconscious; Reflective Thinking; Resilience; Second Nature; Self-Esteem; Servo-Mechanism.

Most of our limitations are self-imposed.

Main Concepts

The most important ideas and insights I have gained from this session are:

Choice Of Activities

A few of my current limitations are:

I would like to eliminate these limitations by:

DAY 8
Comfort Zones

At home, one thing I have become used to is:

My reason for changing this is:

At work, one thing I have become use to is:

My reason for changing this is:

DAY 8
Comfort Zones

Affirmations

Write your own Comfort Zone Affirmations using your ideas gained from this session, your review of related information and notes, as well as affirmation ideas from your Video Resource Guide.

- Refer to the Action/Emotion Word List on pages 173 through 175 for appropriate words.

- Review the Affirmation Checklist on page 171 to be sure you are writing them effectively.

It may be helpful to write down the current reality first, and then describe what it would be like when it is fixed. Use this as the basis to write your affirmations. Transfer your completed affirmations to 3 x 5 cards and place them in your Affirmation Folder.

My Affirmations

Assimilation

Read
▼
Picture
▼
Feel

Refer to the Affirmation Imprinting Reminders on page 194 as you go through your affirmations.

I get a clear and vivid picture in my mind and I feel the wonderful emotion and mood of already achieving my goal. I dwell on this feeling of achievement, which gives life to my affirmations. I do this for each affirmation. I set aside time at least twice daily to imprint them.

DAY 8
Comfort Zones

Journal

DAY 8
Comfort Zones

Audio Summary

In order for us to really accomplish, we're talking about change inside of ourselves. Changing what? Changing habits? Changing attitudes, routines, and ways of doing things. What many of you are going to need to do, in order to really accomplish more, is to get people to help you. How do you feel about that? How do you feel about having somebody to help with the house, if you need more time? How do you feel about someone helping you with the garden, if you need that? How do you feel about somebody doing some of the things that you're presently doing, like driving your children to school, if you need to? How are you feeling about whatever? Some of those things really need to be examined in your reflective thinking to release this potential. The affirmation process will change the habit. It will change the attitude. And as you put this goal in, you're trying to do things on the conscious level, but you have these old patterns holding you back.

Years ago, when I was teaching high school, we were always looking for ways to raise money for certain projects. It could have been for new equipment or new something to do. So, when I had a lot of these young people around me, I would come up with ideas about what could we do to raise money. We could sell cupcakes, you can hold a bake sale, you can wash cars. I mean there are all kinds of ways of raising money for what projects they wanted, which are fun things to do. I remember one time, when I was looking for a way for them to make money, I said, "Here's an idea." When we have these parades and carnivals and events going on during the summertime in the community where we were living, which was Seattle, there are a lot of opportunities for you. If you will go out and invest in a container of helium gas and get some penny balloons and some string, and then you just fill the balloons full of helium, tie some string around them, and go to the parade. If somebody is selling them for a dollar, sell them for 75 cents. If somebody is selling for 75, sell them for 50 cents. If somebody is selling for 50, sell them for a quarter.

Have you ever been around people when you offer opportunities there's always this "yes, but?" Yes, but, and they try to tell you why it won't work. Yes, that's a good idea, but. Have you run into those lately? Well, here I was giving them these ideas about selling balloons, and this one kid raised his hand, and he said, "Yes, but what if we're selling these balloons and the police come and we don't have a license?" Holy cow! I looked at this kid, and I said to him, "Well, you have two handfuls of balloons. If the police come and you don't have a license, all you do is go, 'What balloons?' And open your hands and let go of the string."

Now, I only use that to illustrate how many of you, should I make a lot of suggestions about what is possible and what you could be doing with your future, you keep going "Yes, but; yes, but; yes, but. The "Yes" is to shut me up and the "but" is to change the subject. It's an interesting thing that sometimes you need to let go of what you're holding onto. You need to let go of all the reasons why something won't work.

I used the story from a lady that used to work for us. When she was being raised as a child in one of the New England states of the United States, coming from a Catholic family, she was the

DAY 8
Comfort Zones

only girl. When she was about 19 years old, her mother was always fussing over her, worried and concerned, she said, "Mother, I'm going out tonight," and mother said, "Well, where are you going?" "Well, I'm going to the dance." "What time are you going to be home?" "Well, I'll be home at 12 o'clock or 1 o'clock." "How are you going to get there?" "Oh, I'm going to drive the car." And mother says, "What if you're driving the car and you get a flat fire and it's 12 o'clock?" Something to be concerned about, really, and she replied, "Well, I'll stop and get the spare tire out and fix the tire." Mother said, "But if you're by yourself and somebody comes, what are you going to do? What if you're changing the tire and somebody comes and attacks you?" She said, "I'll hit them with the jack handle." Mother said, "But what if he's bigger than you?" And she said, "Then I'll run." "What if he's faster than you?" She said, "You're right, I shouldn't go."

How many of you "what if" yourself or someone else to death, or allow somebody else to "what if" you to death and you get caught up in it? Let go of the balloons. Option think. Let go. What do you need to let go of? Not just now, but this must be a way of your life. This needs to be second nature. What are you hanging onto that's holding you back?

Remember the story about the farmer who brought a pumpkin, like a squash, to a county fair. And it was unusual because it was the exact size and shape of a two gallon jug – the same shape as a jug with a handle and kind of a mouth to it. He won some blue ribbons, and people would go by and "ooh" and "ah" about the pumpkin. They'd say, "How in the dickens did you ever grow a pumpkin like a two gallon jug?" The farmer said, "Well, it's easy. As soon as the plant started to blossom, I just stuck it inside of a two gallon jug. Then it just grew to be the exact size and shape of the two gallon jug. As soon as it was grown, I broke the glass, and here it is."

Ah, I thought, that's what we do with our creativity, with our ideas, with our lives. We build a container of "can'ts," "they won't let me's," and "it's not possible." We build the container within which we build our business future, our life. Some of us build a container the size of an aspirin bottle, and we put our whole life into a small container. Now, what is the container? It's our imagination. It is that imagination that is allowing your mind to wonder, allowing your mind to expand, to explore. It's an aspiration. It's an ideal. It's an vision. It's a, "I wonder what I could be. I wonder what I could do. I wonder where I could go." I wonder. I wonder. And watch out for the "what ifs." Watch out for the "shoulds" and "hold onto all the balloons" and "what if the police come."

Many of you talk yourself out of things. Now, why do we do that? Ah, you remember. When you look forward out of your comfort zone and you see something that is dangerous that might occur, your subconscious, without asking it, stimulates negative creativity. Most of these people are out of their comfort zone. And when you're out of your comfort zone, you don't ask for it, but your subconscious gives you three reasons why it won't work; or 30 reasons why it won't work; or 300 reasons why it won't work. First of all, if you're going to do something, you need to ask yourself, "Do I want to?" If you don't want to, forget about it, because you're going to come up with why it won't work. You'll talk yourself out of it. Quit talking yourself out of your future and your potential. The first thing you need to do is decide, "Why do I want it? Why would it be per-

DAY 8
Comfort Zones

sonally profitable to me? Why would it be beneficial?" Think about why you do want it, because if you don't want it, your whole creativity will talk you out of it. Just the opposite, if you do want it and you do see you want it, your subconscious stimulates positive ideas about how to get it, how to do it. See how important it is to control your forethought? See how important it is to allow yourself to think expansively, creatively?

So as you keep growing on the inside with your affirmations, and building your strength, with your flick-back and flick-up, and with all the things that you've done well and all the resiliency that we've talked about, what it does is it seems to put the lid on that negative creativity and get you to start thinking about constructively how to do it and why to do it. See you soon.

DAY 8
Comfort Zones

DAY 9
Attitudes

Key Concepts

Affirmation; Attitude; Comfort Zone; Creative Subconscious; Goal; Potential; Reflective Thinking; Self-Talk; Visualization.

Attitude awareness through reflective thinking.

Main Concepts

The most important ideas and insights I have gained from this session are:

Choice Of Activities

My attitude about being a "morning" or "evening" person is:

How does this attitude of mine affect my day and the accomplishment of my goals?

DAY 9
Attitudes

As I prioritize my day, my goals (in order of importance) are:

The goals that are easy for me to accomplish are:

The goals I creatively avoid are:

My attitude is:

An individual with whom I have trouble working is:

What is my attitude?

This week I will change my attitude and look for positive things that he or she does.

DAY 9
Attitudes

Affirmations

Write your own Attitudes Affirmations using your ideas gained from this session, your review of related information and notes, as well as affirmation ideas from your Video Resource Guide.

- Refer to the Action/Emotion Word List on pages 173 through 175 for appropriate words.

- Review the Affirmation Checklist on page 171 to be sure you are writing them effectively.

It may be helpful to write down the current reality first, and then describe what it would be like when it is fixed. Use this as the basis to write your affirmations. Transfer your completed affirmations to 3 x 5 cards and place them in your Affirmation Folder.

My Affirmations

Read
▼
Picture
▼
Feel

Assimilation

Refer to the Affirmation Imprinting Reminders on page 194 as you go through your affirmations.

I get a clear and vivid picture in my mind and I feel the wonderful emotion and mood of already achieving my goal. I dwell on this feeling of achievement, which gives life to my affirmations. I do this for each affirmation. I set aside time at least twice daily to imprint them.

DAY 9
Attitudes

Journal

DAY 9
Attitudes

Audio Summary

I wonder where this negative self-talk comes from. Are you hanging around people who are telling you why things won't work? And even within yourself, where does your negative self-talk originate? How does it get there? Well, it could be habitual, but it could be because you're forcing yourself out of your comfort zone. It could be because, as you take yourself out of your social comfort zone, your subconscious is telling you why you shouldn't go. Your children need you or you have too many other things to do. "I've got some work to do."

You see, negative creativity is best stimulated when you drop yourself into a situation where you're intimidated by it. And when you're intimidated by the situation or the event or the investment or the work, your subconscious starts figuring out avoidant behaviors. Now, that's something to be guarded against; that's what you use your reflective thinking for, to capture that. Now, I don't want you to bully yourself into it. I don't want you to force yourself into it. What I want you to do is use your affirmation process to stretch your comfort zone, to visualize yourself into the next plateau safely. "Next plateau" meaning into that social situation or into that business situation; into that trip or into that world where it's so different – that different restaurant, that different store, that new process at work.

You look at what is it that is intimidating, and you need to be subtle about this, not to make yourself look weak or cowardly. When I'm talking about intimidating, you know what I'm talking about. It gets inside you. You can see yourself or hear yourself in your own mind come up with reasons why you ought to avoid. That's why you use your reflective thinking, because I want you to go back each day and see what it is you're avoiding. How come you can't get yourself started? How come you get started, but you get diverted? How come you're getting off track? How come you can't stay focused? How come you can't concentrate? "I think what I need is to work on my day planner more." "I think what I ought to do is really lock into this." "I've got to get my routine down." What you need to do is to get your attitude right. You need to get your mind right about what you're going after. That's where your negative creativity is being stimulated; your negative self-talk is coming from; and you also become very susceptible to other people. It doesn't take much for them to talk you out of going.

What if you have a whole group around you that needs to move forward at work and you're all talking yourself out of it because you're all frightened of the future? Now, have a good talk. You need to take care of your own mind, your own thinking, your own future. So this negative self-talk, coupled with old negative attitudes, wow. Remember, attitudes are not positive or negative until you set a new goal, and let's go back to the definition of positive and negative. Positive means moving towards. Negative means moving away, or avoidant.

So here we are, sometimes talking about we're going to go after this, going to go after that, and I'm going to do this and I'm going to be that. You really mean it while you're sitting here and it's safe. But as you start pursuing the outcome or the goal, you just can't get yourself to do it. Now,

DAY 9
Attitudes

you don't necessarily tell yourself not to do it. You engage in avoidant behavior or avoidant activities. You find yourself getting off the path, off the track. Instead of going directly – forcefully, creatively, assertively – towards the outcome, you find yourself filling your day or your week with things that don't need to be done.

I would guess that many of you are so busy not because you are so busy, but I would guess that many of you are busy avoiding what it is that you don't want to do. So much of what you're doing isn't because you need to do it. Much of what you're doing, I would guess, is to keep you from doing what you don't want to do. Think about that and write that down. Now, what are you going to do? Give up on your goal or change your attitude? Change your attitude. This is a lifetime process, particularly if you're going to keep growing, continually setting new goals. Many of the old attitudes were absolutely fine for the old goals or the way we're doing life now. But as I set new aspirations and new goals, my old attitudes jump right out.

How do you recognize an attitude? That is what you need to do with your reflective thinking. You need to look and see, "Today, how come I didn't do what I set out to do?" "Well, the reason is," go ahead and believe it, if you want; it may be true, may be an accident and something did interrupt, and that could very well be. But day after day? Is this just bad luck, or do you really need to examine the attitudes you have? I've needed to examine attitudes all the time on myself in order to let myself grow.

Now, hear what I'm saying? Letting myself grow. I needed to change attitudes. I always need to change attitudes. I don't know when I got some of them. I know when I get them now. When I use the affirmation process, I assimilate new attitudes in me. So many of the attitudes I had, I just picked up sloppily, casually, kind of by osmosis – hanging around the people I'm hanging around, reading what I'm reading, doing what I'm doing, listening to what I'm listening to. These attitudes were just picked up. I didn't really set out to get many of them. It wasn't like I decided, "This is the one I want and this is the one I want," until I knew this information.

Going forward, there's more to it than like this ad that we see by this sporting shoe manufacturer, "just do it." "Just do it" isn't that easy, because you can't override and overpower that subconscious will to avoid danger, fear, or unpleasantness. You're too inventive and too creative. Your subconscious will work to get you out of it and hold you back from being what you're capable of being.

It's very important that once you discover the attitude, that's where you're going to use the affirmation process. Get to work on the attitude, and then release the potential that's inside of you and make some wonderful changes that you're capable of making. Otherwise, forget your goal. You're not going to do it. You just might as well forget it. You're not going to do it.

Willpower cannot override that subconscious power of avoidance and creativity. You're not tough enough to overcome that subconscious trying to get you out of something that's unpleasant trying to use willpower and discipline. All it's going to do is put you into a double bind.

DAY 9
Attitudes

You're going to be working back out of it, stronger than you're going forward. You just keep saying, "I've got to get tougher." No, no, no. You need to change the attitude, change the routines. Don't give up on your goals. Give up on outdated attitudes. See you soon.

DAY 9
Attitudes

DAY 10
Self-Esteem

Key Concepts

Attitudinal Balance Scale; Assimilation; Credibility; Sanction; Self-Esteem; Self-Talk; Subconscious; Truth.

The word "esteem" comes from the verb "to estimate."

Main Concepts

The most important ideas and insights I have gained from this session are:

Choice Of Activities

Some of the negative or limiting estimations I, and others (parents, teachers, managers, colleagues), have made about me are:

Which are true?

What have I done about the ones that were true?

I am going to get rid of the false ones that I have accepted up until now by:

DAY 10
Self-Esteem

People whose judgment of me I respect are:

What can I do to make their wisdom more available to me?

A list of my achievements of which I am proud is:

DAY 10
Self-Esteem

Affirmations

Write your own Self-Esteem Affirmations using your ideas gained from this session, your review of related information and notes, as well as affirmation ideas from your Video Resource Guide.

*   Refer to the Action/Emotion Word List on pages 173 through 175 for appropriate words.

*   Review the Affirmation Checklist on page 171 to be sure you are writing them effectively.

It may be helpful to write down the current reality first, and then describe what it would be like when it is fixed. Use this as the basis to write your affirmations. Transfer your completed affirmations to 3 x 5 cards and place them in your Affirmation Folder.

My Affirmations

Read
▼
Picture
▼
Feel

Assimilation

Refer to the Affirmation Imprinting Reminders on page 194 as you go through your affirmations.

I get a clear and vivid picture in my mind and I feel the wonderful emotion and mood of already achieving my goal. I dwell on this feeling of achievement, which gives life to my affirmations. I do this for each affirmation. I set aside time at least twice daily to imprint them.

DAY 10
Self-Esteem

Journal

DAY 10
Self-Esteem

Audio Summary

Let's talk about self-esteem in this segment. First of all, a really interesting way of thinking about self-esteem, very simply, is what is your estimation of your own worth? If we were going to sell a piece of property – let's say you had a house or a vacant piece of property someplace and you were going to sell that vacant piece of property – would you go to your best friend and say, "Tell me what it's worth?" Or would you go to, say, just a neighbor and say, "Tell me what it's worth?" Would you get somebody off the street and say, "Please, just tell me what it's worth, because I'm going to sell my piece of property?" Would you perhaps at work say to somebody you know well at work, and you like what they do, and say, "Tell me, what's this piece of property worth?" Well, there might be a better way. As you ask what it's worth, are they a credible expert in evaluating this piece of property? They may be a good doctor, they may be the best that you have on the job. It may be your best friend, but do they really know the value of property?

So an estimator is someone who needs to have some background or credibility in what they're estimating. What we do if we're not careful, though, is go around and we ask people what they think of us, or what do you think of my chances in this career or in this job? Please give me an estimation of my worth; my worth personally now, my worth in the future, and so on. And I don't think that you would be well advised in the first place, if we were talking about a piece of property, to go to your neighbor or your friend. But how many times do we allow other people to give us an estimation of our own worth? Stop it.

Really ask the question. They may be wonderful people, but do they really know me? Do they really know what I want to be? Do they really know this information? Do they know what I know presently, now that I've gone through this curriculum? Do I really know that I need to be careful how I even evaluate myself? Am I qualified to estimate my own worth? Well, I'm probably as well qualified as a lot of them, but not if, in fact, I don't think well of myself.

See, one of the things we find in estimating our own worth, is we don't respect our own opinion enough. Let's be silly and you might say as you go out – because you're not so sure, not confident about how you look, you're a little unsure of yourself – you're going to go someplace for an interview or you're going to go someplace that's special or you're going to give a talk someplace or you're going to some special occasion. So you say to your friend or your spouse or somebody, "Well, tell me, how do I look?" Well, why would you ask them? You want their estimate of how you look. "Do I look all right?" Oh, no, you look a mess. You look terrible. Why your hair is – oh, no. "Well, I'm sure glad I asked you, because I almost went out looking like this."

See, what we're doing constantly is asking others' opinions of ourselves and what they think. Why? Because we're not sure of our own worth appraisal. It seems when you gain in self-esteem or feeling of self-worth, you no longer need to be constantly eliciting the approval or the estimate of another person. That's where I want to get you. It doesn't mean that we don't ask for

DAY 10
Self-Esteem

advice or ask for some mentoring or criticism. But we stop being vulnerable to the opinions, the comments, the estimates, if you will, of just anybody off the street, or anybody at work.

Now, one of the challenges seems to be – and when I say this, I want you to take it the way it's meant – be most careful about the people who you respect the most around you, and be most careful about the people that you are closest to, because I think those are the ones you will give sanction, more than likely, to their opinions than you would a stranger. And they can be the ones that would be the most damaging, because you really do value what they think. Keep in mind now, it doesn't make any difference what comes your direction. It's only when you give sanction or approval or agree with them.

We can become so vulnerable, can't we? Particularly when things aren't going right for us, or something is not going well at work, or something's not going well at home. We become more susceptible and unsure of ourselves. So you need to watch those vulnerable moments when you're more susceptible to the approval or the comment of another. Remember now what you're doing is building your own self-esteem with your own appraisal or your own self-talk. You don't need to be harsh and critical and negative towards the other person. One of the things that you must learn is to really become a good appraiser of the comments that are being directed your way. Watch for all the negative weights that people are trying to put on your attitudinal balance scale. They don't mean to, it's almost thoughtless or careless. It's almost like it's freely given. It's almost like they really don't know what they're doing. But you know what effect it will have on your own sense of value, your own sense of worth, if you give sanction to it.

Now, as you start building your self-esteem, your performance seems to follow. The stronger the self-worth, then what do you do? Well, you draw people to you, business opportunity to you, friendships to you, that you feel worthy of receiving. And if, in fact, you've spent a good week or two, or a month or two, or a year or two of lowering your own self-esteem, you can see it by the kind of opportunity, the kind of friends, the kind of relationships and so on that are coming your way. Now, do you sit and wait for the outside to change, or do we change the inside? Try it. Change the inside. Speak well of yourself. Think well of yourself. Tell yourself, "Yes, that's like me. Yes, I am good at that. Yes, I am a person of high value." See you soon.

DAY 11
Changing Habit Patterns

Key Concepts

Affirmation; Attitude; Belief; Fear; Forethought; Habit; Internal Standard; Potential; Second Nature.

We rarely exceed our inner standards.

Main Concepts

The most important ideas and insights I have gained from this session are:

Choice Of Activities

Three habits, routines or internal standards I admire in others, which I think would help me in the achievement of those goals that I have chosen to pursue, are:

DAY 11
Changing Habit Patterns

As I study my habits and routines for a week, the ones that would be of benefit to modify or change are:

My habits and routines that I have kept out of fear are:

DAY 11
Changing Habit Patterns

Affirmations

Write your own Changing Habit Patterns Affirmations using your ideas gained from this session, your review of related information and notes, as well as affirmation ideas from your Video Resource Guide.

- Refer to the Action/Emotion Word List on pages 173 through 175 for appropriate words.

- Review the Affirmation Checklist on page 171 to be sure you are writing them effectively.

It may be helpful to write down the current reality first, and then describe what it would be like when it is fixed. Use this as the basis to write your affirmations. Transfer your completed affirmations to 3 x 5 cards and place them in your Affirmation Folder.

My Affirmations

Read
▼
Picture
▼
Feel

Assimilation

Refer to the Affirmation Imprinting Reminders on page 194 as you go through your affirmations.

I get a clear and vivid picture in my mind and I feel the wonderful emotion and mood of already achieving my goal. I dwell on this feeling of achievement, which gives life to my affirmations. I do this for each affirmation. I set aside time at least twice daily to imprint them.

DAY 11
Changing Habit Patterns

Journal

DAY 11
DAY 11
Changing Habit Patterns

Audio Summary

Let's take the issue of working harder, trying to get more done; getting more done with less help or less resources; or getting things done in what seems to be a shorter day. People are demanding more of us in some way. Oh, dear, how are we going to do it? Well, again, is it a matter of using more discipline on yourself? Or is it a matter of working harder on yourself, or maybe changing some attitudes? Is it a matter of changing some of the patterns that we call habits? Is it a matter of really changing inside myself some beliefs that become an internal standard, of which I can't seem to get past?

Well, I don't know if you have any potential inside yourself, because that's up to you. I would suggest that you say you do and that it is possible to be much more effective. To get 10 times more done than you're presently getting done, or even a hundred times more or 500 times more, how in the dickens could we do that? Well, it isn't going to be by staying up later or getting up earlier, although that might help. It's really going to be to take a look at some of the patterns – where I'm spending my time – and then to observe how others, who are doing those kinds of things that I admire or would like to be doing. Then, to use the affirmation process to change my pattern of what I do with my time or my work or my day.

It's a matter of observing another who seems to be successful in the work that you would like to do, and then you write out that pattern in affirmation form. In the comfort of your own living room or a chair, wherever you seem to be comfortable, take yourself through the new routine. In your mind, just go through it. Change the pattern.

See, until you can get yourself into a new groove and let yourself flow, you might only do this one time on this day. Tomorrow you'll be right back where you were. It's a matter of reprogramming the way you work, what you do with your morning, what you do with your evening; what you do on a Wednesday, what you do on a Friday; what you do each month. Observe the pattern you're doing now and say, "Well, that was all right, but now that I have new goals or I have new objectives. I'm not getting it done with the old pattern. What new pattern do I need?" And that's where you use the affirmation process to groove in a new routine.

When you groove in the new routine, you cannot use fear. Don't bully yourself. Don't use fear. If you use fear to pattern yourself, then it's hard to change in the future. So, it needs to be constructive input. It needs to be one that will allow you to let go of this pattern, because in several months, you're going to groove a new one. In areas where you have difficulty grooving new habit patterns, it could be that those were put in with a fear feedback loop.

That's the way we used to coach when I was coaching football. You would punish people or you would yell at them or you would scream at them. If they didn't do things right or step correctly, you would make them do push ups or run a lap or get angry with them, or embarrass them or ridicule them. So they get grooved in their pattern very well, and they function with that technique or that offensive pattern or that movement very well. But the problem is, when you try to

DAY 11
Changing Habit Patterns

bring in a new pattern or change them, they'll fight you to the death. It isn't because they are too stubborn, it is that to deviate from a fear imprinted habit pattern takes a lot of courage.

Some of you are so grooved out of a fear feedback process that you won't allow yourself to undo the habit pattern you're caught up in. You want to look: were you frightened, or were you around a manager who was angry, or who would perhaps withhold your future if you made a mistake? You did get the pattern down so well, but now you're so grooved with that fear feedback, you won't allow yourself to deviate from it. It's almost as if it's sinful. It's almost like it's immoral. But it really isn't; it's just the patterns you've been grooved with.

Examine why you won't let yourself into new routine, into new habits, into new patterns, then use the affirmation process – once you decide the new pattern that would be beneficial – use the affirmation process in a constructive way to groove it so that you flow as it is needed. When it isn't needed, discard it and move on. As we set new goals, as we grow and change our career path, as we change the size of our business and change what we want to do during the week, the month or the year, we can't do it the same old way. So, you need to use this process every time you want a new second nature, a new free flowing of the way you want your week, your day, your month, and then be willing to let it go. The other issue, of course, was the attitudes. We'll pick up attitudes in the next segment. So see you soon.

DAY 12
Attitudes Review

Key Concepts

Affirmation; Attitude; Creativity; Emotion; Energy; Flick-Back/Flick-Up; Forethought; GI/GO; Goal; Habit; Visualization.

Attitudes can help us reach our goals, or they can block us.

Main Concepts

The most important ideas and insights I have gained from this session are:

Choice Of Activities

Which current attitudes do I have that will hinder the achievement of the goals that I have chosen?

Which attitudes would it benefit me to modify and which should I get rid of?

DAY 12
Attitudes Review

Some people I know to be highly effective are:

The attitudes that they possess that contribute greatly to their achievements are:

My library of positive emotions, to flick-back to, includes:

DAY 12
Attitudes Review

Affirmations

Write your own Attitudes Review Affirmations using your ideas gained from this session, your review of related information and notes, as well as affirmation ideas from your Video Resource Guide.

- Refer to the Action/Emotion Word List on pages 173 through 175 for appropriate words.

- Review the Affirmation Checklist on page 171 to be sure you are writing them effectively.

It may be helpful to write down the current reality first, and then describe what it would be like when it is fixed. Use this as the basis to write your affirmations. Transfer your completed affirmations to 3 x 5 cards and place them in your Affirmation Folder.

My Affirmations

Assimilation

Refer to the Affirmation Imprinting Reminders on page 194 as you go through your affirmations.

I get a clear and vivid picture in my mind and I feel the wonderful emotion and mood of already achieving my goal. I dwell on this feeling of achievement, which gives life to my affirmations. I do this for each affirmation. I set aside time at least twice daily to imprint them.

Read
▼
Picture
▼
Feel

DAY 12
Attitudes Review

Journal

DAY 12
Attitudes Review

Audio Summary

Can we discuss the necessity of changing habit patterns? So few people really do that and then the stress occurs of trying to jam more into their day, or take a conscious control over their pattern at the present moment. Like somebody who uses martial arts or an astronaut or someone who would be an elite strike force person, what they do is they build simulations, sometimes in simulators, and they take themselves through in their mind. They groove their pattern over and over, with the proper emotion, until it flows smoothly.

Remember the example I where we talked about an airliner that I was on? When the tires blew out, the pilot put the nose back down and kept us on the runway without killing anybody. You see, what happened is he had grooved that pattern, that habit pattern of what to do when this emergency exists. You don't look it up. It's already grooved. It's habitual.

So, you look forward and see the patterns you need three months from now, seven months from now. When this occurs, "This is the way I'll behave." When this occurs, "This is what I'll do." Now, that's not enough, because we also need to know that we have attitudes or emotional patterns that are grooved. Those are habits of emotion, if you will. Some of those are very constructive and they save our lives, and they cause our lives to go well. But some of those attitudes interfere with allowing ourselves to use the potential, or seek out new opportunity or new goals. They help us engage in creative, avoidant behavior, as opposed to behavior that would cause us and stimulate us to move forward.

Let's take a look and review what attitude is. It's just the direction in which you lean. In aeronautical terminology, if you remember, an attitude was the wings of the airplane in relationship to a fixed point like the horizon. What you say is, does it lean? In a sense, the way that it leans is what they call the attitude of the airplane, the direction in which it is leaning. A positive attitude then, if we're going to use that, means that you're leaning toward the goal, toward the social situation, toward the financial situation, toward what it is that you see would bring you some value. That's a positive attitude, and you feel good about it. It brings up a positive emotion that's attractive. It causes you to be drawn toward it, and it stimulates subconsciously the creativity that gives you the ideas of how to possess it.

What if, in your forethought, you perceive something that would be uncomfortable. It might be something embarrassing, something that would be painful, something that would be awful; and you have that grooved. Not necessarily because of what this new situation might be, but because of something in your history – your individual personal history – your image of reality keeps throwing that emotional, negative feeling back at you every time your eyes or sense of smell or other senses detect an opportunity or a situation. You say to yourself, "What is this leading me toward?" And you say, "Nothing good." Now, remember, negative doesn't mean bad. It means avoidant. It means moving away. It stimulates your creativity to move back, to move away from that which you perceive as being unpleasant.

DAY 12
Attitudes Review

I want to encourage you that, as you set all these new goals for yourself – whether it be career or social, financial, all the things that you want – when you set a new goal, some of the old attitudes that served you well in your old comfort zone will no longer serve you well. As you try to pursue a new career, a new occupation, or a new education or new social strata – whatever it might be that you're going after – your old attitudes will jump out at you. You need to be consciously aware of them. Are they leading me towards what I want or are they causing me to engage in avoidant behavior? And if I'm engaging in avoidant behavior, do I give up on my goal or do I change my attitude? It's your choice. I have my own choices to make, and if I'm smart about it, I want to change my attitude. I don't want to change what I've said would be of value for me or my family or my career or my business. See? But, how many people do you know that just give up on their goal? Changing an attitude is the affirmation process.

You must get rid of the old garbage-in, no longer valuable, negative, upheaval emotion that comes to you. You do so not by just willing it, but by taking the affirmation process; writing an affirmation, and visualizing the positive response that you want when the situation occurs. If you need to, use the flick-back/flick-up technique to find a positive emotion in something similar. Then, you visualize the something similar, let the emotion build up in you, and then drop it into what you are currently avoiding or whatever is causing you to move away from it. You don't just do it once; you may need to do it a hundred times. It may need to be 200 times. I don't know how many times. Nobody does. It has a lot to do with the vividness with which you're doing it.

Build up from your history a library of very successful, positive emotion that you can borrow from. Then, just drop that into whatever is causing you to avoid, causing you to not be or to have that which you really deserve. Very important, you won't get this feedback of negative attitudes while you're sitting here listening to me; and you won't get it even while you're in a safe environment. It's when you put yourself out into the business community, or the social community that you've been avoiding all this time, that you're going to start becoming aware of the attitudes that are holding you back. That's why you need to do that reflective thinking that we keep insisting on. Capture those attitudes. Examine, then make the affirmations to release the wonderful potential and achieve those goals that you're capable of achieving.

DAY 13
Invest In Yourself

Key Concepts

Affirmation; Current Reality; Goal.

Balance keeps our wheels running smoothly.

Main Concepts

The most important ideas and insights I have gained from this session are:

Choice Of Activities

Where am I in relation to my potential in each aspect of my life?

Is my life balanced?

DAY 13
Invest In Yourself

Where do I need to improve?

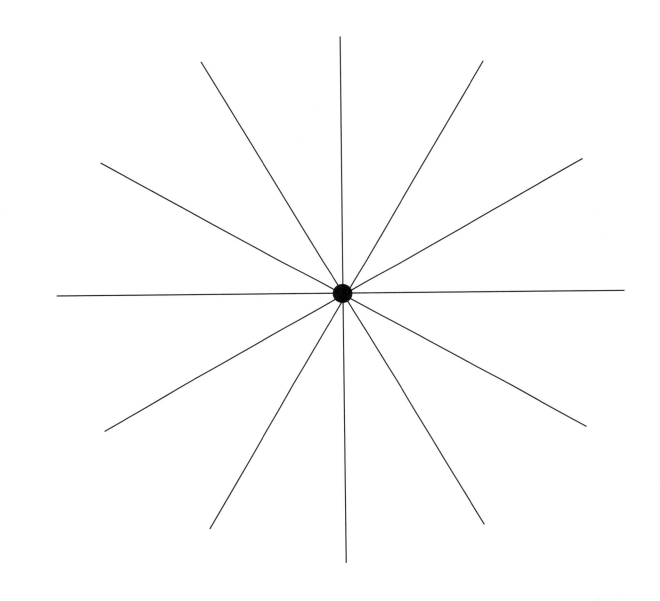

- Family
- Personal
- Community Service
- Education
- Health/Physical

- Health/Mental
- Recreation/Leisure
- Spiritual
- Relationship/Friends

- CareerJob/Vocation
- Sports
- Social
- Other

DAY 13
Invest In Yourself

Affirmations

Write your own Invest in Yourself Affirmations using your ideas gained from this session, your review of related information and notes, as well as affirmation ideas from your Video Resource Guide.

- Refer to the Action/Emotion Word List on pages 173 through 175 for appropriate words.

- Review the Affirmation Checklist on page 171 to be sure you are writing them effectively.

It may be helpful to write down the current reality first, and then describe what it would be like when it is fixed. Use this as the basis to write your affirmations. Transfer your completed affirmations to 3 x 5 cards and place them in your Affirmation Folder.

My Affirmations

Assimilation

Refer to the Affirmation Imprinting Reminders on page 194 as you go through your affirmations.

I get a clear and vivid picture in my mind and I feel the wonderful emotion and mood of already achieving my goal. I dwell on this feeling of achievement, which gives life to my affirmations. I do this for each affirmation. I set aside time at least twice daily to imprint them.

DAY 13
Invest In Yourself

Journal

DAY 13
Invest In Yourself

Audio Summary

This time let's take a look at another principle, the principle of we move toward and we become like that which we think about. Now, let's add another one, that our present thoughts determine our future. Okay. The basis of this is that you're teleological in nature. What that means is that as a human being, you're goal oriented. You need an idea. You need something focused in your mind, like a target or an object to achieve. Then physiologically, psychologically, and emotionally, you're drawn towards what you concentrate on or what you focus on or what you have your mind on.

Remember, you think in pictures. The language that you use triggers the picture. You'll hear people say, "Oh, I have an idea. I have an idea of what I want to do with my life." Hmm, well, that's beneficial. Some people don't have that, of course. They haven't taken the time to think it out or they haven't quite made up their mind yet, which is all right. Some people say, "Well, I have an idea what I want to do for my weekend." Some people, though, can't think that far ahead, because it's only Wednesday. Some people say, "Well, no, I have an idea what I want to do when I get home," and they can think that far ahead. Some people don't even know what they want to do when they get home until they get home. Can we take this whole process of what we're talking about and see what is the furthest out that we can extend what we want to move toward? What is the biggest object or ideal that we can think of right now, of what it is that we want to have happen in our life?

We move toward and we become like that which we think about. Our present thoughts determine our future. See, if we get caught in current reality, talking about how things actually are around us – on the job financially, socially, in our marriage, spiritually, health wise – and we think that we're really realists, then remember that tomorrow looks like today. If that holds true, that we move toward and become like what we think about, our thinking is pretty well dominated by our sensory perception around us. We're dominated by who we listen to, who is in our environment, the quality or quantity of the environment at the present moment. You're not deliberately causing yourself to think forward out of your comfort zone or out of your current reality, so change doesn't happen very fast for you, or doesn't happen in any great amount. You're not allowing yourself to think past your sensory current reality, what you're reading in the newspaper, the reality of your present financial situation.

If we're moving toward and becoming like that which we think about, and if our present thoughts determine our future, it is the affirmation process that helps you deliberately project into your future. It's not me to decide for you. It's you to decide for you. If you only do it twice a day, dog-gone it, that's good enough. That's better than what you were doing it. But what if you do it three times, five times, seven times a day? Of course, if you make too many affirmations and you can't repeat them, you really don't have enough time. You have other things to do. But yet, again, we need to have balance in our life, as we set our affirmations and goals. If we don't and we're just using our affirmations for our income increase or our vocational increase, and we just really

DAY 13
Invest In Yourself

spend our focused time on, say, that issue, that area, your subconscious will steal time from your family or from your social life. You'll become so narrow and so obsessed about this one thing that you're going to leave the other parts of your life behind.

Does that make sense when you understand the gestalt inside yourself? When you throw your system out of order, you're going to re-create the order, and you're re-creating order in only one direction, in one area on one issue. But if, in fact, you can set goals with some balance, which we're encouraging you to do, then you're creative enough to achieve it all and not become obsessive or narrow in your life or your thinking.

Maybe you want to select five or seven or eight areas of your life, and don't try to make too many affirmations in each one, because then you won't give it the focused time. I don't know how long it takes each one of you to make an affirmation, but let's say each affirmation takes a minute, and you've got 10, that's 10 minutes, and if you've got 20, that's 20 minutes. Well, if you're ever going to invest, invest the 20 minutes, invest the 30 minutes. 30 minutes in the morning, and the 30 minutes in the evening, and it doesn't need to be 30. If you don't have 30, then make it 10, make it 15 minutes, but do it five or ten times a day. Couldn't be a better investment than the investment in yourself through this affirmation process.

You move toward and become like what you've deliberately decided that you've chosen to become. You've written them properly, so it affects the neuron of your brain correctly. See, you're thinking future in the present tense. So the reason you write it out is so it becomes accurate, so it becomes focused, so it becomes detailed, so it becomes clear. It's something that you have deliberately and intentionally decided. It's premeditated. (You know, if you were committing a murder and somebody said, "Well, was it accidental or was it premeditated?") Well, why would you get more of a punishment if it was premeditated? Because you did it deliberately, that's why. And that's what I'm telling you, do it deliberately, premeditated. Think about it. Does that make sense?

DAY 14
Go After What You Really Want

Key Concepts

Adventure; Affirmation; Creativity; Current Reality; Efficacy; Emotion; Energy; Forethought; Goal; RAS; Resilience; Subconscious; Visualization.

We get what we expect, not what we want.

Main Concepts

The most important ideas and insights I have gained from this session are:

Choice Of Activities

A dream I have decided to go for is:

My dream, in the present tense, is:

DAY 14
Go After What You Really Want

Putting the details of "how-to" aside, what three things would I really like to have, do or be?

1.

2.

3.

Visualizing these as if they have already been achieved makes me feel:

DAY 14
Go After What You Really Want

Affirmations

Write your own What I Really Want Affirmations using your ideas gained from this session, your review of related information and notes, as well as affirmation ideas from your Video Resource Guide.

• Refer to the Action/Emotion Word List on pages 173 through 175 for appropriate words.

• Review the Affirmation Checklist on page 171 to be sure you are writing them effectively.

It may be helpful to write down the current reality first, and then describe what it would be like when it is fixed. Use this as the basis to write your affirmations. Transfer your completed affirmations to 3 x 5 cards and place them in your Affirmation Folder.

My Affirmations

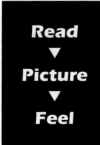

Read
▼
Picture
▼
Feel

Assimilation

Refer to the Affirmation Imprinting Reminders on page 194 as you go through your affirmations.

I get a clear and vivid picture in my mind and I feel the wonderful emotion and mood of already achieving my goal. I dwell on this feeling of achievement, which gives life to my affirmations. I do this for each affirmation. I set aside time at least twice daily to imprint them.

DAY 14
Go After What You Really Want

Journal

DAY 14
Go After What You Really Want

Audio Summary

Let's take a look at what happens when our expectations aren't met. A lot of things happen. One of the things that happens is you're disappointed. You had an appointment with your future, and you are disappointed, it didn't happen. Now, what happens if you really wanted it and really committed to it, it's like the death of a loved one. So what you do is you may safeguard yourself from feeling this way by not setting a high expectation for yourself or going after what you really want. You go after something you settle for.

What kind of car would you really like to have? What would be the ideal car for you? Hmm, think about that. Well, maybe you ought to settle for something just about half as good. What kind of a career would really be ideal for you? Well, don't expect that much. You'd only be disappointed. Maybe we should settle for something about half as good. What kind of a family would you really want? Well, let's not be thinking about that. Let's just settle for something about half as good.

"Be happy with what you have, my dear." You've heard that from a lot of people, haven't you? "Because if you get your hopes up and it doesn't happen, you'll be dashed, you'll be so sad. And it's because I love you that I'm really talking to you this way; because I don't want you to start thinking big ideas and then having these big ideas not materialize." Good words from parents who love their children. "Oh, don't run for president. Why don't you just run for secretary? Nobody else wants the job, and you'll get is easily." I don't want to be secretary. I want to be president. "Well, don't get your hopes up." See, constantly settling for second best because you're using your forethought to anticipate forward and seeing the loss, you're cushioning yourself from the loss of what you really want. You don't go after it with the fervor and the drive. If you wanted to be president, why not go after president? If you wanted to go after secretary, go after secretary. But if you wanted to be president and you're settling for secretary, watch. When you were in high school or grade school, you didn't even make a poster. You didn't even campaign. How come? "I don't even want the job. What I really wanted was president."

Go after what you really want. You're more likely to get what you really want than settling for something that you only half want. Build up your resiliency inside yourself, that tenacity and drive inside yourself, knowing that if you aren't successful and you do get knocked down, you'll feel like anybody who wanted something greatly and you didn't get it. It just knocks the wind right out of your sails. It makes you sick at your stomach. It drops you to your knees. But know you can recover from it. Also know that if you don't expect it, you won't get it. It will only be luck, it will only be circumstance outside yourself. So it's all right to expect. In fact, you get what you expect. You don't get what you want.

Everybody wants to live well. Some of them don't expect it. Everybody wants to have a wonderful job and a wonderful marriage and a wonderful life around them. They just don't expect it, and they've learned not to expect. Shoot for the stars. No. People say, "Why don't you just aim for an eagle and maybe you'll hit a pigeon. Don't think too big, you know. Why don't we just settle for

DAY 14
Go After What You Really Want

. . ." Maybe a lot of times they fool themselves and they say, "Well, I'm going to really think big, because I know I won't get it. I'm going to get something a little less, but if I don't think really big, then I probably won't get this little piece." Why don't you just think big?

Now, remember, big for you is relevant. Just design the life you want, design the career you want. But, hey, current reality denies that it's possible right now. Just remember the power of the subconscious. Remember to develop your efficacy. You're not qualified now for what you really want. In fact, if you know how to get what you really want, you're not stretching enough. You already know the process. You already know the way. If you already know how you're going to do it, you probably aren't stretching yourself enough. Why don't you put a dream out there you don't even know how to get right now. See if you can't use your reticular activating system to discover knowledge, to discover information and resources and people that can get you there. Why don't you do that so you stimulate that creativity inside yourself that comes up with the ideas. Why don't you make life an adventure and a surprise to yourself and have it unfold with wonderful surprises. You're causing it with your intent, you're causing it with your awareness, you're causing it with your readiness to seize opportunity.

So you set a goal far beyond, based upon what it is that you want with your life. It's a dream. Dare yourself to dream. Allow yourself to dream. Allow yourself to know the difference between a declaration of possibility and a promise. You're not promising right now. You're only envisioning. Just get yourself to envision, to envision, to dream. Don't hold yourself to it right now. Don't set the dream and then force yourself to do it. Here comes the "have to" again. Set the dream and allow it to happen. Set the dream and relax. Set the dream, and then just flow. Set the dream. Go after it. Go after it. Don't force it. Visualize it. Create the drive. Create the excitement; create the want. Allow yourself to get inventive and creative, and it may come as an entirely different surprise for you.

For instance, I always wanted to be a football coach. I always wanted to coach. But as I didn't play college football, I only coached when I was in college. I coached at a very good high school and so on, and I still wanted to be a football coach. I became a football coach in high school, and then I became a head coach. I probably would never be able to coach in the pros because you would have to have played at that higher level and so on, or you wouldn't get the opportunity.

Well, still wanting to be a football coach, I came to the realization that I coach the best coaches in the world, and I didn't go through the ordinary way. I didn't go through working my way up through high school coach and then on up into a college coach and then on up into maybe the pros and then on up. No, but I still have what I want. I still coach. I coach people who are the best coaches, in hockey, basketball, football – and I don't even need to go to practice. I don't need to do all that stuff. I'm just coaching the guys that coach. And I enjoy and live vicariously through their success. See how it comes out?

Sometimes it comes out different. I wanted to be a teacher. I am not a teacher in the classroom, but my classroom is all over the world. So envisioning what I really wanted, my subconscious

DAY 14
Go After What You Really Want

invented things that are much better – and not the ordinary, not the routine, not the way that you presently see it. Not the way that I presently planned it. But it comes out even much better oftentimes. So allow yourself to dream. Don't get all caught up in whether you're qualified right now, and don't get all caught up in whether you know the process. The important thing is to dream as though you have it. Dream in the present tense. Dream you in it, not someone else in it. Dream correctly. And to control your dreams, write your affirmations. Don't just write them; use your affirmations to control the dream.

DAY 14
Go After What You Really Want

DAY 15
I Have a Positive Expectancy Of

Key Concepts

Affirmation; Goal; LO/LO; Pygmalion; Resilience; Self-Esteem; Self-Talk; Subconscious.

Setbacks are temporary.

Main Concepts

The most important ideas and insights I have gained from this session are:

Choice Of Activities

Today I will add this affirmation to my affirmations:

"I have a positive expectancy of _____ and I take every setback as temporary."

DAY 15
I Have a Positive Expectancy Of

Three events from my past where I overcame setbacks and achieved my goals were:

I overcame them by:

DAY 15
I Have a Positive Expectancy Of

Affirmations

Write your own Positive Expectancy Affirmations using your ideas gained from this session, your review of related information and notes, as well as affirmation ideas from your Video Resource Guide.

- Refer to the Action/Emotion Word List on pages 173 through 175 for appropriate words.

- Review the Affirmation Checklist on page 171 to be sure you are writing them effectively.

It may be helpful to write down the current reality first, and then describe what it would be like when it is fixed. Use this as the basis to write your affirmations. Transfer your completed affirmations to 3 x 5 cards and place them in your Affirmation Folder.

My Affirmations

Read
▼
Picture
▼
Feel

Assimilation

Refer to the Affirmation Imprinting Reminders on page 194 as you go through your affirmations.

I get a clear and vivid picture in my mind and I feel the wonderful emotion and mood of already achieving my goal. I dwell on this feeling of achievement, which gives life to my affirmations. I do this for each affirmation. I set aside time at least twice daily to imprint them.

DAY 15
I Have a Positive Expectancy Of

Journal

DAY 15
I Have a Positive Expectancy Of

Audio Summary

A quality that I would like to encourage all of us to develop more is the quality of resiliency; a characteristic of tenacity within us. I guess what we're talking about is being tough, but too often we've made the mistake of thinking tough might be beating up on somebody with a chain or pushing somebody around or whatever. Really that's not necessarily what toughness is. Toughness seems to be the quality of being able to lock onto a goal or an end result of a project or a task, and to be able to take disappointment, to be able to take setbacks and blocks as only temporary and not as final. It seems that we lose when we give up on the picture. So the only time you become a loser is when you say," The heck with it" and give up on it.

Well, my question to you might be: Are you using your potential or do you have any of your potential you're not utilizing? Would it be personally profitable for you to grow or expand in that characteristic or quality? Well, let's examine some people. You take a person like Edison, who invented the filament for the lights that we're using. If you go back and see, he was a very, very creative, a very natural kind of a person. You know, he had over 3,000 temporary setbacks before he got the project completed; over 3,000 failures before he got the task done. See, he was able to lock on to an end result and take all setbacks as temporary. There was a guy by the name of Lou Brock who, awhile back, broke a world's record for stealing bases. In the same doggone year, he set another record. Do you know what that was? Being thrown out for trying to steal bases the most times. You see, he also set a record for failure at the same time.

So we look at being tough, and it doesn't mean that everything is going to go well for you. Hey, if it was easy, what you're doing, everybody would be doing it, okay? So somewhere you have a tremendous quality already of tenacity. Let's talk about building it up. Let's talk about being tough a little bit.

I think if I was to use a person who we would all be familiar with, who has that quality or characteristic, I would think it would be somebody like Rose Kennedy. I understand that as she first started out raising her family that she had a child who died, and then she had another child who was born retarded, and she bounces right back. She has another child who was killed in the war, and she bounces right back. She has a son who is assassinated, and she bounces right back. And she has another son assassinated, and she bounces right back. She has a husband die, and she bounces right back. She has another son scandalized, and she bounces right back. She has a grandson with a leg amputated, and she bounces right back. Some people would say, "Ah, the heck with it, I quit." The message is, that's okay. You see, she had a positive expectancy of winning, and she takes every setback as temporary.

That's a quality you want to develop within yourself. How many no's can you take? How easily are you intimidated? How easily are you intimidated by others around you, or by failure or by blocks when things don't go right? Intimidation is in your own mind, Pygmalion. You mustn't allow other people to intimidate. You mustn't allow other circumstances to intimidate you. But you

DAY 15
I Have a Positive Expectancy Of

can build that quality of tenacity within you. It doesn't make any difference whether we're white or black or red or yellow, male or female, whether we're big or little. That is the quality that I find most people who are super at winning have.

Now, how do we go about developing that quality of tenacity within us? You can use imagery to do so. Remember your subconscious doesn't know the difference between vividly imagining experiences or whether you're actually experiencing it, having handled it successfully. Then, as you accumulate, over and over and over, experiences in your mind, you build that opinion that this is like you.

What I would recommend is that you design an affirmation, and use something quite similar like this: You could visualize yourself, perhaps, in a well, and it's very dark in there. You reach to get out and somebody strikes your hand and you pull your hand back in because it's painful. You put your hand out, and somebody strikes you, and you pull it back in because it's painful. You keep putting your hands out and pulling them back in, and as you pull them out, that person who is striking your hands – the setback, so to speak – gets more tired and the striking becomes further and further apart. Pretty soon, you feel that one more time and you're out. You just come right out of that hole a winner, and you build that quality that nothing can keep you in — nothing.

You see, it doesn't need to be coming out of a well. You can be going after a job or going after a sale or raising a child or holding your marriage together. I will work with young athletes. As we would work with football players, I would ask them to visualize themselves running through the woods at night and it's dark. There are a tremendous amount of trees, and as you run, you strike a tree, and it's painful. But instead of just sitting down and crying and whimpering and making excuses, just slide to the side and work toward the next on. You hit the next one, you bounce back; and you strike another one, you bounce back. You strike another one, you bounce back. Nothing is going to keep you from the end result.

As you build that quality of tenacity within you, you walk around like you're a pretty tough person, knowing that you can keep your marriage together, that nothing will cause it to be destroyed. You know that when you go after a task in your corporation or your company, that nothing can keep you down. You know that you are such a winner that nothing – nothing – will keep you from achieving the goal that you want. I would recommend that you take and build that tremendous quality of tenacity and resiliency within you to where you can go after the goals that are vitally important for you in your marriage and in your company and in your life.

DAY 16
Goal-Setting/Life Style I

Key Concepts

Belief; Comfort Zone; Efficacy; Environmental; Goal-Set; Magis; Philosophy of Life; Potential.

Who am I? Why am I? Where am I going?

Main Concepts

The most important ideas and insights I have gained from this session are:

Choice Of Activities

Who am I?

Why am I?

Where am I going?

DAY 16
Goal-Setting/Life Style I

The best ideal Sunday would be:

Five things that make me happy are:

DAY 16
Goal-Setting/Life Style I

Affirmations

Write your own Goal-Setting Affirmations using your ideas gained from this session, your review of related information and notes, as well as affirmation ideas from your Video Resource Guide.

* Refer to the Action/Emotion Word List on pages 173 through 175 for appropriate words.

* Review the Affirmation Checklist on page 171 to be sure you are writing them effectively.

It may be helpful to write down the current reality first, and then describe what it would be like when it is fixed. Use this as the basis to write your affirmations. Transfer your completed affirmations to 3 x 5 cards and place them in your Affirmation Folder.

My Affirmations

Read
▼
Picture
▼
Feel

Assimilation

Refer to the Affirmation Imprinting Reminders on page 194 as you go through your affirmations.

I get a clear and vivid picture in my mind and I feel the wonderful emotion and mood of already achieving my goal. I dwell on this feeling of achievement, which gives life to my affirmations. I do this for each affirmation. I set aside time at least twice daily to imprint them.

DAY 16
Goal-Setting/Life Style I

Journal

DAY 16
Goal-Setting/Life Style I

Audio Summary

Up until now, we've spent most of the time working on growing on the inside, and you never want to let that go. That's not ever to be let go. You always want to hold onto the development on the inside. One reason why, is there's a direct relationship between the way you think on the inside and the way your world looks on the outside. How many people, though, sit around waiting for the world on the outside to change, and then they're going to improve or get better? Most people. If what we're saying is true, then we need to, inside of ourselves, develop our efficacy, which you already know about. You need to then work on those core beliefs that maybe hold you back, and releasing those. This is always ongoing.

Now, let's talk about the physical – the environmental comfort zone, or the environmental reality. Some of you may think, of course, it's money, and in most cases much of it is. Some of you may think in terms of, "Well, there's a lot of other things," other resources and so on that are necessary in order to achieve the goals that we want – relationships and teamwork and technology and all kinds of things, and all that is true.

But let's just talk about how can we get past this week, this month, the next five months, and really start goal setting to alter – dramatically alter – the physical world around us, if that's what we desire. Here's one way that's essential: Again, I want you to develop for yourself, if you will, a philosophy of where you're going and why you're going there. "Going." What does that mean? Well, what are you doing with your life's energy? What are you alive for? Why don't you just pack it in right now? Why don't you just finish it off? What are you doing hanging around on earth for? Those are interesting questions. What do you really want to be when you grow up? What are you doing and what is your purpose? Those kind of questions need to be asked.

The questions, "Who am I? Why am I? Where am I going?" seem never to get past just asking. You must answer them. Who am I? Why am I? Where am I going? Okay. Now, when you develop a philosophy about what you want to be doing with your life's energy and what you're trying to create, I think then what we want to do is to design for ourselves a style of life. Start looking at, "What is my style?" Is it going to be working with people or is it going to be working by myself? Is it going to be involved travel, or is it going to involve pretty much staying at home? Is it going to involve both? Is it going to involve working for myself or working for another? Is it going to involve no work at all? Is it going to be working to maybe do something very spectacular with my life, or is it just being a good person, hanging around my family and my friends and so on, is that enough?

So what are all these things? What do I want to do? Now, it seems very difficult to do unless . . . For me, it was, unless I just broke it down into something ordinary like a day. What do I want to do if I was going to design the best Sunday? Okay. What best Sunday in the winter? What would be best Sunday in the summer? What would be best Sunday in the spring? What would be best Sunday in the fall? Because, they might be different. So you just start with a Sunday, and allow

DAY 16
Goal-Setting/Life Style I

yourself to dream and think about Sunday. Then what you want to do from there is to say to yourself, "Am I talking about Sunday morning or Sunday afternoon or Sunday evening?" Would I be doing the same thing all day? Who would I have around me? Where would I be placing myself? What would lunch look like? What would dinner look like? What would it be like after dinner? What about a Monday, what would a Monday look like?

Well, as we were messing around with this one time, Diane and I, a Sunday we had was on a ranch. But, we lived in the city, so we had to figure out a ranch. I was working in the city, so how am I going to get to work? Maybe I don't go to work. No, you go to work. Well, how you going to get there? I guess I need to fly. Well, I don't fly. Well, do you want to fly? No, I don't want to learn to fly. Okay, then what you need to do is hire somebody or hire an airplane to take you back to the city, don't you? Hmm. Yes, but that gets expensive. I guess you better earn more money, hadn't you?

Then, what do you say to yourself? "Well, I'm not worth that much." Well, that's true. So what you need to do now is you develop yourself. If we're going to design this, don't worry about whether you're presently qualified, because once we design it, then we're going to get presently qualified. Then we're going to get qualified.

So I designed the best Monday in the fall, the best Monday in the summer, the best Monday in the winter. Then take a Wednesday, take a Saturday, take a Friday. Then take the best week in the spring, the best week in the summer, the best week in the winter. What would it look like? What would be ideal? And you just allow yourself to start designing the ideal of where you want to be, how you want to travel, who you want around you, the kinds of people. As you do that, you write all these weird ideas down, and you do it over and over, and you do it with the people you really care about. If it's your spouse or your family or if it's people at work, you start designing the ideal. What would be the ideal way?

And then, remember, you're presently not qualified, more than likely presently not qualified. In fact, if you are presently qualified, I doubt if you're stretching yourself, because you are already pretty closely doing what it was that you're describing. Ah, that's too close. Diane and I, one time, decided we wanted a ranch, but we didn't want to live on the ranch all the time. We just started designing a ranch. We didn't really have any financial resources to bring it about at the time, but you start designing it anyway. Even the home that we presently live in, we've lived in it for 20 some years. When we decided that, we were just out of high school teaching, and we had many children to take care of.

One time, going from the Oregon coast up to Seattle we had the kids design – and these were little kids, some of them were five, some of them were nine, some of them were twelve – what you do want in a home. No restrictions, just tell us what you want. Oh, gee whiz, they wrote 170 some things down that they wanted, and among them were sunken garbage cans, because the dogs kept knocking them over and their job was to pick up the garbage. The other things they wanted were, oh, swimming pools, and they wanted eagles and they went on and on and on – jukeboxes,

DAY 16
Goal-Setting/Life Style I

and they wanted pool tables – they just kept going. They wanted to be on a lake and they wanted a boat. Keep in mind, we did this, and we didn't have the money. But we found a home with at least half of what they asked for, including the jukebox, and the pool table, and many of the other things were in the home that we found.

Now, several years later, I don't know how many, let's just say almost 10 years later, Diane found the list. It was a list with misspelling, you know, it was 160, 170 some things, whatever it was. We came to the realization, "I think we have them all now," and we weren't consciously going after it. It was something that just happened. Now we do have a ranch, and with that ranch we have eagles; we do have barns; we do have horses; we do have all the other things that they put on their list; but we didn't get it in one place. We got it in two, and we had no conscious level intent to do so. But we were so dead serious about the style in which we wanted to live, the environments that we wanted to create, and we allowed our imagination to invent it before we ever had the resources. And, sure enough, there it is.

Now, we haven't done that again like that, although we do when we build our office or we build other things. We do allow ourselves to think outrageously, or magis. You just let yourself think it. You don't know how you're going to do it. Keep in mind, again, you're not presently qualified. That's why you keep working on the inside. You get qualified. Now, in the next audio, what we're going to do is talk more about goal setting and how you get that inside change so the outside occurs.

DAY 16
Goal-Setting/Life Style I

DAY 17
Life Style II

Key Concepts

Affirmation; Comfort Zone; Creative Subconscious; Creativity; Future as Now; Reality; Servo-Mechanism; Subconscious; Visualization.

Deliberately designed for fulfillment.

Main Concepts

The most important ideas and insights I have gained from this session are:

Choice Of Activities

The lifestyle I would like to create is:

DAY 17
Life Style II

What additional resources would I need to make this level of achievement normal?

What do I expect right now?

DAY 17
Life Style II

Affirmations

Write your own Life Style Affirmations using your ideas gained from this session, your review of related information and notes, as well as affirmation ideas from your Video Resource Guide.

- Refer to the Action/Emotion Word List on pages 173 through 175 for appropriate words.

- Review the Affirmation Checklist on page 171 to be sure you are writing them effectively.

It may be helpful to write down the current reality first, and then describe what it would be like when it is fixed. Use this as the basis to write your affirmations. Transfer your completed affirmations to 3 x 5 cards and place them in your Affirmation Folder.

My Affirmations

Assimilation

Refer to the Affirmation Imprinting Reminders on page 194 as you go through your affirmations.

I get a clear and vivid picture in my mind and I feel the wonderful emotion and mood of already achieving my goal. I dwell on this feeling of achievement, which gives life to my affirmations. I do this for each affirmation. I set aside time at least twice daily to imprint them.

DAY 17
Life Style II

Journal

DAY 17
Life Style II

Audio Summary

I have a lot of goods friends who, I think I mentioned before, were generals in the Army. They retired in their early 50s, and when they retire, they usually go and look for a job where there's a defense contract. This isn't out of the ordinary, because they get hired by the firms that manufacture a lot of the supplies that the military would use. I was talking to this one lovely couple; they were in their late 40s and looking forward to retiring in about a year and a half. And I said, "Well, what are you going to do?" They were going to go to Dallas to go to work – I think it was for Ross Perot in one of the companies he had there – and she was saying, "I really don't like Dallas, but we're going." And I said, "Holy cow! Why don't you just stop for a moment, and instead of finding a job and building your life around the job, why don't you design your life and then find the job?" Oh, never thought of that.

That's really what I'm encouraging you to do. Now, I don't encourage you now to leave what you're doing at all, because what you're doing may be exactly what you want to do. But how many people place themselves into a neighborhood or into a job or some kind of a business and they really don't like it? "It isn't what I want to do, but it is the way I make a living." Then what you do is you design your life around the way you make your living. And I would say, let's just play with this. Why don't you just see if you can design your life and then find some way to make enough money to support the way you want to live?

Really, that's about the way Diane and I did it. We knew what we wanted to be doing. We wanted to be teaching, and we wanted to teach this kind of information, but nobody would hire us. I wouldn't have hired myself. With the style of life I was designing, nobody could hire me and pay me that much money to be able to support that life style. So what I needed to do was create the life style and then to develop myself and develop a business and develop income that would support the life style. So that's really what I'm encouraging you to do: design the style and then develop the income stream.

Let's go back to how the subconscious works and how the creative subconscious works, and let's talk a little bit about tithing. Tithing is an interesting concept. You give perhaps 10% to charity or 10% to the church. But in tithing, it's the first 10%, and not the last 10%. That's an interesting concept, because if you waited to give what you had left over, it would be like some of you who save what you have left after you pay your bills, or you invest what you have left after you've paid your bills. Quite frankly, you're living right now to the max, and so you don't have enough to save. You don't have enough to give to the church, you don't have enough to give to charity. Oh, but some day, you're going to.

Keep in mind, I think your subconscious is a lot like your children. If you told them to wash the dishes, they would, but not the pots and pans and not the silverware, not the cups and saucers. They do exactly what they're told. So the creative subconscious does exactly what it's told. And it will create enough income to support not what you wish for, but what you've come to

DAY 17
Life Style II

expect. Inside your expectation level of what you know your life style is, "I don't expect to give any money to the church right now. I want to some day." So your subconscious says, "Well, okay, we'll figure out enough ideas. We'll develop you sufficiently to create the income, not for what you want in the future, but for what you expect right now – what you expect right now, what you expect right now, what you expect right now.

That's why the affirmation process is so essential. You must change what you expect right now, then you get creative to earn the income. It's not extra money that's necessary. Your creative subconscious does what's necessary. So you need to, in your mind, create the environment, create the life style, and live it in your mind over and over. Give yourself feedback through your senses to the contrary. "Hey, we're not living that way." Your creative subconscious now will correct for the mistake. It solves the problem. It creates the energy. It may cause you to increase your business. It may cause you now to get out of the location you are and become worldly, because there's not enough income where you're sitting. You may need to expand your product. You may need to create a new one. What it will do, it will give you enough creativity and drive to consistently earn the income that you've come to expect or that you need, not what you want.

What if we create the need first, but not by going out and buying something you can't afford, not by placing yourself in debt. There's an interesting saying by a lot of car salespeople that we hang around, if you don't have a wolf at your door, maybe it would pay you to go out and hire one. It's like you ought to put yourself in debt, buy something big so now you have to sell something. No, no, no, that's not what I'm talking about. I'm talking about really visualizing the style of the home and create in your mind first the necessity. It isn't a want. It isn't a wish. It isn't what I hope to be. It is really "I expect to do this."

So let's go back to tithing. If you expect to give 10% of your income to the church, you say, "Well, wait a minute. I wouldn't have enough money to pay the electricity bill." Well, "then earn more," your subconscious says. It isn't just "give them if we've got it." You give it, and then you get it. So, if you're going to save, you need to expect to save. And if you're going to invest, you must expect to invest. And as you start increasing the expectation of the style of life, there is no pressure. It isn't now a matter of being uptight about earning the money. It becomes automatic. It just comes to you. It isn't just like, "Oh, I just sit and it comes to me." It means I study, I develop, I create the work, I create the business, I create the income. I create the income stream to support my life style. I always have. Now, saving is a part of it. Investing is a part of it. Living and traveling the way I travel is a part of it.

What I need to do then is to somehow create the business around me, and sometimes I can't find it in Seattle. Sometimes I need to go to Guatemala or I need to go to Europe or I need to go to Asia, so that becomes a part of it. I just get inventive. You become inventive to support the life style. Create the life style. That's what you visualize, not the process, not the method, and you don't worry about the money to start with. You create the ranch. You create the home. You create the style of travel, the vacations, the security financially, whatever it is that you want.

DAY 17
Life Style II

You create that in your mind, not just by thinking about it once, but actually living in it in a first person present tense, living as though the future is right there now. You place yourself in it and you have a good time in it.

And what you're going to find is, "I'll be darned, I seem to be expanding my business. I'll be darned, my income is really increasing, isn't it?" Remember now, your subconscious has an idea of how much money you need to support your life style. Not what you wish for, not what you want. Your creative subconscious stimulates enough drive and energy to earn the money to support your internal reality. Change your internal reality, and you'll earn more money.

DAY 17
Life Style II

DAY 18
What's Good Enough?

Key Concepts

Aspiration; Creative Subconscious; Creativity; Energy; Goal; Potential; Self-Talk.

Goal-set up to, and through.

Main Concepts

The most important ideas and insights I have gained from this session are:

Choice Of Activities

An example of where, in the past, I have Goal-Set To but not Through is:

DAY 18
What's Good Enough?

Examples in the media of athletes, politicians and others who Goal-Set To but not Through are:

One goal I have set now that I need to Goal-Set Through and beyond is:

DAY 18
What's Good Enough?

Affirmations

Write your own What's Good Enough Affirmations using your ideas gained from this session, your review of related information and notes, as well as affirmation ideas from your Video Resource Guide.

- Refer to the Action/Emotion Word List on pages 173 through 175 for appropriate words.

- Review the Affirmation Checklist on page 171 to be sure you are writing them effectively.

It may be helpful to write down the current reality first, and then describe what it would be like when it is fixed. Use this as the basis to write your affirmations. Transfer your completed affirmations to 3 x 5 cards and place them in your Affirmation Folder.

My Affirmations

Read
▼
Picture
▼
Feel

Assimilation

Refer to the Affirmation Imprinting Reminders on page 194 as you go through your affirmations.

I get a clear and vivid picture in my mind and I feel the wonderful emotion and mood of already achieving my goal. I dwell on this feeling of achievement, which gives life to my affirmations. I do this for each affirmation. I set aside time at least twice daily to imprint them.

DAY 18
What's Good Enough?

Journal

DAY 18
What's Good Enough?

Audio Summary

One of the things that I think stops you or me the most isn't that we don't have the resources, it's that we don't have the idea. We don't have the dream. We don't have the aspiration. One of the things I think that stops us is that we've arrived at something that we felt was as much as we ever deserved or as much as we would want. You know, when we've done so, we've hit against that concept that I've shared with you. Once you arrive at a goal that you set, remember what happens? You lose your drive, you lose what we call energy, and you lose your creativity.

Now, you don't lose it, you keep enough energy to sustain the status quo. In other words, you work hard enough to keep it as it is. You get enough ideas to keep it looking about the way that you see it, but no more. Now, how much potential do you have? Who knows? That creative subconscious is a genius. But remember, the creative subconscious only does enough to sustain the picture that you hold in your mind of what is good enough. Remember the example I said, if you told your kids (and your kids would be like the creative subconscious) to wash the dishes, they would, but not the pots and pans, because you didn't say pots and pans. You didn't say silverware. It does what it's told to do. It has potential to do the pots and pans, but not if you don't ask, not if it doesn't become expected. So once you arrive at a goal that you set, you exert only enough energy to sustain that status quo, to sustain that level of performance.

I've seen so many people whose goals might have been to, say, as a doctor or as a dentist, open a practice. Now, look at the fallacy. If you listen to them, open a practice they did. Go out of business quick they did also. They only opened the practice, they didn't grow the practice. Now, can you see so many examples of where your business has flattened out? You must take this concept and see inside, in listening to your people or listening to your own self-talk and going back and reflecting. Where have you stopped you? Where have you arrived at, as far as your career, as far as your income, as far as your environment, as far as where you allow yourself to take vacations? What have you come to expect? That's what you get.

So once you arrive at the goal that you've set, your energy and your drive doesn't take you past that. I think there was a saying in the old days that was called the Peter Principle. It was a psychological phenomenon where people said they reached the level of their incompetence. Well, that's probably true. But, you see, is it because they don't have the potential? Oh, yes, because in many of those days, could you believe they thought people were born with only a certain capacity? Well, they may be. But that was a good excuse for not setting a new goal and growing beyond it, wasn't it? Because if you're born that way, or if you really viewed your own people and your own organization as not really having the capacity to go beyond or grow, well, of course, now I don't need to mentor or coach or manage you past that expectation. Okay, so it's very important that Peter Principle is true, but it doesn't need to be.

I would think in most cases there was still more to develop, but the problem was they didn't see past that horizon. They didn't see past that fixed point. So, do you wait until you achieve that

DAY 18
What's Good Enough?

fixed point before you set a new horizon? A lot of people do. But if you want sustained momentum and sustained growth, then you set the aspiration out about as far as you can see yourself having the refrigerator, and then you don't wait until it's completed. What you do is, as you approach that aspiration or goal, wouldn't you think that that would be the time to start projecting into the future?

Now, goal-setting isn't a once in a year kind of a process. It maybe once a year in some areas of your life, but it might be every three months in some others. What you need to do is really have some good talks with yourself. What is it that I really want? How far do I want to go? And then you need to set your aspirations past that fixed point of setting up a practice or a business. "No, that's not what I really wanted."

I remember when I first started many years ago, I didn't know anything about selling. So what I'd do is I would set goals to go call on important people, and I would. But I didn't have any business from it. I remember walking down Fourth Avenue in downtown Seattle by the Olympic Hotel, and I said, "My goodness, I know what I was doing." My goal was to call on them, and I was. I didn't at all tell myself the goal really was to get them engaged in our curriculum and have them pay for it and then have them grow from it and have them refer new business. All I was doing was setting a goal to call on important people. I changed my mind, and it changed my business. Isn't that amazing? Now, how many times have you done the same thing? I don't know. But I would guess that you stop you more than anybody else or any other circumstances. That is the one concept that stops most companies and most organizations, most people, most armies.

If you go back and study in the Revolutionary War, there was a great study done about somebody whose goal it was to take a bridge. They got to that point, and they stopped. If they had only marched further, they could have perhaps won the war, but they didn't. They achieved the objective and quit, and got clobbered.

You can look at this all over, especially little kids. Listening to them, what is their aspiration, what is their goal? As a mentor, as a coach, knowing this principle, you just talk them past their stopping point. "Oh, I want to make the team." Does that mean you just want to be on the team, or do you want to start on the team? And do you want to then win or just make the team and start? Do you want to go past winning and do you want? Really, it's just a matter of listening carefully, knowing these objectives. You can do it with a little kid or you do it with big kids in your business. This is a liberating principle. It liberates within you that prison that you put yourself in by reaching the objective that you set and not setting another one. Turn yourself loose.

DAY 19
Visualize the New

Key Concepts

Current Reality; Creativity; Energy; Goal; Goal-Setting; Potential; Visualization.

Small beginnings.

Main Concepts

The most important ideas and insights I have gained from this session are:

Choice Of Activities

My current top three small goals are:

If I imagined I was asked to share my goals with a group of fifty people, using as few words as possible, what words would I choose?

DAY 19
Visualize the New

Where do I feel dissatisfaction because I visualize my goals vividly and emotionally?

What new small or medium-sized goals could I set for myself now to practice?

DAY 19
Visualize the New

Affirmations

Write your own Visualization Affirmations using your ideas gained from this session, your review of related information and notes, as well as affirmation ideas from your Video Resource Guide.

- Refer to the Action/Emotion Word List on pages 173 through 175 for appropriate words.

- Review the Affirmation Checklist on page 171 to be sure you are writing them effectively.

It may be helpful to write down the current reality first, and then describe what it would be like when it is fixed. Use this as the basis to write your affirmations. Transfer your completed affirmations to 3 x 5 cards and place them in your Affirmation Folder.

My Affirmations

Read
▼
Picture
▼
Feel

Assimilation

Refer to the Affirmation Imprinting Reminders on page 194 as you go through your affirmations.

I get a clear and vivid picture in my mind and I feel the wonderful emotion and mood of already achieving my goal. I dwell on this feeling of achievement, which gives life to my affirmations. I do this for each affirmation. I set aside time at least twice daily to imprint them.

DAY 19
Visualize the New

Journal

DAY 19
Visualize the New

Audio Summary

Okay, in this goal-setting process, we must make the new image – the new vision, the new idea, or generally in the style of life that you want – so dominant in our mind. We want to live in it so dominant in our mind that the environment in which you are presently placed becomes irritating in a sense, almost irritating. It almost catapults you out of the environment. "I'm out of here," you've probably heard people say; that freedom from, which we've discussed a little bit already.

When I left high school teaching, you need to understand that this was where I wanted to be, from the time I was nine. Leaving something that I had set so seriously in my mind and prepared everything for, it was almost unthinkable in my mind to allow myself to even dwell on being outside of that structure of teaching in a high school. But I started to visualize a different style of life, of being still a teacher, but teaching in a much different way and in a different environment. As I started letting my mind see the freedom, the income, the results that I was accomplishing, only in my mind instead of with kids, it would be with business leaders or government leaders or community and so on.

As I would do that over and over, it got to the point where I could not stand to go to another faculty meeting. It drove me nuts. I hated the bells. When the bells rang, every 45 minutes or every hour, you'd have the first bell and the second bell, the bells were literally driving me irritably nuts. And the kids that I cared about, that I was there for, if they knocked on the door and wanted to see me, I would go, "What do you want?" I was so irritated in that environment that I couldn't wait to get out. I found every reason. It was just, "When am I going to be out of here?" Had I not visualized the new and made myself feel – I know the principle, but I was really experiencing – so uncomfortable, I would never have left. It would have been too scary. I would have stayed right where I was.

So remember the principle. As you visualize the new, you become dissatisfied with the old. That could be a car, or it could be a career. It could be the next level of development for yourself. As you visualize the new, you become unhappy or dissatisfied with the old. Don't burn the bridge behind you though. Don't go out, you know, complaining about everybody. Don't think that all of a sudden everybody just kind of fell apart and it got ugly around you. No, it was always that way.

That environment, that school environment, didn't change. I changed. As I visualized myself into a better environment for me – not better environment but better environment for me – I started noticing blemishes all over the place. If I hadn't noticed the blemishes, I would have been too comfortable there. I would have allowed myself to stay right there with another excuse not for leaving. So allow yourself. See how this process works. It takes some time. You must visualize yourself into that new level of environment, the new level of performance, the new level socially or whatever it might be, and then you'll notice you become inside yourself dissatisfied with your present job or your present income status. I mean, you become almost stagnant in your social life. I mean, these are the same people we've seen over and over. I mean, they're nice people. "I

DAY 19
Visualize the New

don't want to see them." Was there something wrong with them? No. It's a sign of growth. It's a sign of growth, if, in fact, you're visualizing a better way.

Start causing that inside yourself through the visualizing of a better level of quality in whatever area you're trying to improve – a better area of quality of home environment, business environment, and pretty soon you get dissatisfied with the size of your company. But if you're not dissatisfied with the size of your company, you won't cause the growth in it. If you're not dissatisfied with the product that you're delivering, you'll keep delivering the same product.

You need to feel toward the product or toward the size of your company, or whatever you're doing, the same way I felt about being in Kennedy High School. And Kennedy High School is Kennedy High School. It didn't fall apart. It's been going pretty good since I left it. But I needed to cause myself to leave it; and I did, and I was happy to get out. But you know what was going through my mind? "Well, in case this business doesn't work out, I could always go back to my old job." This was in February, and the year wasn't going to be complete until June. But when I left, they immediately hired a new coach and a new teacher. "Oh, no. Now I can't go back." That seemed sad, but that was great. I had no option to return, no option. Now, the only thing I could do was make it.

I didn't have a lot of money either, which, when I look back, wasn't so bad. Because if I had had a lot of money, I would have probably used the money before I became effective. But I needed the urgency of making it happen now. That urgency inside oneself is not a badness that you feel. See, it is that drive that causes you to take the right kind of action. Don't leave where you are in what you're doing until you've created enough dissatisfaction – with where you presently are or what you're presently doing – that will drive you with enough drive and creativity to go forward. It isn't just jump from where you are into the new, because I think you'll find yourself not knowing if you want to go back, go forward, go back.

So somehow use this process, not in something so huge for you or something that's the greatest challenge of your life, but use it with your lawn mower. Get unhappy with your lawn mower, pushing it, and find one you can ride. I mean just something simple, something dumb. Pretty soon this lawn mower, you might even make it fall apart, if you don't like it. You could ruin it. Do the same with your car. You'll find your car will fall apart on you. You want to just find some things, and then say, "Now, what could I do with other parts of my life?" See how you do that?

DAY 20
Power of Your Word

Key Concepts

Affirmation; Integrity; Magis; Spirit of Intent; Trust.

Trust is reliance on the integrity of others.

Main Concepts

The most important ideas and insights I have gained from this session are:

Choice Of Activities

Recent promises I have made to myself, both big and small, are:

How many have I kept?

What does this tell me about my word?

What does this tell me about my spirit of intent?

DAY 20
Power of Your Word

Promises I have made, and not kept, to others are:

How does this make me feel?

My plan to improve my keeping of promises, to myself and others, is:

DAY 20
Power of Your Word

Affirmations

Write your own Power of Your Word Affirmations using your ideas gained from this session, your review of related information and notes, as well as affirmation ideas from your Video Resource Guide.

- Refer to the Action/Emotion Word List on pages 173 through 175 for appropriate words.

- Review the Affirmation Checklist on page 171 to be sure you are writing them effectively.

It may be helpful to write down the current reality first, and then describe what it would be like when it is fixed. Use this as the basis to write your affirmations. Transfer your completed affirmations to 3 x 5 cards and place them in your Affirmation Folder.

My Affirmations

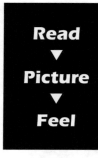

Read
▼
Picture
▼
Feel

Assimilation

Refer to the Affirmation Imprinting Reminders on page 194 as you go through your affirmations.

I get a clear and vivid picture in my mind and I feel the wonderful emotion and mood of already achieving my goal. I dwell on this feeling of achievement, which gives life to my affirmations. I do this for each affirmation. I set aside time at least twice daily to imprint them.

DAY 20
Power of Your Word

Journal

DAY 20
Power of Your Word

Audio Summary

In order for you to really get the value of your affirmations, I want to share with you something I think is very important, and that is to improve the power of your word to yourself. You could hear people give promises like "the check is in the mail," but the spirit behind it wasn't there. Or, "let's get together for lunch some day." That is just a nice thing to say, but you don't really mean it. You hope they don't call.

Sometimes what we do is we say something, "Have a nice day," but we don't really care if you do or not. It's our word that we're giving or the words that we use that have the power. Now, it's very important, I think, that if I would ask you if you gave your word to another person, would you keep it? You would probably say, in most cases, "yes." And I would say, yes, that's true. But now the next statement that I'd like to have you reflect on would be, "Is your word to yourself as good as your word to another?" That's the key. If you tell yourself you're going to do something, do you do it?

I think for me, I am not nearly as strong at my word to myself as I am my word to another. That's really where some affirmations or some work could take place. If you could really get to the ultimate, where you would say, if you were a smoker, "I'm no longer a smoker. I quit," and your word to yourself would be that powerful, so be it. I mean you need a one-time affirmation, and just zap, and you're it. But, for the most part, that's not probable. I really want to encourage you to work towards making your word to yourself as strong, if you can, as your word to another. That's where your power comes from. One time, when we were first in our business with Australia, we promised we would send something to them, and we didn't send it. It got delayed or something. So, I think for $2,500, Diane delivered it in person. She flew over, handed it to them, and flew back. If we tell you it's coming, count on it. Well, that's a nice way to run your business. That's a nice way to run your life. And, again, that's pretty well the way Diane and I are. If we're going to tell you we're going to do something, you can pretty well count on it.

The other thing, though, is I don't know that I'm that strong with myself. See, some days I'll say to myself, "I think I'll lose weight today. Yep, today's the day," I'll tell myself. I'm in the shower, and today's the day. Then what goes through my mind is, "If nothing else gets in the way," and what gets in the way is lunch. I'll get about that far. But the next day with great resolve, I'll say, "Today's the day, if nothing else gets in my way." And what gets in my way is guests and a good bottle of wine. Ah, but the next day with great resolve, "Today's the day." And what happens then . . . One time, I remember Diane saying, you're losing your power if you keep doing things like that. See you're losing your power, because your word to yourself isn't any good.

So you either don't make yourself a promise, or keep it, one of the two. Otherwise, you lose that inner power, that inner strength that I want you to develop. So let's work on that word to oneself, that real intent. It isn't in every part of my life, because in some parts of my life I have fierce resolve, but in some parts of my life I'm weak as the dickens. So it isn't like it's an either/or that

DAY 20
Power of Your Word

this is the way it is. Does that make sense? It isn't like I'm weak in everything at all. You want to keep working in those areas where you are really letting yourself down and watch your inner power come, watch your strength come. Your affirmations works better, your self-talk works better, your life goes better. Your word is just strong that way.

Then there's another problem that we talked about. You won't let yourself think outrageously. You won't let yourself think in magis terms. You won't let yourself think in like declarations of possibility, because if you start thinking in declarations of possibility, you confuse that with a promise. So, if you confuse that with a promise, then you keep your aspirations and your goals pretty close to what you're already doing because you can deliver. Maybe have a good talk with yourself, and say, "Hey, this is a declaration of possibility. It's possible I can lose weight. I don't know if I want it right now. It's possible I could do it, yep." That's a declaration option. It's a possibility, it ain't no promise. Okay, when I make a promise, I'll make a promise.

Now, same with stretching your business, stretching your life. Allow yourself to think that horizon beyond the horizon. Know the difference between a promise and the difference between when you're really exploring with your thinking and you're going to think outrageous. Let yourself think outrageous, but there's a time when you need to make a promise. Then make that promise and keep it inside yourself – yes, it's done.

Now, one of the things that Dr. Matthew Budd has taught me over the last few years is this idea about requests and promises. That idea, very simply, is when you are making a promise to another in an agreement and so on, what you're really doing is you're agreeing to build a future together. See, what you're doing is you're saying, "Let's get together for lunch," and what you need to do then is to set a time frame; put some conditions on it like, "Let's get together for lunch at noon on Tuesday." And that's not enough. Now we need to become more specific in order for it to be become just something that will never occur by saying "where."

Now, to all this, force yourself for clarity in this goal-setting process, because that's goal-setting. That goal-setting to "get together for lunch" was your understanding that the other person is building their future on your promise. They're building their future on your word. They're going to show up. Your reliability of keeping that promise becomes essential. People build the business on promises. That's all. They build a marriage on the promise. They build future on promise. It's a matter now of knowing that there are those specifics that we're talking about that need to be put into it so that you have a greater likelihood of the promise coming to a reality.

So force clarity on this. When people make a statement and you make a statement, force clarity. "Well, what time are we going to gather for lunch?" See the difference? "Let's get together for lunch some day." It ain't gonna happen. But it will happen if you say, "Let's get together for lunch on Tuesday at 12 o'clock at Rosselini's. I'll be there." Now you must show up, because if you don't show up, you make a promise the next time, people won't necessarily want to build their future with you.

DAY 20
Power of Your Word

So that's what business is like. It's a matter of requests and promises and keeping promises and building your competency, building your strength inside yourself, building inside so that you can deliver the promise. Some of you, you may want to keep the promise, but you're not competent. You may care, you may be sincere, but you just don't know how to do it. So it's not only a matter of giving your word, but you need to be able to be competent. Learn the skills, start growing, really develop yourself so that you can deliver on your promise. When you do that, then your promises will get bigger. Does that make sense?

Relevant Biographies

Programs of The Pacific Institute are based on current, highly credible education verified by the most valid, reliable research available.

The Pacific Institute maintains continuing relationships with a number of distinguished human development and social learning theory researchers. We do this to ensure that we are current on important findings related to thought patterns and belief systems – findings that are crucial to our clients. Prominent among these widely respected researchers are the following:

Dr. Albert Bandura

Dr. Bandura is the David Starr Jordan Professor of Social Science in Psychology at Stanford University and one of the most frequently cited psychologists in the world. In a recent ranking of the 100 most eminent psychologists of the 20th Century, Dr. Bandura came in fourth, behind B. F. Skinner, Jean Piaget and Sigmund Freud. He is author of countless articles on a wide range of issues in psychology, as well as seven books, including *Principles of Behavior Modification, Social Learning Theory, Social Foundations of Thought and Action,* and *Self-Efficacy: The Exercise of Control.*

Dr. Bandura has been a keynote speaker at The Pacific Institute's International Conference on several occasions. He has also spent many hours with Lou Tice and key Pacific Institute staff informally discussing the relevance of his work on individual and collective efficacy to our education. These discussions have focused on how efficacy is developed, and how perceived high efficacy changes behavior, concepts central to all programs of The Pacific Institute, including *Thought Patterns for a Successful Career™*.

Dr. Martin E.P. Seligman

Dr. Seligman is Professor of Psychology and Director of Clinical Training at the University of Pennsylvania, where he holds the Kogod Term Professor chair. He is a prolific writer and internationally recognized scholar and researcher. Throughout his career, he has conducted extensive research with grants from the National Institute of Mental Health, the National Institute on Aging, the National Science Foundation, the Guggenheim Foundation, and the MacArthur Foundation. His book, *Learned Optimism: How to Change Your Mind and Your Life,* and his latest work, *What You Can Change and What You Can't,* have received rave reviews. Dr. Seligman has also served as President of the American Psychological Association.

Dr. Seligman's theories of learned helplessness and learned optimism have contributed a great deal to our understanding of human thought and behavior. The Seligman Attributional Style Questionnaire (SASQ) is a widely used tool that measures levels of optimism/pessimism. Dr. Seligman's visits to The Pacific Institute, his keynote presentation at our International Conference, and the time he has spent with Lou Tice at the Tice Ranch, have served to verify and strengthen the conceptual foundation of our curriculum.

Relevant Biographies

Dr. Gary Latham

Dr. Latham holds the Secretary of State Chair, Faculty of Management, at the University of Toronto. His expertise is in personal and organizational goal-setting and performance appraisal/compensation systems and is well acquainted with The Pacific Institute's curriculum. His latest book, coauthored with Kenneth N. Wexley and published in 1994, is entitled *Increasing Productivity Through Performance Appraisal,* a recent edition of an earlier book of the same title. Dr. Latham was elected President of the Canadian Psychological Association in 1999.

Dr. Latham has consulted with Lou Tice and has addressed The Pacific Institute's staff and clients on numerous occasions, primarily concerning practical applications of the scientific principles of goal-setting, feedback, and performance improvement. He is an outspoken and enthusiastic advocate of our educational processes, and has been a speaker at several International Conferences.

Dr. David Matsumoto

Dr. Matsumoto is currently an associate professor in the Department of Psychology and Director of the Intercultural and Emotion Research Laboratory at San Francisco State University. His books and monographs include *Culture and Diversity: A World of Differences* (in preparation) and *People: Psychology from a Cultural Perspective.* He is also preparing a video presentation entitled *Culture and Diversity: A World of Differences.* He is the author of more than 50 articles and related symposia presentations throughout the world. As a prior keynote speaker at our International Conference, Dr. Matsumoto consults with The Pacific Institute on matters of cultural diversity – with particular focus on how culture influences behavior and how to manage cultural diversity within organizations.

Leon Festinger

In 1954, Leon Festinger developed a concept he called "Cognitive Dissonance." He used it to explain the discomfort he observed in human test subjects when they held two conflicting thoughts at the same time. This discomfort was observed to cause some action: the subject either moved toward one thought or the other. Both thoughts could not be held at the same time.

Rather than see this as a negative situation, Lou takes the idea of cognitive dissonance and uses it as a springboard to create positive change and growth. Since change requires some form of movement, we intentionally create cognitive dissonance in an area where we wish to grow. We make the picture of where we want to be so bright and vivid, that we move toward it, thereby returning harmony.

Relevant Biographies

Dr. Viktor Frankl

Distinguished philosopher and author of several books on purpose in life, including *Man's Search for Meaning*. In this book, Dr. Frankl, a concentration camp survivor, relates that the men and women who were best able to survive the terrible physical and psychological deprivation were those who were determined to stay alive because of some reason bigger than themselves. In some cases it was their families. In other cases, it was important work they wanted to continue. And in some instances, it was the services and support they were providing for fellow prisoners.

Richard Gregory

Distinguished psychologist and author of numerous publications. His area of expertise is the cognitive process, especially the relationship between perception and intelligence.

According to the dictionary, intelligence is the capacity for learning and understanding.

Gregory once told Lou that intelligence is simply the "art of guessing correctly." Anything we can do to improve our guesswork is going to make us more intelligent.

Dr. Wilder Penfield

A cognitive scientist, and author of *Speech and Brain Mechanisms*. During exploratory surgery on a conscious epilepsy patient, with a portion of the skull removed, Dr. Penfield noticed that as he touched the temporal cortex of the patient's brain, the patient relived an experience that had happened years before. As they did further experiments, Dr. Penfield discovered that the information, the individual's version of the experience, was stored in the temporal cortex – never to be lost, never to be forgotten.

Norbert Wiener

"Founding Father" of the computer, and co-author of the book, *Differential Space, Quantum Systems and Prediction*. Wiener coined the phrase, "Garbage in – Garbage out," in relation to data entered into the computer "brain." Simply put, if you put wrong information into a computer, you cannot get anything but wrong information out of it.

The same thing applies to the human mind. If we accept incorrect information about ourselves into our minds, then we are operating, and making decisions, with incorrect information. We must be careful to accept only correct information, and disregard the incorrect.

Relevant Biographies

Dr. Glenn Terrell

Dr. Glenn Terrell serves as academic advisor to The Pacific Institute in curriculum creations, as well as research into the effectiveness of The Institute's programs. Dr. Terrell earned his B.A. in Political Science from Davidson College, his M.S. in Psychology from Florida State University, and a Ph.D. from the University of Iowa.

Dr. Terrell served as Chairman of the Department of Psychology, University of Colorado, Dean of the College of Liberal Arts and Sciences and as Dean of Faculties at the University of Illinois in Chicago before an 18-year tenure as President of Washington State University. He also served as President of the National Association of State Universities and Colleges, Commissioner for the State of Washington on the Western Interstate Commission for Higher Education, served on the Board for General Telephone Northwest and West for 23 years, was a Fellow for the Society for Research in Child Development, and a Fellow for the American Psychological Association.

Dr. Terrell has received numerous honorary degrees and awards, among them a listing in Who's Who in America: American Men of Science, and Distinguished Graduate of the Department of Psychology, University of Iowa. He has managed multimillion dollar technology transfers and faculty and student exchange programs throughout the world. Dr. Terrell's publication, The LETTER, is published quarterly by The Pacific Institute.

A Brief Bibliography

On Cognitive Theory and Research applicable to The Pacific Institute's services

General

Ashton & Webb (1986) *Making a Difference: Teacher Efficacy and Student Achievement.* Monogram. White Plains, NY: Longman.

Bandura, A. (1986) *Social Foundations of Thought and Action: A Social Cognitive Theory.* Englewood Cliffs, NJ: Prentice Hall.

Bandura, A. (1988, Dec) "Organizational Applications of Social Cognitive Theory." *Australian Journal of Management Review,* (Vol. 13, 2, 275-302). The University of New South Wales.

Bandura, A. (1989) "Human Agency in Social Cognitive Theory." *American Psychologist,* (Vol. 44, No. 9, 1175-1184). The American Psychological Association, Inc.

Bandura, A. (1991) "Self Efficacy Mechanism in Psychological Activation and Health Promoting Behavior." *Neurology of Learning Emotion and Affect.* (J. Madden, IV, Ed. 229-270) New York: Raven Press.

Bandura, A. (1991) "Self-Regulation of Motivation through Anticipatory and Self-Regulatory Mechanisms." In R.A. Dienstbiere (Ed.), *Perspectives on Motivation: Nebraska Symposium on Motivation* (Vol. 38, 69-164). Lincoln: University of Nebraska Press.

Bandura, A. (1994) "Self-Efficacy." *Encyclopedia of Human Behavior.* (Vol. 4) Academic Press.

Bandura, A. (1997) *Self-Efficacy. The Exercise of Control,* Freeman, New York, N.Y.

Bandura, A. (2001) "Special Cognitive Theory: An Agentic Perspective." *Annual Review of Psychology.* (52: 1 to 26)

Bandura, A., Barbaranelli, C., Caprara, V., and Pastorelli, C. (2001) "Self-Efficacy Beliefs as Shapers of Children's Aspirations and Career Trajectories." *Child Development,* January/February (Vol. 12, 187-206)

Bandura, A., Caprara, V. and Zsolnai, L. (2001) "Corporate Transgressions Through Moral Disengagement." *Journal of Human Values,* 6.1

Bandura, A. (2004) "Health Promotion by Social-Cognitive Theory." *Health Education and Behavior.* (Vol. 31, 143-164)

Barling, J. & Abel, M. (1983) "Self-Efficacy Beliefs and Performance." *Cognitive Theory and Research.* (Vol 7, 265-272).

Barling, J. & Beattie, R. (1983) "Self-Efficacy Beliefs and Sales Performance." *Journal of Organizational Behavior Management.* (Vol. 5, 41-51).

Dembo & Gibson (1984) "Teacher Efficacy." *Journal of Educational Psychology.* (Vol. 76, 569-582).

A Brief Bibliography

Gardner, H. (1985) "The Mind's New Science." *In A History of The Cognitive Revolution.* New York: Basic Books.

Goldman, D. (1995) *"Emotional Intelligence."* New York, N.Y., Bantam Books

Mahoney, M. (1978) *Cognition and Behavior Modification.* Cambridge: Ballinger.

Clinical Applications

Beck, A. (1979) *Cognitive Therapy and Emotional Disorders.* New York: New York Anniversary Library.

Beck, A. (1991) "Cognitive Therapy: A Thirty Years Retrospective." *American Psychologist.* (Vol. 46, No. 4, 368-375).

Beck, A., Emery, G., & Greenberg, R. *Anxiety Disorders and Phobias: A Cognitive Perspective.* New York: Basic Books.

Beck, A., Rush, J., Shaw, B., & Emery, G. (1979) *Cognitive Therapy of Depression.* New York: Guilford Press.

Ellis, H. (1975) *A New Guide to Rational Living.* North Hollywood, CA: Wilshire Books.

Niemark, J. (1987) "The Power of Positive Thinkers." Reprinted from *Success Magazine,* September 1987.

Rush, J., Beck, A., eds. (1988) "Cognitive Therapy." in Francis, A and Hales, R., eds. *Review of Psychiatry.* (Vol. 7). Washington, DC: American Psychiatric Press.

Seligman, Martin, E.P. (1990) *Learned Optimism.* New York: Pocket Books (Simon & Schuster).

Goal-Setting – Performance Evaluation

Latham, G.P. & Wexley, K.N. (1994) *Increasing Productivity Through Performance Appraisal,* 2nd Edition. Reading, Massachusetts: Addison- Wesley Publishing Company.

Locke, E.A., & Latham, G.P. (1984) *Goal Setting: A Motivational Technique that Works.* Englewood Cliffs, NJ: Prentice-Hall.

Publications Which Are of Significant Value to The Pacific Institute

Bennis, Warren. (1994) *On Becoming A Leader,* Perseus Publication. Greenwald, Tony. (1995) *Implicit Social Cognition: Attitudes, Self Esteem and Stereotypes Through Social Support Training.*

A Brief Bibliography

Psychological Review (102) 4-27.

Levin, Henry (1995) "Accomplishments of Accelerated Schools." National Center for Accelerated Schools Project, Stanford.

Marlatt. (1992) "Substance Abuse: Implications of a Biopsychosocial Model for Prevention Treatment and Relapse Prevention." Psychopharmacology. Smoll, Frank (1993) "Enhancement of Children's Self Esteem." *Journal of Applied Psychology.*

Zigler, E. (1993) "Using Research and Theory to Justify and Inform Head Start Expansion." *Social Policy Report, S.R.C.D.* (Vol. VII #2).

A Brief Bibliography

Key Concept Glossary

V = Video Unit   A = Audio Assimilation Unit   B = Bonus Materials

Achieve – To accomplish goals. *A 13, 16, 18*

Accepting Credit – To agree that one has done something well.

Accountable/Accountability – Responsible; answerable for an outcome. *V 4, 14, 16, 19*

Accurate Thinker – One whose thoughts are accurate.

Actualize – To make happen.

Adventure – When one deliberately takes oneself out of one's old comfort zone, safely imprinting the new into one's subconscious, life becomes an adventure. *A Overview, 2, 14*

Affirm/Affirmation/Affirmation Process – A statement of fact; an internal, cognitive act that establishes a specific course, direction, outcome, or state of being for the future; a confirmation or ratification of a truth. *V 7, 9, 11, 13, 14, 15, 17, 18, 19, 21 A 1, 2, 3, 4, 5, 6, 8, 9, 11, 12, 13, 14, 15, 17, 18, 20 B Overview, 1*

Aggressive-Aggressive – A personality trait; extraordinary ascendant.

Ah-ha – An insight; sudden realization of new information. *V 3*

Alpha State – A state of physical and mental relaxation, while still being aware of what is going on around us. An ideal state for synthetic thought and creativity. *A 1*

Anxiety/Tension – An unpleasant emotional state of apprehension, dread, or distress that exists oftentimes with no objective. *V Overview, 12, 15, 18, 20*

Appetite For Growth – Desire for improvement and self-development.

Appraisal – Analysis of the worth of self, others or other events.

Aspiration – Desire, hope, goal toward which one strives. *A 18*

Assimilate/Assimilation – The incorporating of an idea or thought into the subconscious; the absorption or process of incorporating something external into one's body or cognitive processes; making new visions a part of our lives; e.g., one learns and can behaviorally manifest mastery of fundamental mathematical processes. *V 7, 9, 13 A 1, 5, 6, 10*

Associate/Association – Any learned, functional connection between two or more elements; a particular psychological experience evoked by a stimulus or event. *V 6*

Attitude(s) – A consciously held belief or opinion; easiest to visualize if we picture ourselves leaning toward those things we like (positive) and away from those things we dislike (negative). *V 7, 10 A 4, 5, 8, 9, 11, 12 B 21*

Attitudinal Balance Scale – A cognitive means of assessing one's positive or negative acts; e.g., positive self-talk (I am a capable person and people like me.). *V 9, 19 A 10*

Authentic – Genuine.

Key Concept Glossary

Autopilot – An instrument that guides a ship or airplane, without active participation of a human pilot.

Avoidant/Avoidant Behavior – Response of moving away from undesirable events. *V 20*

Awareness – An internal, subjective state of being cognizant or conscious of something; alertness; consciousness. *V 4, 10*

Balance – Appropriate attention to desirable values in one's life.

Behavior(s) – In terms of human activity, any measurable response of a person. *V 5, 13*

Belief(s) – An emotional acceptance of a proposition, statement, or doctrine. *V 1, 3, 4, 5, 6, 8, 9, 10, 13, 16, 20 A 5, 6, 11, 16*

Belief Without Evidence – Conviction; confidence in a truth; a faith in the ability to establish a goal without first considering the means whereby it will be achieved. (The means to an end follows the establishment of the end.) Once a goal is set, the RAS will actively seek opportunities/means to reach the goal.

Beta State – A state of being consciously alert; a general state of consciousness.

Blind Spot – see Scotoma.

Capable – mentally, emotionally and physically able to succeed at a task or challenge. *V 1 B 1, 18, 20*

Captain of the World – An obsessive, compulsive behavior displaying a pervasive pattern of perfectionism and inflexibility; preoccupation with rules, details, lists, and schedules to the extent that the major point of the activity is lost.

Causative/Causative Power – A person's ability to make happen, which can influence or determine behavior.

Central Cortex – That portion of the brain associated with intellect, rather than emotion.

Change Beyond Pretense – Change driven by genuine desire only.

Check and Balance System – A distribution of power or influence, where each part keeps all other parts in check.

Choose-To – A voluntary act as opposed to a required act. *V 14*

Coaching/Managing Backwards – A system of beginning with a behavior of those being managed.

Co-Creativity – Mutual or joint activity that transcends the ordinary and brings into being original ideas or outcomes.

Coercive Motivation – A drive based on fear and/or authority; a have-to. *V 14*

Key Concept Glossary

V = Video Unit   A = Audio Assimilation Unit   B = Bonus Materials

Cognitive Dissonance – An emotional state where two simultaneously held attitudes or cognitions are inconsistent, or there is a conflict between belief and overt behavior; thought conflict; the uncomfortable psychological condition created when a person experiences contradictory or conflicting opinions, beliefs, or attitudes at the same time. The resolution of this conflict is assumed to serve as the basis for attitude change, in that belief patterns are generally modified to be consistent with behavior. We can hold different attitudes without emotional disharmony as long as a situation does not occur where these attitudes are brought into direct confrontation with one another. *V 2*

Collective Truth – ideas or beliefs held to be true by a group, team, or organization. *V 3, 4*

Comfort Zone – A limited area of perception and association wherein the individual/group can function effectively without experiencing uneasiness or fear; a limited, defined physical or psychological area in which a person feels at ease; self-regulating mechanism; anxiety arousal control. *V Overview, 12, 15, 16, 17, 18, 20 A 6, 8, 9, 16, 17 B 1, 2*

Compliant – the state of bending one's own will to the wishes of another; going along with or agreeing with. *V 14*

Compulsive – Super conscientious.

Condition/Conditioning – A predisposition to a mode of behavior given the appropriate stimulus. *V 1, 2, 3*

Confidential – (Lat. confidere: to trust) A matter not to be divulged.

Conflict – (Lat. conflictus: to strike together) Incompatibility arising from opposing demands or impulses. *V 15*

Conscience – One's inner beliefs of right and wrong.

Conscious – The aspect of mind that encompasses all that one is momentarily aware of; that is, those aspects of mental life that one is attending to. *V 5, 6, 7, 11, 13, 15*

Constructive Motivation – A positive and free-flowing drive on a want-to basis. *V 14*

Co-Responsibility – Mutual or joint accountability; an obligation to act responsibly; shared responsibility for the outcomes of an act.

Create/Creativity – The quality of being creative; the ability to create. *V 7, 10, 12, 15, 17 A 12, 14, 17, 18, 19*

Creative Avoidance – A movement away from an object or goal by means of the imagination with the intent of anxiety reduction. Procrastination is one way to creatively avoid a situation. *V 7, 14*

Creative Energy – The drive or associated stimulus to change, originating in the creative subconscious.

Key Concept Glossary
V = Video Unit   A = Audio Assimilation Unit   B = Bonus Materials

Creative Genius – The inherent ability to find solutions, theories, and ideas.

Creative Implementation – The act of implementing solutions to a challenge or problem; vital step in the creative process.

Creative Subconscious – The source of mental processes that leads to solutions, ideas, conceptualizations, artistic forms, theories, or products that are unique and novel. *V 5, 6, 13, 15, 17 A 8, 9, 17, 18*

Credibility – Worthy of belief; sufficiently good to bring esteem or praise. *A 10*

Critical Listening – Careful observation; hearing.

Culture – An organization's cumulative values, attitudes and beliefs.

Current Reality – All that which forms an integral part of what an individual believes to be real at the moment. *V 16, 18 A 3, 7, 13, 14, 19*

Decision-Making – The act of arriving at a course of action. *V 6*

Dignity and Respect – Highly valued descriptions of a person. *V 11 B 19*

Discrepancy Production (Out of Order) – To increase differences or inconsistencies; to deliberately attempt to create conflict. *V 16*

Discrepancy Reduction (Into Order) – To decrease differences or inconsistencies; to increase levels of agreement; to move toward consistency. *V 16*

Dispute – Disagreement, conflict

Dissonance – A state produced by two opposing views; see Cognitive Dissonance.

Diversity – Variety; not the same.

Dominant Idea – The prevailing view; the strongest picture; a ruling view or belief that is primary.

Downward Spiral – A pattern of belief in which one feels life is hostile, hopeless, and worthless.

Drive – A motivational state learned through association and directed toward a particular goal or objective; an inner urge that stimulates activity or inhibition. *V 18*

Effective/Effectiveness – The ability to cause a result or outcome.

Effectiveness Zone – An area of thought or life where one feels confident, or at home.

Efficacious – Result producing behavior, able to gain ends through efficient means.

Efficacy – The power to produce results; a generative capability in which cognitive, social, and behavioral sub-skills are organized into integrated courses of action to secure innumerable purposes. *V 16, 20 A 2, 14, 16*

Emotion – An experience of feeling as opposed to thinking. *V 7 A 1, 12, 14*

Key Concept Glossary

End-Result Thinking – End-result oriented, without knowing the "how" at the present moment. *V 18* *B 3*

Energy – A force that drives one to a goal. *V 10, 14, 15, 17, 18* *A 12, 14, 18, 19* *B 2, 16, 18, 19*

Environment – The combination of external physical surroundings that affect and influence the growth of organisms; the social and cultural conditions that affect the nature of an individual and community. May be a positive or negative environment. *A 16*

Environmental Comfort Zone – The kind of environmental conditions to which we have been accustomed; e.g., the kind of clothes we wear, the car we drive, the home we live in.

Environmental Self-Image – A self-image relating to the current environment. This self-image may change with differing environments.

Escalate – To raise higher.

Evaluate/Evaluation – The determining of the value or worth of something; generally measured against a previous experience. *V 6*

Expectation – The prospect of a future embodiment of an abstract idea; an anticipation.

Experiential – A state or activity through which one has learned and gained knowledge. Some (experientialists) argue that experience is the only or principal basis for knowledge. *V 17*

Familiarization Process – A procedure designed to learn something. *V 19*

Fascination – A strong feeling about something.

Fear – An emotional state in the presence or anticipation of a dangerous or noxious stimulus; an internal subjective experience that is often physically manifested. *V 14* *A 11*

Feedback – Psychological or sensory information about an event that modifies or reinforces future behavior; a reaction from the environment (including people) that serves as a basis for future action; generally, the functioning of one or more components of a system. A smile is an example of positive feedback; a frown, an example of negative feedback. *V 12*

Feedback Loop – An operational mode/system that provides information about an ongoing operation or the state of the system at a point in time that may serve as a basis for future action or modification.

Feel – Sense of touch; an emotional awareness.

First Nature – Genetically inherited tendencies and traits. *V 8* *A 5*

First Person – A grammatical state in which a speaker (writer) refers to himself or herself or to a group including himself or herself. *V 18*

Flatten Out – Behavior, performance or a view related to life that seems to be constant, continuing, and unchanging. *B 16, 18*

Key Concept Glossary

V = Video Unit   **A = Audio Assimilation Unit**   **B = Bonus Materials**

Flexibility – Pliable, a willingness to change. *A 7*

Flick Back/Flick Up – To borrow from a past, positive experience and bring the feeling into your present visualization of your affirmation; systematic desensitization. *A 8, 12*

Forecast – To predict.

Forethought – Thinking ahead. *V 17, 20 A 1, 2, 3, 5, 6, 7, 8, 11, 12, 14 B 2*

Four Levels of Happiness – Activities, in ascending order, of joy: H1 – self; H2 – competition; H3 – the good of all; H4 – the ultimate.

Four Levels of Self-Talk – 1) Negative resignation; 2) "I should . . ."; 3) "I quit . . ."; 4) "I intend to . . ." *V 10, 19*

Freedom For – Choosing to do something, or make decisions, without fear of possible outcomes.

Freedom From – Choosing to do something, or make decisions, based on fear of possible outcomes.

Free-Flow – Unimpeded flow of thought and action coming from the subconscious.

Free Will – A state wherein one can make choices.

Fulfillment – The state of mind following the achievement of goals.

Future as Now – Seeing the future end-result as already having happened. *A 17*

Generativity – Giving of oneself unselfishly, without needing to control; guiding and directing the next generation toward the fulfillment of sound goals.

Gestalt – Human beings are always working to complete the incomplete, working for closure; discrepancy production, discrepancy reduction; a view that psychological phenomena could only be understood if viewed as organized, structured wholes (Gestalten). The Gestalt point of view challenged the idea that phenomena could be introspectively broken down into primitive perceptual elements, for such analysis left out the notion of the whole unitary essence of the phenomena. *V 9, 10, 15, 17*

Getting Used To – Satisfied with the current state of affairs.

GI/GO (Garbage In/Garbage Out) – Meaningless or unwanted data. In the world of computers, if one puts misinformation into a computer, the only thing that can come out is the wrong answer. The subconscious mind functions in the same way. It does not make value judgments about what the programmer (or conscious mind) wants to put in. *V 5, 6 A 12*

Goal(s) – A sought end that may be actual and objective, or internal, subjective and operational; conceived future; distal goals are end-results, targets; proximal goals are near-term means to the end-result. *V Overview, 2, 4, 13, 14, 15, 16, 17, 18, 19, 20 A 1, 2, 3, 5, 7, 8, 9, 12, 13, 14, 15, 18, 19 B Overview, 1, 9, 11, 18, 20, 21*

Key Concept Glossary

Goal-Seeking Mechanism – The process of setting goals. As humans, we are goal-seeking by design.

Goal-Setting – The act of establishing what we want. *V 7, 10, 15, 16 A 19 B 16, 18*

Goal-Set Through – Goal-setting beyond more proximal goals. *A 16*

Grooved Behavior – Actions that become automatic; patterned.

Growth Change – The result of a process whereby development or progression has occurred; e.g., increased understanding.

Habit(s) – A learned act; a pattern of activity that has, through repetition, become automatic, fixed, and easily and effortlessly carried out. *V 7, 19 A 5, 7, 8, 11, 12*

Half-Step Method – Achieving a goal by two stages. *A 3*

Happiness – The possession or attainment of what one considers to be good.

Have-To – Motivation by threat, fear or coercion. *V 14*

Hesitation/Doubt – A state brought about by indecision.

High-Performance People – Individuals who are analytical and skeptical of information (truth) that comes their way, accept accountability for their own thinking and what goes on around them, and really feel they can make a difference in the world; scotoma busters. *V 9, 11*

Hopeless – Having no hope; refer to Downward Spiral.

Hostility – Anger, expressed or released.

Humility – A trait characterized by lack of pretense. *V 9*

I x V=R – Imagination times vividness equals reality (in the subconscious). *V 8, 16, 19 A 5*

Idea(s) – A product of thought. *V 7*

Ideal(s) – Values about a perfect world.

Image of Reality – A cognitive process that operates as if one had a mental picture that was a representation of a real world scene; a construction; a picture in the mind.

Imagery – The formation of mental pictures through the use of the imaginative faculty.

Imagination – The ability to envision creative solutions. *V 12, 15, 17 A 2*

Imprint(ing) – To establish firmly or impress on the mind or memory; a kind of restricted learning that takes place within a relatively compressed time span, generally is exceedingly resistant to extinction and reversal, and has a profound and lasting effect on later social behavior with respect to the stimulus objects for the behavior; an acquired behavioral response that is difficult to reverse and is normally released by a certain triggering stimulus or situation.

Key Concept Glossary

V = Video Unit   A = Audio Assimilation Unit   B = Bonus Materials

Incubation – A period of time during which no conscious effort is made to solve problems, but which terminates with a solution for the subconscious.

Inefficacious - Behavior that does not produce results.

Inhibitive Motivation – A kind of restrictive motivation; a habit of acting on an, "I have to...or else something awful will happen to me," fear-pattern basis.

Inner Concept/Construct – Self-image; ideas or beliefs that come from within.

Inner Strength – A trait that comes with resilience.

Insight – Sudden comprehension, an "ah-ha."

Integrity – Adherence to moral and ethical principles; whole; sound; unimpaired. *A 20*

Internal (inner) Standard – Your internal idea of who you are; that point at which you self-regulate your behavior, actions and performance. That which is "good enough" for you. *V 5, 15 A 11*

Invent the Future – To determine one's own desires for what lies ahead.

Invent the "How" – To determine how one's desires are to be achieved.

Isolation – A separateness, a feeling apart from others and events.

Level of Expectation – Our view of what we are capable of accomplishing.

Literal Mechanism – Actual meaning of words; not figurative.

Logo Psychology – A distinctive trademark of psychology.

LO/LO (Lock-On/Lock-Out) – An act whereby one has a limited perception of possibilities, problems, or solutions; a restricted, narrow, or singular view of alternatives. When we lock-on to an opinion, belief, or attitude as being the truth about something, we build scotomas to, or lock-out, contrary or different information. This is a defense mechanism that helps us to survive and provides security, but it also works against us when change and flexibility are needed. *V 3, 4, 18 A 3, 15 B 3, 21*

Locus of Control – The degree to which an individual feels that he/she has control over the events that impact his/her life. A person who believes in self-reliance and self-centered accountability is said to have an internal locus of control. Conversely, one who feels victimized or not accountable for events professes an external locus of control.

Magis – Outrageous, forward thinking. *A 16, 20*

Maintain Reality – Being aware of the current state of affairs, and working to keep this current state the same.

Mental Discipline – Ability to think straight under all conditions.

Mentor – Someone who advises and supports another to assist in their development. *V 17*

Key Concept Glossary

V = Video Unit   A = Audio Assimilation Unit   B = Bonus Materials

Mindset – A pattern of thought. *V 2, 14*

Motivation – A need or drive to action based on incentive value of the goal or the expectation of reward or punishment. Emotional states have motivational properties. *V 14, 19* **B** *Overview*

Necessity – An imperative or indispensable requirement; an unavoidable need.

Negative Attitude – A pessimistic view; leaning away from something.

Negative Creativity – Ideas that come from your creative subconscious when you want to avoid something. *V Overview, 20* **A** *2*

Negative Forethought – Pessimistic thinking ahead

Negative Ideas – Prone to pessimistic thoughts.

Negative Picture – A view of oneself that is reinforced by negative self-talk, resulting in a diminished self-image.

Negative Self-Talk – Conversation with one's self that is self-criticizing. *A 4*

Negative Wizard – One who claims authority in making pessimistic pronouncements. *V 21*

Neuron – A nerve cell. *V 5, 13, 15, 16*

Newtonian Point of View – Sir Isaac Newton, an English physicist and mathematician, was a key figure in the scientific revolution of the 17th century. Often called the father of modern physical optics, he also originated the three laws of motion and devised calculus. His view of creation is that all matter in the universe is subject to unchanging laws. When applied to the human condition, the conclusion is that man's destiny is limited. Newtonian leadership is a style that suggests that God created a perfect world with the exception of human beings.

Normal/New Normal - The way things usually are. A "new" normal is the new way things are. *B 19*

Option Thinking – Thought which includes two or more interpretations.

Order and Consistency of Goals – The stability of life's goals; prioritizing what is important.

Or Else – Implicit threat for failure to act according to dictates.

Out of Order/Into Order – Discrepancy production/Discrepancy reduction. *V 15, 16, 17*

Override – To establish one dominant belief in place of another.

Paralysis of Will – A state brought about by inability to act.

Passive-Aggressive – Aggressive behavior that appears to be benign.

Past/Present/Future Time Frame – The three areas of time in which humans can choose from to create their realities. *V 10*

Perceive – An awareness that comes about through sensory or extrasensory processes. *V 7*

Key Concept Glossary

V = Video Unit   A = Audio Assimilation Unit   B = Bonus Materials

Perception – Those mental processes that give coherence and unity to sensory input; a conscious event initiated by some external or internal event; an organized complex dependent on a host of other factors (attention, constancy, motivation, illusion, etc.). *V 2, 3, 4, 5, 6, 15*

Performance – An act or behavior of any kind.

Performance Reality – How one acts and performs based on one's currently dominant self-image. *V 13*

Philosophy of Life – A set of assumptions about one's purpose in life. *A 16*

Picture(s) – A detailed vision of current affairs or the future.

Positive Attitude – An optimistic view; leaning toward something.

Positive Motivation – Moved to action by an optimistic view of life.

Positive Self-Talk – Conversation with one's self that stresses good qualities, characteristics, and achievements. *A 4*

Positive Wizard – A "who-said of the greatest magnitude" who supports and encourages. *V 21*

Possibility Thinking – A cognitive, reflective, and creative process by which one considers all alternatives of a given situation. This process may also include an assessment of the reality, veracity, impact, and relative weight of all elements that compose a situation or condition.

Post-Dissonance – An emotional state of uncertainty as to the merit of an act following its completion; sometimes referred to as buyer's remorse.

Potential – Having the strong possibility for development into a state of actuality; possible or in the making; latent. *V Overview, 1, 2, 3, 5, 6, 7, 9, 12, 13, 15, 16, 17 A 5, 6, 9, 11, 16, 18, 19*

Pre-Dissonance – An emotional state whereby one is disposed to act; however, movement toward, or the completion of, the act is dissuaded by uncertainty as to the merit therein or the benefit thereof. Generally, constant overriding reassurance from an external source is required to complete the act.

Present Reality – The way things are perceived to be in the current time frame.

Present Tense – Current state of being or existence, usually expressed in grammar by the use of a verb ("I am a considerate, loving person."). Stating the future as now.

Pressure – see Anxiety; Tension. *V 6*

Problem – A challenge, difficulty needing a solution.

Process of Thought – The interaction of the conscious, subconscious, and creative subconscious.

Procrastination – To defer action or delay; prolong; postpone; a type of creative avoidance. *V 14*

Progressive – Actions generated by new and better ideas.

Key Concept Glossary

Psycholinguistics – A study of the relationship between language and the cognitive or behavioral characteristics of those who use it; the power that words have on our behavior.

Purpose In Life – Reason for existing.

Push-Push Back – When one is pushed, one unconsciously pushes back. *V 14*

Pygmalion Effect – The effect by which people come to behave in ways that correspond to others' expectations concerning them. *A 1, 4, 5, 15*

Quality – An attribute; a degree of excellence.

Read-Picture-Feel – Three concepts important to effective affirmations; critical components to effective imprinting of affirmations or ideas.

Realistic – Conforming to a common-sense notion of what is possible.

Reality – All that forms an integral part of what an individual believes to be real; the perception and assessment of the environment in ways that coordinate with one's social and cultural schemes and values; an awareness of the environment and the need to accommodate to the demands thereof. *V 3, 5, 6, 9, 15, 17 A 6, 17*

Reflective Thinking – A casting back or returning to a thing; an introspection; a reflection on a previous experience or event and its significance. *A 3, 8, 9*

Reiterate(ing) – To repeat; the action of repeating. *V 9*

Resilience – Ability to bounce back in the face of adversity. *V 20 A 8, 14, 15 B 9*

Respect – See Dignity *V 11 B 19*

Restrictive – Whatever blocks the ability to see beyond current reality

Restrictive Motivation – Motivation by threats, fear, or coercion; have-to or else. *V 14*

Restrictive Zones – Subjective areas of thought processes that interfere with and limit rational thought or action.

Reticular Activating System (RAS) –A network of neurons in the brainstem involved in consciousness, regulation of breathing; the transmission of sensory stimuli to higher brain centers; a primary alert to awareness network that may function differently in varying degrees of consciousness. *V 4, 18 A 4, 14*

Risk Avoidant – A trait of a person or group to steer clear of risk.

Rite of Passage – An event or ceremony with significant internal meaning and associated belief. A one-time affirmation. *V 21*

Root Cause – Primary cause, or causes, of a specific behavior patterns that are reflected in performance.

Key Concept Glossary

V = Video Unit   A = Audio Assimilation Unit   B = Bonus Materials

Routinize(d) – To make a course of action habitual.

Sanction – To give approval to; to agree with. *V 2, 8 A 4, 10*

Sanity – A mental state whereby one is capable of adequate, adaptive functioning on a day-to-day basis; soundness of mind and judgment. *V 5*

Sarcasm – A caustic remark. *V 8*

Scotoma – An expression to indicate that one fails to see or is blind to alternatives and therefore can see only limited possibilities; a sensory locking out of information from our environment. We develop scotomas to the truth about our world and ourselves because of our preconceived ideas, other people's preconceived ideas (flat worlds or cultural trances), and conditioning. We do not see or are blind to certain things. *V 1, 2, 3, 4 A 2 B 3, 20*

Second Nature – Acquired habit or tendency, so deeply ingrained as to appear automatic. *V 8 A 4, 5, 6, 8, 11*

Selective Information Gathering – A process involved in situations whereby attention is focused on positive or negative stimulus input; assumes a predisposition toward the stimulus based on preconceived value judgments.

Selective Perceiver – Someone whose perception of an event or person is governed by personal attitudes.

Self-Actualize – Resorting to initiative.

Self-Concept – One's opinion of self-worth.

Self-Correct – To adjust one's own behavior.

Self-Determined – To decide, take control, of one's own being and actions. To make one's own decisions about the future. *V 19*

Self-Efficacy – One's appraisal of one's own ability to cause, to bring about, make happen; one's own power or capacity to produce the desired effect; a combination of one's self-esteem, skills, and resources; task specific.

Self-Esteem – The degree to which one values oneself; the worth/value of the picture. *V 11, 14, 16, 17 A 4, 8, 10, 15 B 2, 11, 19, 21*

Self-Examination – The process one uses in arriving at one's worth or one's opinion.

Self-Fulfilling Prophecy – A phenomenon wherein one's prediction about the future may come to pass, because of the belief that underlies the prediction. *V 2*

Self-Image – The accumulation of all the attitudes and opinions one has perceived about oneself that form a subconscious picture of oneself; the imagined self; the self that one supposes oneself to be; the picture; self-regulation. *V 5, 8, 9, 12, 13 A 1, 5 B 21*

Key Concept Glossary

Self-Motivation – Energy for action comes from within.

Self-Regulation – Adhering to and following an internal standard. *V 5, 8, 12*

Self-Sabotage – To contribute to one's own downfall.

Self-Talk – An act whereby one evaluates or assesses one's behavior; how one talks or reaffirms to oneself when one reacts to one's own evaluation, or others' evaluations of one's performance. Self-talk may have an affirming influence in establishing self-image. *V 2, 8, 9, 10, 11, 12, 13, 14, 15, 20 A 8, 9, 10, 15, 18 B 1, 2, 10, 11, 19, 21*

Sense(s) – To become aware of something. In humans, to perceive through sight, sound, smell, touch and taste.

Serendipitous – Come upon by accident rather than by design. *A 7*

Servomechanism – An ability to evaluate behavior in order to make adjustments designed to exercise desired control. *A 8, 17*

Setting Priorities – To develop a plan of attaching relative importance to actions to be taken.

Significant – To make a difference; may be positive or negative. *V 4*

Skeptical – Being wary of something done or said. Discriminating, as in "skeptical listener." *V 2*

Smart – Possessing intelligence; ability to think and learn. *V 1 B Overview, 20*

Solve Conflict – To eliminate or resolve; completing goals.

Spirit of Intent – The intent or motivating force behind one's acts, words, or deeds. *A 20*

Stability – A steady, predictable state of affairs.

Standards – A degree or level of requirement, excellence or attainment; what you perceive the level of quality or excellence to be. It is critical for organizations to clearly articulate and define their expectations or standards, because not everyone will operate from the same level if their picture is not clearly defined. *A 6*

Stress/Tension – A state of psychological tension produced by physical, and social forces and pressures. *V 6*

Structured Affirmation Process – A well-ordered plan for one's goal-setting and goal achievement.

Structured Process – A system for accomplishing one's activities.

Stuck / Unstuck – To be imprisoned, resulting in inaction followed by thoughts or actions that move one forward. *V 1, 2*

Key Concept Glossary

Subconscious – The level of mind through which material passes on the way toward full consciousness; an information store containing memories that are momentarily outside of awareness but that can easily be brought into consciousness. *V Overview, 1, 2, 4, 5, 7, 8, 9, 10, 11, 12, 13, 14, 15, 16, 17, 18, 19* **A** *8, 10, 14, 15*

Subconscious Reality – Real circumstances of which we are unaware.

Sub-Goals – Goals of current, lesser, immediate importance whose accomplishment is required for main goals to be achieved.

Success/Successful – The state of reaching goals; goal achievement.

Superstition – Belief in something that has no basis in fact. *A 7*

"Sure Enough" Principle – By believing something will happen, it will. "You expect a bad day and, sure enough, you get a bad day." *V 4, 9*

Systematic Desensitization – A technique used to reduce fear (or other maladaptive response) by frequent and organized exposure to the feared object.

Teleological – A doctrine or belief that a final cause exists, that there is a purpose to being, that all move toward a goal or final destination, and that order in the universe is not random. *V 10, 13* **B** *10*

Tension – An emotional state characterized by restlessness and anxiety; a mental state where one is thwarted from achieving an end. *V 11, 12, 15, 18*

The next time . . . – A vow to better performance at the next opportunity.

Third-Party Affirmation – To verbalize good opinions about a person, in the presence of another person.

Thought Patterns – Organization of thoughts, reflected in actions and performance.

Threat – Words or actions that frighten or imperil.

Three Dimensions of Thought – Human beings think in three dimensions: words, triggering pictures, which cause emotions.

True (Truth) – A characteristic of a proposition, statement, or belief that corresponds with reality, as it is known, possibly based on an earlier evaluative process. *V 1, 2, 3, 5, 6, 8, 9, 12, 13, 17* **A** *10* **B** *20*

Trust – Belief in the honesty and good intentions of others. *A 20*

Under-Living – Not living up to one's potential.

Unwarranted Self-Esteem – Self-esteem not based on the actual value of the self.

Key Concept Glossary

Value(s) – Quality of worth, merit; custom or ideal that people desire as an end or means of itself; something of excellence or importance.

Vision – A dream, aspiration, goal, or aim relating to the future. *V 18 A 3 B 1*

Visualize (Visualization) – To recall or form mental images from the imagination; to make perceptive to the mind; forethought; mental stimulation. Creative visualization is often a means of unblocking or dissolving barriers that we ourselves have created. *V Overview, 7, 10, 12, 15, 16, 17, 18, 19 A 2, 9, 12, 14, 17, 19 B 11, 19*

Vivid – Bright; intense; living; lifelike.

Vow – A solemn pledge, promise, or commitment of oneself to an act, service, or condition. *V 21*

Want To – To desire to do something. *V 14*

Warranted Self-Esteem – Self-esteem based on the actual value of the self.

Whiteheadian Point of View – Alfred North Whitehead, an English philosopher and mathematician, taught philosophy at Harvard in the 1920s and established a reputation as a critic of scientific materialism that he retained until his death. His approach to human behavior suggests that man is not locked in to a condition, but can co-create, with God, a better life through the exercise of free choice. Whiteheadian leadership is based on this belief that creation is ongoing.

Who-Said – An authority figure to whose word you give sanction. *V 21*

Words-Pictures-Emotions – Three critical components to the affirmation process. *V 8, 19*

Worthless – Having no worth; being worth "less" than before.

Zone of Proximity – Nearness in time or distance (with reference to goals).

Key Concept Glossary

V = Video Unit   A = Audio Assimilation Unit   B = Bonus Materials